Studies in Writing & Rhetoric

Other Books in the Studies in Writing & Rhetoric Series

Minor Re/Visions

Minor Re/Visions

Asian American Literacy
Narratives as a Rhetoric
of Citizenship

Morris Young

SOUTHERN ILLINOIS UNIVERSITY PRESS

Carbondale

Publication partially funded by a subvention grant from The Conference on College
Composition and Communication of the National Council of Teachers of English.

Library of Congress Cataloging-in-Publication Data

Young, Morris, 1967–
    Minor re/visions : Asian American literacy narratives as a rhetoric of citizenship
/ Morris Young.
        p. cm. — (Studies in writing & rhetoric)
    Includes bibliographical references (p.) and index.
    1. English language—Rhetoric—Study and teaching—United States. 2. American
prose literature—Asian American authors—History and criticism. 3. Asian Americans—Biography—History and criticism. 4. Asian Americans—Education—Language arts. 5. Asian Americans—Intellectual life. 6. Asian Americans in literature.
7. Biography as a literary form. 8. Citizenship—United States. 9. Literacy—United
States. 10. Narration (Rhetoric). I. Title: Minor revisions. II. Title. III. Series.
PE1405.U6 Y68 2004
808'.042'071073—dc21
ISBN 0-8093-2554-3 (alk. paper)   2003014187

Printed on recycled paper. ♻

Contents

Acknowledgments

As the narrative I have constructed in this project may reveal, writing this book has been in many ways a struggle as I have experienced both the anxiety and nostalgia of literacy. Perhaps the anxiety is my own as I asked myself often what I could possibly contribute to a discipline that has addressed in powerful and meaningful ways issues concerning educational inequity, the literacy practices of diverse communities, and the importance of teachers, students, and classrooms, to name just a few of the areas where we engage in necessary work. But the generosity and support from friends and colleagues have made it clear that I can offer something even if just a tiny bit. And the nostalgia is my own as well when I reflect on the role literacy and language has played in my life, creating connections with family and friends and helping me to understand the meaning of community.

And it is friends and family who have played the largest part in shaping my life as a researcher and teacher and in helping me to complete this project. The people most responsible for suggestions and revision for this project, Barry Chabot, Kate Ronald, and Keith Tuma, read either parts or the complete manuscript and provided critical comments and encouragement at a crucial time; and Mary Jean Corbett read the entire manuscript with a careful eye and careful pen, insightful comments, and plenty of excellent advice about both the book and the profession. The guidance of Robert Brooke, editor of the Studies in Writing & Rhetoric series, has been invaluable in helping me to reframe this work and to clarify my ideas. The comments and suggestions of reviewers Stuart Ching, Juan Guerra, and Lad Tobin, as well as anonymous reviewers, have helped me to understand the place of this work in our discipline. The first versions of this work emerged when I was a graduate student at the University of Michigan in the Joint Ph.D. Program in English and

Education. Anne Ruggles Gere encouraged this work and helped me to understand the many ways literacy infiltrates and fulfills our lives. Steve Sumida provided an example of the crossing of disciplinary and geographical boundaries that I attempt to do here and that he does so well. As readers, Jonathan Freedman, Gail Nomura, and Arlene Keizer provided generous comments and useful advice. Karl Kageff of Southern Illinois University Press has made the publication process an easy one. Some of this work appeared in different forms previously: "The Anxiety and Nostalgia of Literacy: A Narrative about Race, Language, and a Teaching Life" was first published in *Personal Effects: The Social Character of Scholarly Writing* edited by David Bleich and Deborah Holdstein (Logan: Utah State UP, 2001. 296–316). "Standard English and Student Bodies: Institutionalizing Race and Literacy in Hawai'i" was first published in *College English* 64.4 ([March 2002]: 405–31). Copyright © 2002 by the National Council of Teachers of English. Reprinted with permission.

My professional life at Miami University has been a wonderful blending of teaching and research. I am thankful for the research time and funding provided by the university and the support of my department chair, Keith Tuma, past chair, Dianne Sadoff, and assistant chair, Jerry Rosenberg. My colleagues in the Department of English have provided many useful conversations about the issues discussed in this project and about teaching and the profession in general. For their generosity and advice I thank Paul Anderson, Don Daiker, Jennie Dautermann, Mary Fuller, Katharine Gillespie, Cheryl Johnson, Katie Johnson, Frank Jordan, Rodrigo Lazo, Cindy Lewiecki-Wilson, Jean Lutz, Laura Mandell, LuMing Mao, Tim Melley, Max Morenberg, Kerry Powell, Diana Royer, Michelle Simmons, Jeff Sommers, and Whitney Womack. The Department of English office staff—Jackie Kearns, Trudi Nixon, Kathy Fox, and Debbie Morner (who has been invaluable in helping me to understand how to direct a graduate program)—have been wonderful in assisting with the many organizational and everyday details that are part of research, teaching, and the profession. Mary Cayton, Bill Gracie, Bill Hardesty, Carolyn Haynes, Sally Lloyd, Ron Scott, Peggy Shaffer, and Bill Wortman have been very supportive of my efforts to introduce Asian American topics at Miami. Kate Rousmaniere has provided needed conversations and information about the history and state of education on numerous occasions. I have also worked with many fine graduate students at Miami, but I have been particularly fortunate to work with Brenda Helmbrecht, Connie Kendall, and Michelle Weiner. The many students I have worked with in Hawai'i, Michigan, and Ohio always teach me what is important about the classroom and provide me with many more insights about my research and teaching than I could ever discover on my own—for these experiences I am grateful.

I also express my appreciation to friends and colleagues at other institutions who have provided useful inspiration and advice. Though some of the people I name here may be surprised to find themselves listed, I have found that even the slightest gesture of encouragement or the time to listen when we see each other at a conference have been invaluable. For their generosity, I thank Arnetha Ball, David Bleich, Stuart Ching, Nancy Cho, Caroline Clark, Janet Carey Eldred, Keith Gilyard, Cheryl Glenn, Doug Hesse, Susan Jarratt, Bob Johnson, Paul Matsuda, Debbie Minter, Terese Monberg, Renee Moreno, Peter Mortensen, Gail Nomura, Emily Nye, Gail Okawa, Grace Pang, Cris Paschild, Jay Robinson, Randall Roorda, and Margaret Willard-Traub. My early training at the University of Hawai'i prepared me well for graduate school and the work I do now. I thank my teachers at UH, in particular, Jeff Carroll, Arnie Edelstein, Tom Hilgers, Craig Howes, and Joy Marsella, as well as Elton Fukumoto and J. Kastely, who have moved on to other positions.

Caroline and Ted Clark (and now Emma) have always welcomed me as part of their family: first, when we were graduate students in Ann Arbor, and now in Ohio where we teach and work. Their generosity and good nature have reminded me of the importance of friendship. My own family has been a constant source of support and love. While I have chosen to live away from Hawai'i for now, I always remember growing up there with parents and siblings who shared in a love of reading, culture, and family. My parents, sisters, and brother were my first teachers. My nieces and nephew remind me of the importance of teachers. I continue this work with them in mind.

Note on Hawaiian Words and Usage

In writing about Hawaiʻi and its peoples and cultures, it is necessary to use and present terms and concepts as they are used in Hawaiʻi. For guidance in the use of Hawaiian words, I have consulted Stephen Sumida's note "About Spelling and Capitalization" from his book *And the View from the Shore: Literary Traditions of Hawaiʻi* and the *University of Hawaiʻi Style Guide* for university publications. Necessary to the spelling of Hawaiian words are the *ʻokina,* or glottal stop, which appears as a single open quotation mark (ʻ), and the *kahako,* or macron (-), to indicate elongated vowel duration. When I have quoted Hawaiian words from published texts, they appear as originally printed. In my own text, I spell Hawaiian names and words with the diacritical marks. When Hawaiian words are Anglicized, these marks are generally not used: for instance, the ʻokina is not used in the word *Hawaiian,* which is considered an English word. However, the *University of Hawaiʻi Style Guide* advises that the use of an apostrophe and an *s* is acceptable in forming English possessives of Hawaiian singular nouns *(Hawaiʻi's people).*

As is the practice in Hawaiʻi, I reserve the word *Hawaiian* to identify Native Hawaiian (i.e., Polynesian) people and culture, though I will typically employ the term *Native Hawaiian.* For a non-Polynesian, I use *Hawaiʻi person.* In this usage, then, *the Hawaiian sovereignty movement* refers to a political movement by Hawaiʻi's indigenous Polynesian people, while *Hawaiʻi writer* refers to a writer who locates himself or herself in Hawaiʻi but whose background is not Native Hawaiian.

Minor Re/Visions

Introduction

Let me begin a narrative here. Before I started kindergarten, I often attended story hour at the neighborhood public library, where I would receive a handmade program that listed the stories for the day and an animal shaped name tag (artifacts that my mom has saved to this day). I remember when I was about five or six having to go off to some faraway school classroom on a Saturday morning, where a young teacher (I assumed) asked me to identify objects, read a few simple words, and practice my *S* and *T* sounds as well as other phonics exercises. I later learned I was being evaluated by a speech pathologist because I did not enunciate my words clearly. On a family vacation when I was twelve, I found myself in New Orleans at an open market looking at some used comic books (my passion at the time) when the burly man who ran the stand looked at me accusingly and said in a gruff voice, "Don't you understand English?" as he pointed aggressively to a "no reading" sign. I only stared at him and thought, "Of course I understand English. Why else would I be looking at the comic book?" I am not sure why these memories stay with me. Perhaps because these were encounters with language, I have internalized them and have become aware of the everyday uses of language and their contexts. Or I recall these experiences now because at the time they occurred I didn't understand their implications. Wasn't story hour just fun? What was a speech pathologist? Did I look as if I didn't know English? Did I look foreign? Though these encounters were not especially dramatic or traumatic life-changing experiences, they were significant because I became aware at an early age of the emphasis our culture places on language.

As a graduate student, my encounters with language continued and seemed to become progressively stranger and more significant. For example, in the span of three days one summer in the 1990s, the various fragments of my dissertation research were brought together into one site of discussion at a hotel in Washington, D.C., through a series of coincidences. It was May, and I was attending the annual meeting of the Association for Asian American Studies. At the meeting there were a number of sessions and papers about the historical and theoretical constructions of Asian American citizenship, a key term that continues to inform my work. At the same time of this meeting and at the very same hotel, the National Spelling Bee was being held. That year the championship was won by Wendy Guey, a tiny, bespectacled, Chinese American eighth-grader from Florida. This coincidence is important because I will suggest that the demonstration of a person's literacy—and a spelling bee championship is such a demonstration—has been key in the construction of a person's identity, legitimacy, and citizenship when that person is racially marked as Other. Here is the next coincidence: On the last day of the meeting as I rode on the underground metro back to the hotel with some friends, a well-dressed young white man asked for the time and I obliged. He then proceeded to speak to me in what I recognized as Japanese, asking if I spoke Japanese (I think). "No," I answered, not to the specific question but to his attempt. Then he tried a Chinese dialect. "No," I answered again, "English only." The irony of my "English only" response partly escaped me at the time as I felt my face flush and as my friends stared at him with annoyance. But now that I think about it, I am even more convinced that ideology and literacy are connected and are deeply embedded in our culture, so much so that even a person like myself, devoted to raising awareness about diverse literacy practices and to recognizing the value and history of diverse language traditions in our country, can utter "English only."

I reflect on these experiences not for the sake of authorizing this study with a personal experience or to invoke identity politics in the following discussion about the intersections among literacy, race, and citizenship. Rather, I read these events as the preconditions for considering the position of Asian Americans within larger American culture and within the site of my professional life, the academy, and specifically in the study of literacy. While Wendy

Guey's spelling bee victory was most often reported matter-of-factly —noting the winning word ("vivisepulture") and her plans for the prize money ("spend it!")—a subtle construction of her also took place as news accounts mentioned her family's move from Taiwan to the United States ten years earlier. This daughter of immigrants, who in her words "studied a lot . . . really wanted to win . . . and prayed a lot," was able to show America her facility with and legitimacy in using English (Malkin B4). Wendy was not only a true American success story, she confirmed America's expectation of Asian Americans as studious, intellectual, and hard-working—she became hyper-literate to dispel any question about her Americanness. In the other instance, the assignment of foreignness to my Asian body seemed to be "natural" to that young white man. The expectation that I would know Japanese or some dialect of Chinese also came naturally to him, ignoring the fact that at the time I was having a lengthy conversation in English with my friends (though perhaps with a bit of a regional Hawai'i accent) and answered him in English. And my response of "English only" perhaps also came naturally to me as I—now to my disappointment—answered this challenge to my "legitimacy" by invoking this counterintuitive term to end the conversation.

My stories are not uncommon. In his introduction to *A Different Mirror: A History of Multicultural America*, Ronald Takaki recounts his own experience with being "foreign":

> I had flown from San Francisco to Norfolk and was riding in a taxi to my hotel to attend a conference on multiculturalism. Hundreds of educators from across the country were meeting to discuss the need for greater cultural diversity in the curriculum. My driver and I chatted about the weather and the tourists. The sky was cloudy, and Virginia Beach was twenty minutes away. The rearview mirror reflected a white man in his forties. "How long have you been in this country?" he asked. "All my life," I replied, wincing. "I was born in the United States." With a strong southern drawl, he remarked: "I was wondering because

your English is excellent!" Then, as I had many times before, I explained: "My grandfather came here from Japan in
the 1880s. My family has been here, in America, for over a
hundred years." He glanced at me in the mirror. Somehow
I did not look "American" to him; my eyes and complexion
looked foreign. (1)

Why is there an expectation of foreignness? If we were to continue
Takaki's story, the cab driver, now defensive, might insist that he
does detect an accent since traces of Takaki's Hawai'i accent may
slip through. However this would open up another set of expectations and constructions as the trope of Hawai'i relocates Takaki to
that distant paradise that is quasi-foreign in the American imagination. The Asian markings of Takaki's body define him as foreign despite any other signifier that would mark him as American. His use
of Standard English, his credentials as an academic at an elite university (the University of California, Berkeley), his expertise in
American history, seemingly will not supersede his racialized body.

Here is another example. When United States Senator Alphonse
D'Amato mocked Judge Lance Ito on a radio talk show by using an
exaggerated Asian accent reminiscent of Japanese villains in old
World War II movies, he displayed an attitude that often constructs
Asian Americans as less than literate and as less than full citizens in
America. The *New York Times* reported:

In a rapid-fire conversation with the radio talk show host
Don Imus on Tuesday, Mr. D'Amato sharply criticized and
belittled Judge Lance Ito over his handling of the Simpson
case and used an exaggerated Asian accent, like that of vil-
lainous Japanese characters in old World War II movies,
in talking about the Judge . . . "Forever and ever, because
Judge Ito will never let it end," Mr. D'Amato said in his
version of a Japanese accent. "Judge Ito loves the limelight.
He is making a disgrace of the judicial system. Little Judge
Ito. For God's sake, get them in there for 12 hours; get this
thing over. I mean this is a disgrace. Judge Ito will be well

known. And then he's going to have a hung jury. Judge Ito
will keep us from getting television for the next year." (Van
Gelder B1, B7)

While we might give the cab driver in Ronald Takaki's story the
benefit of the doubt since his interaction with Takaki was probably
limited and overdetermined to start, it is harder to dismiss D'Amato's
willingness to construct Ito as a Japanese caricature with a pro-
nounced "foreign" accent. Ito had been seen and heard on television often. His position as a judge seemingly provided an authority
and legitimacy that located him securely as an American citizen.
And yet D'Amato felt he had license to portray someone with an
Asian body as a foreigner with a recognizable marker of foreignness, an accent, as well as the use of "Yellow English."

A more recent example illustrating the status of Asian American citizenship occurred in May 2001. On 25 May 2001, David Wu,
a member of the of the U.S. House of Representatives from Oregon,
stood on the floor of the House chamber and described an encounter he'd had:

> Mr. Speaker, an odd thing happened to me 2 days ago on
> my way down to the Department of Energy. I was going to
> give a talk to employees there, and I was stopped by the
> guards when I was trying to enter the building and I was
> asked repeatedly, my staffer and I were asked repeatedly,
> whether we are American citizens. This occurred both be-
> fore and after I presented my congressional identification
> card. . . . The ultimate irony is that I went to the Depart-
> ment of Energy 2 days ago to give a talk, at their request,
> about the progress of Asian Americans in America as part
> of Asian Pacific American Heritage Month celebration ac-
> tivities by the employees there.[1]

The resistance to his American citizenship that David Wu encoun-
tered is just another recent example of the struggles Asians and
Asian Americans have faced regarding their status in the United

States for the last hundred years. Whether it was immigration policy that kept Chinese from entering the country,[2] or laws that kept Asians from being naturalized as U.S. citizens,[3] or the internment of Japanese Americans during World War II,[4] Asians and Asian Americans have been regarded as less than potential citizens (sojourners who only intend to return to an Asian "homeland") and as less than full citizens (people unable or unwilling to leave a "home" culture behind).

I offer these different scenes and begin to narrate my own experiences as an introduction because they illustrate the complicated relationship among literacy, race, and citizenship that exists in our culture. The ability to participate in public discourse, to be perceived as fully literate (and without an accent) often becomes a marker of citizenship and legitimacy. Our culture's discourse of literacy (the ways in which we talk about and deploy literacy), its inherent construction of race, and the implications for the teaching of writing are problematic not just because literacy is often constructed in uncomplicated terms, as an unquestioned public good; rather, the discourse about literacy is also problematic because it is often a coded way to talk about race, citizenship, and culture in America by raising the specter of crisis. As John Trimbur argues, the "discourse of crisis" about literacy is often invoked to provide American dominant culture with a way to express its anxiety about a changing America (through immigration, globalization, and other economic and social pressures) and to become nostalgic for an imagined time when literacy would regulate the citizenry, provide hope for the less-literate and confirmation for the literate, and sustain the nation not only in material ways but also in symbolic ways (285–86, 293).

This book is about this tension between the anxiety and nostalgia of literacy, and the tensions that exist between competing beliefs and uses of literacy among those who are part of dominant American culture and those who are positioned as minorities. Perhaps the most obvious tension is between those who are constructed as the majority and those who are constructed as the minority, and in the United States this is often correlated to racial and ethnic difference.

Another tension is between those who are constructed as literate and those who are constructed as illiterate or less-literate, though this is often determined through a person's facility with Standard English and is another way of marking membership and status within the community, and in providing educational and cultural capital. Located in these categories of racial subjectivity and literacy are tensions between the public and the personal, between the public uses of literacy to enact citizenship and the personal uses of literacy in the construction and expression of identity. For example, we see in these tensions the anxiety and nostalgia of literacy, where individuals fear that a perceived lack of literacy will exclude them from the community—and in the case of Asians and Asian Americans "confirm" their status as "foreign"—and yet remain nostalgic for the promise of literacy, a belief that literacy will easily (and even magically) confer membership and perhaps erase the differences that mark them. One of the major aims of this book is to explore the conditions under which these tensions emerge by examining specific social and personal histories, which provide a broad field for understanding the uses of literacy and its intertwining with individual lives and cultural groups.

More specifically, *Minor Re/Visions* examines the ways literacy and race intersect in American culture, in particular, the ways the perception of a person's citizenship is overdetermined because of competing ideological constructions about literacy and race. The processes of reading and writing literacy narratives is one means for people of color to develop and articulate their negotiation of citizenship, in particular by arguing for "cultural citizenship," a term suggested by Renato Rosaldo, which attends "not only to dominant exclusions and marginalizations, but also to subordinate aspirations for and definitions of enfranchisement" (37). I think of these processes as "minor re/visions," invoking the irony of the term as we consider the major revisions that must take place within American culture to account for the literacy and rhetorical practices of people of color. While being a minority in America is often a label about race and ethnicity or about political power (if these things can be separated), to be "minor" is a position, described by Gilles Deleuze and Felix Guattari (and extended by Abdul JanMohamed and David Lloyd), that deterritorializes dominant discourse, connects the individual to political immediacy, and provides a collective, even revolutionary, enunciation (Deleuze and Guattari 18). This book examines the "minor" positions of people of color, especially Asian Americans, and how their narratives act to disrupt dominant discourses about literacy and race, create the possibility of political action, and offer collective (but not representative) experiences to complicate expectations about the "minor."

Re/vision (a term familiar to writing teachers) is another key process in thinking about the connections between literacy, race, and citizenship, where on one level we work with existing material, negotiating ideas and arguments, but also work to re/vision what these ideas and arguments can be, what they can teach us and others. This is the sense and trope of re/vision that Nancy Sommers articulates when she describes it as "the lyrical dream of change, of being made anew, always believing that a new vision is possible" (26). On another level, the work of re/vision in this book is to challenge the binaries and categories that continue to organize and domesticate American culture. As Sommers argues, "these either/or ways of seeing exclude life and real revision by pushing us to safe positions, to what is known" (29). Re/vision is a way to bring in multiple voices, to connect the public and personal, to view uncertainty as possibility, to work, as Sommers suggests, "between the drafts." This trope is particularly important to people of color whose visions of America are often "between the drafts" and in the margins rather than being a commonly told tale of America.

As a way to work "between the drafts" and to move beyond the "safe" stories that might be told about literacy, race, and citizenship, I turn to the writing of my own literacy narrative to provide the personal experiences that result from, are a continual part of, and inform larger structural and cultural histories and narratives. For example, how has Hawai'i's literacy history and legacy of English Standard schools in the early twentieth century affected my life in the late twentieth and early twenty-first centuries? Or how do the explicit literacy representations and expectations created of Asian Americans contribute to my position as a teacher and researcher: the use of "Asian American English" or "Yellow English"; the social hierarchies marked by Pidgin; the silent Asian American student? I also choose to weave my narrative into the narratives of others in order to move beyond two dominant discursive models: telling either the representative story for all Asian Americans or people of color, or the exceptional story which signals to dominant American culture that literacy and hard work alone are enough to overcome racism.

Through my own narrative and the engaging of other narratives, I want to offer scenes and experiences that capture specific moments when literacy, race, and citizenship come to an intersection where we gain an understanding of how literacy and race have shaped our and their lives. In many ways, this book is a collection, a montage of scenes I have come across in my life, which have troubled me, pushed me to think beyond simple binaries, forced me to learn the hidden histories about Asian Americans, and moved me to complicate literacy and citizenship beyond their promise for the American Dream. Though the scenes I read in this study are often part of full-length narratives, I focus on what I see as key moments in a subject's life, when he or she must grapple with the promise and peril of being literate and of living in America as a person of color. My method here is, perhaps, idiosyncratic, as I move between narratives that are organized loosely around what they offer in terms of their readings of culture and citizenship and the uses of literacy. My method is also in-process as I read and write narratives to draw upon current discussions about literacy, race, and citizenship but also to fill in gaps in these discussions, which often are underdeveloped and undertheorized in bringing together these areas of examination, especially concerning Asian Americans. Thus, I see these scenes and narratives as pieces of a larger picture—perhaps titled too ambiguously, "Literacy"—which I am composing through my own narrative, a bit at a time, always changing, and always present.

As Deborah Brandt has suggested, "to think of literacy as a staple of life—on the order of indoor lights or clothing—is to understand how thoroughly most Americans in these times are able to take their literacy for granted" (1). But, as Brandt continues, literacy also "has proven to be a difficult and contentious topic of investigation because its place in American culture has become so complex and conflicted" (2). The largeness of literacy and the power we attribute to it is one of the driving forces for this book. Why do we so easily view literacy as an unquestioned public good? Why have we taken literacy for granted? How do we see literacy beyond the skills of reading and writing? How do people, especially people of color, transform literacy to their own purposes beyond the ideologically infused belief (or faith) in its transformative power?

In this project I attempt to answer these questions in specific contexts, examining the uses of literacy in the lives of Asian Americans and in relation to the exemplary literacy narratives of other overdetermined subjects. Part of the work of *Minor Re/Visions* is to provide some contextual background for reading the literacy narratives of Asian Americans. As Brandt has explained, a contextual perspective on literacy can bring "attention to specific material facts of people's experiences with literacy" (4). With this in mind I offer a broad definition of literacy as a starting point with the belief that the specific conditions and work of each narrative that I discuss here provide its own nuanced definition of literacy and offer a clear purpose for that writer and text. Here I suggest that literacy is the creation and use of texts (in a most general sense) in our everyday lives. Such an understanding of literacy is influenced by Brian Street's definition of literacy practices which "refers to both behaviour and the social and cultural conceptualizations that give meaning to the uses of reading and/or writing" (2). Because of my own interest in examining the literacy practices of diverse communities, I have found the work of Anne Ruggles Gere particularly informative. Gere's argument in *Intimate Practices* that clubwomen enacted important cultural work—the insertion of themselves into civil society—through their literacy practices provides me with a conceptual framework as I examine the type of cultural work enacted by

Asian Americans through their literacy practices (2). In Robert Yagelski's *Literacy Matters*, I find a useful working definition:

> Literacy . . . is at heart an effort to construct a self within ever-shifting discourses in order to participate in those discourses; that effort is always local in the sense that any construction of a self within discourse, although inherently social, is mediated by a variety of factors unique to a specific act of reading and writing within a specific situation. (9–10)

And from the work of Jay Robinson, I adopt a commitment to social justice through the teaching and enactment of literacy when he envisions literacy as the

> means for students to connect what is deeply personal with what can be made deeply and meaningfully public in attempts to make and remake public spaces of dialogue and possibility—places where we can meet one another, perhaps as friends, even as we act out in words and actions our own peculiar identities, obligations, and responsibilities. (5)

Because of these influences, I offer a broad sense of what the purpose and cultural work of literacy can be because I hope to illustrate in this book that literacy, as Street, Gere, Yagelski, and Robinson have suggested, is more than demonstrating "schooled literacy," those acts of reading and writing that have become accepted as the credentials for full and active citizenship. What I hope to suggest in *Minor Re/Visions* is that living a life filled with literacy is full of both pleasure and pain. Pleasure from those first scribbles with a crayon to the self-awareness of reading a book for the first time to the exchange of intimate notes with a loved one; and pain from the dirty looks from someone who disapproves of your accent or sees you as uneducated because you use "can" instead of "may" or compliments you on the quality of your English despite your status as a native speaker. Intertwined with these literate acts are social contexts that are inextricably tied to the ways we are perceived to be literate. The pleasure and pain of literacy is both public and private, acting in the construction of a sense of self and citizenship.

In each of the following chapters I examine the uses and cultural work of literacy narratives through the conceptual terms I have briefly outlined here: citizenship and cultural citizenship, the minor, re/vision, and literacy. I want to understand how citizenship and cultural citizenship become important tropes to describe a person's relationship to America, to both strive for full recognition and challenge the requirements for recognition. In these narratives it is important to understand the "minor" positions that are constructed in order to complicate dominant narratives about literacy and race. Understanding citizenship and the "minor" can lead to the re/vision of citizenship and the ways we use literacy to construct citizenship. However, certain terms may be foregrounded more than others as I see a narrative working in a particular way. For example, Maxine Hong Kingston's "Song of a Barbarian Reed Pipe" is an especially effective discussion about the politics of literacy and silence and the position of the minor subject, while Lois-Ann Yamanaka's *Wild Meat and the Bully Burgers* focuses on the connection between literacy and race, and an attendant anxiety about citizenship. While each chapter may focus on particular aspects of literacy narratives, my goal is to put citizenship and cultural citizenship, the minor, re/vision, and literacy in conversation with each other so that we may begin to understand the cultural work performed by people of color, in particular, by Asian Americans. Woven throughout these chapters is my own literacy narrative as I trace my own relationship with literacy, coming to racial and political consciousness, and becoming a teacher and researcher of literacy. By writing my own narrative here, I hope to provide a map for understanding how literacy, race, and citizenship interact.

Chapter 1, "Re/Visions: Narrating Literacy and Citizenship," discusses the ways literacy and citizenship are written by American culture. Through the use of memoir, writers have often narrated their experiences with education both broadly and traditionally conceived, describing institutional and extracurricular sites of learning. But beyond the traditional bildungsroman, a specific genre of memoir has emerged: the literacy narrative. Literacy narratives also trace personal growth and development but with special attention to an individual's relationship to language or literacy. In this chapter, I examine the development of the "literacy narrative" genre as the writing of the American Story. Building upon critical work by Janet Carey Eldred and Peter Mortensen, who provide a taxonomy of the literacy narrative, I extend their discussion to first show why literacy narratives are particularly useful in expressing American citizenship and then discuss why they are key in both form (in their conventional and innovative narrative strategies) and function (for specific pedagogical and political purposes) for writers of color. The use of the literacy narrative is part of the process in becoming minor, a position described by Gilles Deleuze and Felix Guattari and Abdul JanMohamed and David Lloyd. As a way to trace the development of the genre and to illustrate becoming minor, I interject parts of my literacy narrative to provide a specific contextual perspective. Using literacy artifacts from my own literacy history, I begin to read the larger narrative of literacy through my personal texts, examine the impact of American culture in my personal stories, and explore the meanings of citizenship.

Chapter 2, "Reading Literacy Narratives," examines the construction of literacy and citizenship in minor narratives by Richard Rodriguez *(Hunger of Memory)*, Victor Villanueva Jr. *(Bootstraps: From an American Academic of Color)*, Carlos Bulosan *(America Is in the Heart)*, and Maxine Hong Kingston ("Song of a Barbarian Reed Pipe" from *The Woman Warrior*). I focus on these texts here for two purposes: First, I read them as exemplars of the literacy narrative, providing key moments for discussing the personal and public uses of literacy in their formal and extracurricular sites of education. These narratives also clearly connect issues of literacy with issues of racial and ethnic subjectivity and citizenship within the community, illustrating the process of becoming minor. Second, I read these narratives to complicate the American racial landscape, to see discussions about race and literacy beyond the often dominant paradigm of Black and White. By reading Rodriguez and Villanueva, I draw an analogy between the status of Latinos and Asians in America. While these groups have very different histories in America and are even widely heterogeneous within their own racial categories, they are both subject to overdetermined constructions as "foreign" or "alien" as well as non–English speaking, a questioning of their literacy. In reading Rodriguez and Villanueva, I lay a foundation for understanding the particular problems of those whose position in America is brought into question because their status in America as "legitimate" citizens (or at least residents) is in question. I then transition to Carlos Bulosan, whose Filipino background bridges the position between Rodriguez and Villanueva (as subjects of both Spanish and U.S. colonialism) and the place of Asians in America. In focusing on Maxine Hong Kingston's "Song for a Barbarian Reed Pipe," I examine the difficulties faced by the first American-born generation, where silence and literacy operate in the teaching of American citizenship. My discussion here is not meant to be a close reading of these texts alone but rather also a discussion of my encounters with these texts and my reading process. These texts have helped me approach and complicate the reading of literacy narratives by other writers of color and to begin to understand what a rhetoric of citizenship for Asian Americans may look like and how it may work.

Chapter 3, "Reading Hawai'i's Asian American Literacy Narratives," examines a specific context for reading literacy narratives as a response to racism, linguistic discrimination, and other attempts at "othering." In particular, I examine the history of Hawai'i's system of English Standard schools and then turn to two scenes of re/vision where students must confront and respond to the ways they have been constructed as illiterate. Marie Hara and Lois-Ann Yamanaka focus on the anxieties caused by schooling and the politics of Standard English, manifesting a resistant literacy for Hawai'i's Asian Americans in the use of Pidgin. While there is much anxiety about language and the "necessity" of Standard English, Pidgin becomes a language that inverts its "lack" into a "presence" that binds together a community dealing with a legacy of racism and social injustice. The continual debate about Pidgin in Hawai'i illustrates the anxiety that still exists for local residents who still see themselves in tension with the rest of the United States. In these Hawai'i Asian American narratives we see the position of the minor come into play. In their uses of literacy and language, the characters in the narratives by Hara and Yamanaka deterritorialize dominant discourse, move toward political action, and provide collective experiences that complicate dominant narratives about Asian Americans. In these cases, literacy narratives are a way for those in minor positions to re/vision what citizenship and literacy can mean, to provide alternatives to the American Story.

Chapter 4, "Teaching Literacy Narratives," discusses the uses of literacy narratives in our classrooms. While literacy narratives are often employed in the classroom as a way to create pathos and to demonstrate the ethos of writers, to see these writers and their projects as "models" for student writers, they can be even more effective by drawing students into conversations with these narratives. By using the conceptual terms and tropes of citizenship and cultural citizenship, the minor, re/vision, and literacy, students can productively engage the experiences of others rather than simply appropriate or recolonize these experiences. While the material conditions of an individual are affected by social class, gender, race and ethnicity, or other "minor" positions, students can begin to move toward understanding what it means to be minor by both reading and writing literacy narratives that challenge their safe positions. In having students read and write literacy narratives I want to move them toward re/vision, both metaphorically and literally—to have them re/vision their positions in America and to have them re/vision their work in the classroom.

Chapter 5, "Personal/Public/Professional," considers the implications for our research, teaching, and profession as we continue to think about the uses of the personal, what the minor means in our classroom, and how we participate both in and beyond our institutions. As a teacher and scholar of color, I choose to use the personal in my research because it provides a context for understanding how and why I apply specific analytical frames to the subjects I study.

The personal becomes more than ornamentation or a merely subjective point of view. The personal contributes to understanding the multiple locations we occupy as researchers, teachers, and citizens, and we must be willing to interrogate the personal if we are to fully understand the many contexts for the uses of literacy. As a teacher and scholar of color, I also choose to insert the minor into my classroom, to interrogate what a concept like "diversity" means to people today and what it can mean for people in the future. Rather than rely on domesticated meanings of diversity or the minor or race or other categories of difference, I want to use the classroom to re/vision these concepts and to create new meanings that move students and teachers to critical consciousness. And finally, as a person of color, I choose to consider the condition of race because I believe, despite domesticated discourses about the value of diversity and belief in equality, despite rhetoric that suggests race is overemphasized and made into a problem, that race does (as do many forms of difference) have material consequences, a fact often elided in an American Story that tells us that race can be *overcome* in order to achieve our Dream. The key question that organizes this chapter is this: What does it mean to become a public citizen from a minor position? I argue that being minor is in fact already a public act, an act that inserts the minor into the conversation with dominant American culture, which must now account for the array of diverse voices already present.

I end with a coda: "American Re/Visions." This refrain reminds us of why the issues I raise in *Minor Re/Visions* are important in our work as researchers, teachers, and citizens. In the wake of September 11, 2001, thinking about literacy issues and the teaching of writing seemed to be a minor priority. But as electronic discussion groups buzzed with advice on how to use writing as a way to cope with the tragic events, it became clear to me and many others that writing and literacy were central in engaging the dominant narratives about race and citizenship that now fed our anxieties about an uncertain future and the unquestioned (and unquestionable) nostalgia of nationalism. The position of the minor and the need for re/vision is even more critical as we are faced with dominant discourses that construct race and citizenship in even more problematic ways, as official institutions become even more powerful and prevalent in the silencing of minor voices.

Let me continue with my literacy narrative. Perhaps it was just a coincidence that I grew up on School Street, on the edge of downtown Honolulu in the working-class neighborhood of Kalihi. Within two blocks of my home was the neighborhood public library, a Hawaiian history museum, and just one house over, the public elementary school I attended. When I think back over my childhood, I am amazed at these resources that were available to me. The library, museum, and school were not the imposing institutional structures of education that we often romanticize, or perhaps reduce them to. They were the places I played, explored with friends and family, and saw as an everyday part of my life. I was lucky to live on School Street.

However, the meaning of growing up on School Street became more complicated as I pursued a career in teaching and research. I learned the history of the school next door and found out it was an English Standard school during Hawai'i's territorial years, admitting only those students who used "correct" English and spoke with no accent. And the museum down the block is a constant reminder of the struggle of Hawai'i's indigenous people and the immigrants brought in to work the sugar and pineapple plantations. What was a simple memory of childhood has become for me a reminder of the importance of educational opportunity for a wide range of students who may be placed on the margins simply because of their backgrounds. My neighborhood is infinitely more complicated than I ever imagined. But these complications enrich a person's life: the stuff of education is messy and difficult and rewarding and meaningful. Like School Street, my education and my work have become noisy and busy. Like School Street, my teaching and research about literacy issues have become home. Like my memories of School Street, I re/vision my life and literacy and continue to write my story.

1 / Re/Visions: Narrating Literacy and Citizenship

Personal Re/Vision

February 1, 1973: Speech evaluated—Missing central incisors. No apparent speech defect; however omits initial /s/ in blends (st, sw). Difficulty could be due to missing teeth. Good stimulability—Recheck. Waiting list. *J. Takano*, Speech therapist.

I look up from my chair at the stranger who has come to take me to an unfamiliar classroom. My legs dangle over the chair seat, feet not reaching the floor as I prepare to hop off. The building this classroom is in is different from my school— more sterile and hospital-like with the long corridors and chairs placed outside doors along the hall. In the yard there are no swings or jungle gyms to play on (a strange absence, I think now, if this were indeed another school).[1] *As we enter the classroom, I notice the walls are not covered with kiddy cartoon figures or alphabet letters or big funny pictures like my kindergarten classroom. And it's dark. Not pitch black but more gray and gloomy as if a storm were approaching this room alone.*

The walls are hospital green—not quite the blue-green of the ocean but not grass green either; more the pale mint of tooth paste. The furniture is familiar with kid-size tables and chairs. Easels stand on either side of the table—one with a paper pad and markers propped up on it, the other holds a felt-covered board with felt letters, numbers, and shapes that stick to it.

Mom and Dad wait on the other side of the closed door as

I sit across from a young woman. She looks like a teacher but is friendlier than the teachers I knew back at my kindergarten. She asks me questions, has me pronounce words and letter-sounds and read a little. I do as I am told, unsure why I am being drilled this way, especially when everything is so easy. I know my alphabet—A, B, C, D, E, F, G, H, and the rest. I read a little—"See Spot run" or some other simple sentence. And I answer all of her questions—"How old are you?" "I am six. My birthday was last month. I go to Kapalama School." Why was I pulled away from my Saturday morning cartoons (though I remember vaguely being bribed with the promise of a chocolate covered wafer bar)? Why was I in another classroom far away from my regular school that was just next door to my home?

January 1, 1974: Speech eval.: Spacing bet./teeth—Slightly distorted /s/. Often omits /s/ in blends. Difficulty with /l/. Enroll for therapy. *J. Takano,* Speech therapist.

I walk up to the main office building, leaving behind the rest of my classmates in room 34. This has become a weekly routine as I miss story hour every Tuesday to meet with Mrs. S. But Mrs. S is nice and I don't mind talking with her. It's those worksheets that annoy me. Why do I need to fill the sheet with Ls and Ss? Why do I have to practice the ST and SW sounds when I can do them already? But I bring home the worksheets to show Mom. "Look Mom. Listen Mom. S S S S S. ST ST ST ST ST. L L L L L." I continue to practice even when my missing tooth makes the air whistle through the gaps. (Then, I remember, I stop going to speech therapy. I don't know why. It just seemed to stop. I stayed in room 34 and sat for story hour with my classmates on Tuesdays now.) *Sometimes I stop by the main office building on my way home and say "hi" to Mrs. S.*

April 18, 1974: Speech re-eval. No further therapy recommended. *J. Takano.*

I begin with a personal memory, a narrative re/vision of an experience and an identity I will narrate throughout this book. I also begin with a literacy artifact from my life—the speech pathologist reports on my school health card—and a memory of that time (see fig. 1.1). This health card was one of the many artifacts collected by my mother and saved in the file she kept about each of her five children. The file is selective and includes many of the expected things: report cards, notices of achievement, important school and personal records. But then there is also a hodge-podge of items that illustrate a life filled with language and literacy. There are items that reflect the pleasures of language and literacy: a calendar my mom used to track my first year of life and the verbal utterances I made, story hour programs, and my first library card (see figs. 1.2–1.5).

As I reflect back on my life it is not surprising that some of my most vivid memories from my childhood are about language. My opening memory about that Saturday morning speech evaluation is often replayed in my head as I look out at my classes everyday and speak publicly with them. I wonder how much this early experience with language has shaped my life. Is it just coincidence that the study of language has become part of my professional life? Why did

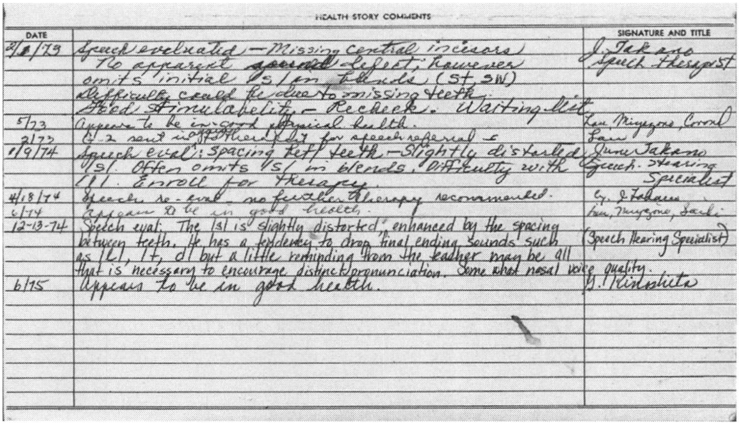

Figure 1.1

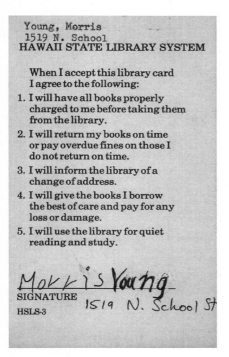

Figure 1.2

I become engaged with language rather than alienated like so many other students who may have had similarly "negative" experiences? Or was it a negative experience? Despite the "scariness" of being evaluated and the potential for resentment as I was sent off by myself on those afternoons, I was comfortable with language and perhaps even amused at the treatment I was receiving. I remember dutifully (perhaps even gleefully) practicing my phonics exercises because I wanted to demonstrate that I was capable, more than capable of acquiring these language abilities. Yet, I still wondered why there was so much interest in me. What about those other kids who seemed to have the same "problems" but did not receive the same attention I did? Was I treated differently because I came from a family familiar to my teachers, teachers who knew that the Young children were studious and "good"?

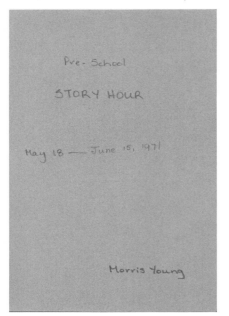

Figure 1.3

Figure 1.4

Figure 1.5

In this memory, I see Sylvia Scribner's three metaphors for literacy—Adaptation, Power, and State of Grace—often the common tropes that drive our narratives about literacy and citizenship. I see Adaptation in my experience with the speech pathologist where I needed (or was expected) to modify and develop my language skills to participate fully in school, to acquire the abilities that would begin to fulfill the promise of citizenship in America. Literacy as Power becomes clear as I unpack the literacy history of Hawai'i's public school system and learn about the linguistic discrimination faced by my parents' generation because their race was often conflated with their literacy levels, discrimination that often kept white Americans and nonwhite Americans separate despite their equal claims to citizenship. And perhaps I am experiencing literacy as a State of Grace now since I am able to make language my career and experience the promise of literacy—a good education and a good job—fulfilling the American Dream and reaping the benefits of American citizenship. There are variations in these stories about literacy, but usually recognizable characters, themes, and actions emerge to create a familiar cultural script. Scribner's metaphors of literacy operate within these stories to naturalize experiences and create master narratives of transformation and success that seem like easily achievable and desirable goals. These stories can evoke nostalgia, recuperating meaning for those who want to remember their literacy experiences in uncomplicated ways and who seek confirmation of their place in society; this is the artifice of literacy. It is through our artifacts of literacy that we can disrupt the nostalgia and begin to unpack the hidden histories about our literacies. And as I consider my own struggles with literacy and citizenship, I can acknowledge the struggles of others who have often found themselves unsure, confused, and immersed in the contradictions of their lives and literacy.

In the rest of this chapter, I will discuss the literacy narrative and its emergence as a genre. I will also consider how "minority discourse" can inform the literacy narrative and begin to read how my own personal literacy narrative converges with public narratives about literacy to suggest a rhetoric of citizenship. In these narratives and throughout this study, I will begin to unpack Scribner's metaphors of Adaptation, Power, and State of Grace and show how they inform my readings of literacy, race, and citizenship. As these personal and public narratives converge, Scribner's metaphors undergo re/vision by minor subjects in order to transform literacy to their own rhetoric of citizenship.

Public Re/Vision

> Literacy, then, as a measure of modernity, on either the individual or the societal level, becomes a symbol—and just as its benefits are located in the areas of abstraction and symbolism, so are its functions.
> —Harvey Graff, *The Literacy Myth*

When change does occur and as the king elides into the president, those who continue to hold power and position

within a society must contrive documents or proclamations that articulate a carefully limited and defined concept
of progress which does not contravene their status: a new
deal, a great society, a light at the end of the tunnel. In a
word, ideology persists and is both less and more than history. It is an attempt to *sell* history, to sell an interpretation
of the time and place in which men and women live their
lives to those same men and women.

   —Cathy N. Davidson, *Revolution and the Word*

[The scholarship boy] would like to be a citizen of that
well-polished, prosperous, cool, book-lined and magazine-
discussing world of the successful intelligent middle-class
which he glimpses through doorways or feels awkward
among on short visits, aware of his grubby finger-nails.

   —Richard Hoggart, *The Uses of Literacy*

Just as the personal memory I began with is a narrative re/vision of
experience and citizenship, I begin a public narrative about literacy
with the above epigraphs because they each describe and critique a
public re/vision of literacy, of the importance that our culture places
on discursive practices, whether it is a set of defined skills known
as literacy (i.e., reading and writing), the construction of sociocultural narratives known as histories, ideologies, and the like, or the
production of material texts such as books and magazines that can
indicate various levels of social status. More simply, though, I find
that these passages also explain our interest in (or our attraction to)
stories about education in general and about literacy and language
in specific—public narratives that inform at least part of a cultural
identity that values literacy. Harvey Graff's suggestion that literacy
becomes a symbol recognizes how much our culture infuses meaning into it: acquiring literacy makes for a good story as our culture
values the rags-to-riches fable of individual achievement through
self-education and hard work. The stories we tell about literacy become, in Cathy Davidson's words, "documents or proclamations
that articulate a carefully limited and defined concept of progress,"

and often act to reinforce the ideologies of Nation, to demonstrate the achievement of democracy. And finally Richard Hoggart's description of the "scholarship boy" illustrates the desire that is cultivated for literacy, not just as a means for education or improved life, but as the means to attain material wealth and social status—the rewards of hard work and a good education. In Hoggart's description, it is the "citizen" who already is the beneficiary of cultural and educational capital. Thus stories about education and literacy are not simply stories about learning to read and write; they are attempts to define who we are and what we want to become, both as individuals and as a community.

In his book *The Call of Stories*, Robert Coles tells us that "one keeps learning by teaching fiction or poetry because every reader's response to a writer's call can have its own startling, suggestive power" (xix). As a teacher, I value the emphasis that Coles places on pedagogy and how a teacher's own learning can inform his or her practice. As a reader and student of literature, I also believe that Coles is right when he suggests that the "call of stories" plays a very important role in a reader's life. When we read stories we attempt, whether consciously or unconsciously, to make a connection between stories and our lives. Those narratives about education, about literacy and language, hold even more sway because our memories about these types of experiences (whether negative or positive) resonate with a bit of "truth," as we can often find at least a glimmer of familiarity and can often read these fictions through our own experiences.

However, as the passages from Graff, Davidson, and Hoggart also point out, there is a danger in the way we use stories. Our attraction to stories is due partly to our attempts to see ourselves or aspects of our lives in them; to read the narrative of another's life is to sometimes read (or attempt to read) the narrative of our own life. But it is this very desire of the reader that can be exploited, providing the possibility that stories may be employed in ideological projects that act to advance particular views rather than allowing readers to transform stories into the self-examination of their own lives.

Harold Rosen suggests that we keep in mind these "basics of narrative" when we read and think about stories:

1. that it matters *which* stories we work with and that remembering and comprehending are especially related to the power of a story to engage with the world of feeling and thought in the listener;
2. that receiving a story is an exploration by the receiver(s), not a set of responses to someone else's questions in right/ wrong format;
3. that we should ask *why* we should remember a story and not simply *what* we remember;
4. that the most constructive way of examining the hold a story has is for it to be presented in a propitious context and to be retold in an equally propitious one. (229)

Rosen's "basics" provide us with not only a way to approach stories, but also with a way to approach the use of story in our culture. In these guidelines he recognizes the interestedness in the telling and use of story. To counter this, he proposes a set of critical methods that *readers* of story must utilize in order to understand how a story is working beyond the narrative structures of plot, character, and setting, and in our own larger structures of culture and society. These guidelines seem like common sense since they build upon a reader's own interest in reading story. And yet the very need to articulate a critical approach to reading suggests that we are more often *uncritical* in our reading, that we easily accept plot, character, or setting because of their familiarity, or transform the elements of story into a recognizable form that relieves the anxiety or discomfort experienced by a reader. Thus, the potential of stories in our lives becomes a danger if it acts to fill a void through diversion, through providing simply entertainment or domesticated knowledge, rather than to help us in creating our own meaningful narratives.

Stories can provide us with a sense of belonging, can appeal to

our desire to belong, or even confirm our belief that we do not quite
fit in. While the power of story is that it can bridge differences and
appeal to many, this is also its danger. As Rosen notes:

> The very universality of narrative contains its own surrep-
> titious menace. Stories are used to manipulate, advertise,
> control, above all to soothe, to massage us into forgetful-
> ness and passivity. They are, in the original sense of the
> word, diversions. (236)

The universality of narrative acts to create a community, but while
community can provide a sense of purpose through the production of common practices and goals, it can also result in a sense of
reality with a very limited view: whatever or whoever falls outside
the parameters of the community simply is not part of the story.
Raymond Williams's definition of community is similar to Rosen's
description of story as soothing, "massag[ing] us into forgetfulness
and passivity." Williams writes:

> Community can be the warmly persuasive word to de-
> scribe an existing set of relationships, or the warmly per-
> suasive word to describe an alternative set of relationships.
> What is most important, perhaps, is that unlike all other
> terms of social organization (state, nation, society, etc.) it
> seems never to be used unfavourably, and never to be given
> any positive opposing or distinguishing term. (*Keywords* 66)

The persuasiveness of story and community can act in the erasure
of subjects who do not fit easily into either the story or community.
In the attempt to create a universal and unifying narrative, stories
can erase those minor narratives that tug and pull at the margins
and bring into question the universality of a story. Minor narratives
are either dismissed as unimportant or too radical, or are "rewritten" to appeal to the larger culture, making sure that the unfamiliar
becomes familiar even if it means relying upon stereotype or other
overdetermined representations. As Jerome Bruner argues, "The

function of the story is to find an intentional state that mitigates or at least makes comprehensible a deviation from a canonical cultural pattern" (49–50). So if a minor subject cannot be rewritten in order to fit the cultural script of the story, then the minor subject must be explained away as unassimilable or even as a threat to the community. Thus in our culture, stories about education and literacy are often read as stories about becoming American, about the transformation from cultural Other into legitimate American subjects. And as Janet Carey Eldred points out, despite the controversy over cultural literacy in curricular matters and readings of conflicts between literacies, "the myths of self-reliance and of the self-made man who transcends his environment, who succeeds despite his origins, *still bolster critical readings*" (696, emphasis added). No matter what ideological or political project is at hand, the trope of literacy as transformation or conversion or State of Grace occupies an important place in the American consciousness because it brings us back to those nationalist fantasies of self-reliance and success through hard work that have been part of our country's imagined narrative history and character. This is the National Symbolic suggested by Lauren Berlant, where the production of fantasy, the use of traditional icons, metaphors, rituals, and narratives "provide an alphabet for a collective consciousness or subjectivity" (20).

With these uses for story in mind, especially in the project of American culture, I want to suggest how literacy narratives in both form and function are used in the process of minor re/vision. I begin by plotting a genealogy of the literacy narrative and then turn to an examination of the process of "becoming minor." Building upon autoethnographic strategies and theories of minority discourse and emergent culture, I suggest that to become minor is an act that creates the possibility for interacting with and responding to dominant culture. Thus, racialized subject positions, as one form of becoming minor, provide a primary condition in the production and emergence of literacy narratives. As those in minor positions produce these literacy narratives, they also begin a discursive process of cultural citizenship, a way to describe the constructed relations between individuals and the larger culture that dictate the ways these minor writers participate in these communities, how these communities construct them, and how these minor writers locate themselves in America. In understanding the form and function of the literacy narrative, and the related processes of becoming minor and cultural citizenship, I move toward minor re/vision, a process that intervenes into existing discourses of power and both acknowledges and rewrites the American story.

Like discussions about literacy, discussions about literacy narratives have seemingly mushroomed overnight. Perhaps as a response to the discourse of crisis that has surrounded public talk about literacy in recent years (but as history shows has always been an issue), stories about literacy seem to be everywhere. For a number of years in literary studies, recuperative projects, especially in African American and feminist literary studies, have brought previously unacknowledged texts to public attention. Often these texts have been autobiographical or narrative in form, which invites particular kinds of readings. For example, bildungsroman, conversion narratives, or memoir are recognized as specific genres but in general are stories that describe an individual's entry and relationship to culture through life experiences that have been educational. Even the recent trend of literary memoir, academic autobiography, and personal disclosure gives attention to narrative and self-reflection and often includes a transformative educational, language, or literacy experience.

Another gauge of the rise in consciousness and study about literacy issues in general and about literacy narratives in particular can be found in a survey of convention programs of the Conference on College Composition and Communication. An examination of programs in the 1990s reveals a steady increase in papers and sessions about literacy, from six and five "Literacy" sessions in 1990 and 1991 respectively to a high of 252 sessions in 1994.[2] There is also a steady increase in papers about literacy narratives. That is, there has been growing attention to the use and reading of narrative as a way of teaching and studying literacy practices. Conference papers range from the study of more well-known narratives by

Frederick Douglass, Richard Rodriguez, and Mike Rose, to the accounts written by our students for first-year composition courses.

In their essay "Reading Literacy Narratives," Janet Carey Eldred and Peter Mortensen discuss the possibilities of a specific area of rhetorical criticism—literacy studies—in the study of literary texts. They see their project moving beyond the initial project of literacy studies to "define and describe literacy in the language of formal scholarship" and toward analyzing literacy as an element and product of culture that is reflected in literary texts (512). As part of this move they introduce a term, "literacy narrative," to describe a particular genre of literary texts that has often been discussed but never named to reflect the explicit aspects of literacy and language acquisition that are central to the story.[3] While Eldred's essay, "Narratives of Socialization: Literacy in the Short Story" is the initial introduction of the term, "literacy narrative," Eldred and Mortensen's essay does the work of sorting out a number of similar and related genres that each use literacy and education broadly defined as central themes:

The *literacy myth* grows out of the easy and unfounded assumption that better literacy necessarily leads to economic development, cultural progress, and individual improvement. For example, while it is often assumed that literacy is a prerequisite to modernization and progressive urban cultures, some studies propose that literacy may actually decline as population density increases. The concept of the literacy myth, then, prompts us to interrogate what are often taken as "natural" assumptions about connections between schooling and social mobility (see Graff).

Narratives of socialization are stories that chronicle a character's attempt to enter a new social (and discursive) arena. Many texts, especially coming-of-age stories that show characters negotiating the world around them, often contain detailed and insightful investigations of how language is acquired and how it creates particular regional and private identities. In these narratives, literacy is a necessary component although it is not emphasized (see Eldred).

Literature of the contact zone is that fiction authored in colonial contexts or out of colonial histories. It studies the particular problems of forcing a sanctioned literacy on colonized subjects and examines, among other things, the role of "autoethnography" in resisting legislated representations (see Pratt).

Finally, what we call *literacy narratives* are those stories, like Bernard Shaw's *Pygmalion,* that foreground issues of language acquisition and literacy. These narratives are structured by learned, internalized "literacy tropes" (Brodkey 47), by "prefigured" ideas and images (see White 1–23). Literacy narratives sometimes include explicit images of schooling and teaching; they include texts that both challenge and affirm culturally scripted ideas about literacy. (512–13)

Eldred and Mortensen are careful to point out that they are distinguishing between similar and related terms "not to stake out definitions for their own sake, but to situate our work and to tease out strands of narrative possibility" (512). I would like to add another term to their taxonomy coined by Alice Yeager Kaplan, "language memoir," which I think also works to develop connections and possibilities among and beyond this subjectively organized body of texts. These connections and "strands of narrative possibility" raise the question of genre: Do these varied stories about literacy constitute a genre? How do these varied stories about literacy constitute a genre?

In her essay, "On Language Memoir," which followed the publication of her self-described memoir, *French Lessons,* Alice Yeager Kaplan discusses the attraction of a genre she calls "language memoir." Kaplan begins her essay by reflecting on what it means to write her own story about learning French and how she becomes aware of the complexities of language and identity. Though the issues of language and identity that she raises from her own experience are different from the ones I have raised thus far or will be examining later (she is an academic at an elite university writing about acquiring French as opposed to learning English or developing literacy from a minor position of race or social class), Kaplan's discussion of "language memoir" is useful in building upon the terms defined by Eldred and Mortensen and as a pretext for the ways I will be discussing literacy narratives.[4] She writes:

> What I was looking for was not theory, but fiction. When I turned to fiction I found, to my delight, that there is an entire genre of twentieth-century autobiographical writing which is in essence about language learning. But it has never been categorized or named as such, either because it is discussed in terms of the history of a specific ethnic or national literature, or because language is understood in these books as mere decor in a drama of upward mobility or exile.
>
> In the genre I am calling "language memoir," the second language is not always a "foreign" language; sometimes it is a new dialect, a language of upward mobility, a language of power or expressivity within the native language. (59)

What I find interesting about Kaplan's description of "language memoir" are the apparent contradictions in her formulation of the genre. She says she was looking not for theory but fiction, and yet I would argue that she does indeed find theory as she names a genre which is specifically about examining how language works in the formation of a self. Kaplan also creates a tension when she juxtaposes the terms "fiction" and "autobiography." While her desire for fiction may be simply a recognition of a postmodern construction of reality and the subjective nature of the autobiographical self in writing such a reality, I also think that this tension illustrates what Thomas O. Beebee has called "generic instability" (27). Kaplan's easy move from fiction to autobiography and her turn away from theory reveals how the generic boundaries between these categories of texts are actually governed by the critical frame perceived by both writer and reader and then applied because it meets his or her "use-value" for the text (Beebee 7). This is why Kaplan is able to "rewrite" those genres of ethnic or national literature and drama of upward mobility and exile as "language memoir": she has a need for fiction because it provides her with the ability to create new selves through language, to construct new stories about a new cultural awareness. For my purposes, I see theory in memoir because it is in the representation and use of language that I find ways to interpret these new selves, new stories, and new cultures. The categories of "fiction," "autobiography," "memoir," "theory," and unnamed others blend, and the distinctions blur until both writers and readers imbue these texts with a purpose and respond with a genre, the identification and application of form and function to carry out their particular project.

The literacy narrative fulfills a particular project: Writers and readers respond to the anxieties and crises that they face in their present cultural-historical circumstances by reading and writing in the genre of the literacy narrative. Whether it is responding to slavery in nineteenth-century America, Americanization campaigns of the early 1900s, or the "literacy crisis" of the 1970s and 1980s, the literacy narrative has emerged in many instances when marginalized peoples have been forced to prove their legitimacy as citizens or potential citizens through a demonstration of their literacy, education, and often a (cultivated) desire to join dominant culture. In each of the subgenres of literacy narrative defined by Eldred and Mortensen and Kaplan we find common tropes that set the conditions for the use-value of the narrative. Sanctioned literacy or language is represented as a goal, and students begin their process of Adaptation. The newly enlightened subject now becomes part of the community and enjoys the rights and privileges of membership (often represented as economic, political, cultural capital), the realization of Power. Through education, transformation or conversion is achieved, and these "citizens" enjoy a State of Grace. While each trope plays upon different expectations to varied degrees—

some tropes being more appealing than others—they all operate in the function of the narrative, as part of the rhetoric that attempts to persuade readers to a particular meaning. The subject position of those who write literacy narratives also contributes to this rhetoric and plays a critical role in determining the use-value of the narrative. The literacy narrative can act to confirm, transform, or even reject a person's participation in culture, raise questions about community identity and membership, or encourage participation of not only the writer but also the reader in making meaning from the narrative.

Though I will develop my discussion of the specific conditions under which literacy narratives are generated and revised by Asian American writers in later chapters, I do want to start here by suggesting that racialized subject positions are one of the primary conditions in their production and emergence. I do recognize that writers who occupy minor positions in other ways (i.e., gendered, classed, queered, Othered, etc.) also produce literacy narratives as responses to the ways they have been constructed by and excluded from dominant culture. However, I consider those who write from racialized subject positions in particular because they find themselves so ideologically infused by dominant culture and carrying so much cultural baggage that they are more susceptible to being read as noncitizens, often as "foreigners" in their own land. Though the expected impulse is to prove proficiency (even expertise) in Standard English, there is also an impulse to resist Standard English, or at least resist the imposition of Standard English. Thus the racialized subject reconfigures the literacy narrative as a strategy for resisting appropriation by a dominant American culture that imagines a unifying narrative of citizenship and culture through the naturalized discourse of Standard English by *denaturalizing* Standard English. In the story written by dominant American culture, racialized subjects are included only marginally, reduced to cultural Other, or presented as "good Americans" who have successfully assimilated. George Lipsitz's concept of "counter-memory" inverts this story, and cultural Others may begin to use local moments in order to critique larger master narratives of history and culture

(213). For Lipsitz, countermemory is a "way of remembering and forgetting that starts with the local, the immediate, and the personal" and "focuses on localized experiences with oppression, using them to reframe and refocus dominant narratives purporting to represent universal experience" (213). Thus in reading the uses of literacy through the local narratives of minor subjects, it is the inversion of Standard English, not the dismissal of it, that begins the process of analyzing literacy tropes and how they operate in literacy narratives. These strategies of recognizing the local, the immediate, and the personal, and how they re/vision dominant narratives guides my reading of the ways literacy, race, and citizenship operate in American culture.

While Eldred and Mortensen have already introduced Mary Louise Pratt's "literature of the contact zone" in their taxonomy, I want to take a closer look at her construction of what she calls autoethnography and discuss its importance as a narrative response to and by racialized writers. When the "contact zone" is invoked, it is often posited as the opposing term to "community" and is often reduced to meaning "conflict."[5] Pratt herself describes the "contact zone" as "those social spaces where cultures meet, clash, and grapple with each other, often in contexts of highly asymmetrical relations of power, such as colonialism, slavery, or their aftermaths as they are lived out in many parts of the world today" ("Arts" 34). Pratt theorizes a space where more complex action occurs and suggests that rather than simple conflict there is a type of collaboration that goes on in the relationship between dominant and nondominant, perhaps unwittingly or unstrategically, but collaborative just the same. An "autoethnographic" moment occurs when those who are in minor positions respond to the ways they have been represented through the production of their own representations. Pratt writes:

> Thus if ethnographic texts are those in which European metropolitan subjects represent to themselves their others (usually their conquered others), autoethnographic texts are representations that the so-defined others construct

in response to or in dialogue with those texts. Autoethnographic texts are not, then, what are usually thought of as autochthonous forms of expression or self-representation (as the Andean *quipus* were). Rather they involve a selective collaboration with and appropriation of idioms of the metropolis or the conqueror. These are merged or infiltrated to varying degrees with the indigenous idioms to create self-representations intended to intervene in metropolitan modes of understanding. Autoethnographic works are often addressed to both metropolitan audiences and the speaker's own community. Their reception is highly indeterminate. Such texts often constitute a marginalized group's point of entry into the dominant circuits of print culture. (35)

For racialized writers, autoethnography becomes a strategy and provides narrative form through which they can respond to the ways they have been represented by dominant culture. However, autoethnography also becomes a way to revise and critique the tropes utilized by dominant culture. While there are variations in the stories we tell about literacy, we usually rely upon (both in writing and reading literacy narratives) recognizable characters, themes, and actions, even employing (perhaps unconsciously) Scribner's metaphors of Adaptation, Power, and State of Grace. On one hand, acting to naturalize experiences, preach transformation, and offer hope, the literacy narrative can provide meaning for those who want to remember their literacy experiences in uncomplicated ways and reinforce their achievement in society. On the other hand, the literacy narrative can often be an unfamiliar story for those who have had very different literacy experiences. The literacy narrative can create anxiety rather than nostalgia because it can further marginalize those who have already been marked as Other by privileging one story over another. As Pratt points out, the reception of autoethnographic texts is "highly indeterminate." This is true of the literacy narrative in its autoethnographic form: these narratives produced by marginalized writers fulfill different purposes and desires for different audiences. However, this "highly indeterminate" status of the text also provides the possibility for re/vision to occur as the minor not only represent themselves but engage the ways dominant culture has constructed them.

Those who write literacy narratives are trying to tell stories that have often been hidden or ignored. But they also tell these stories as a way to create opportunities for engagement and interaction. The literacy narrative is inherently intertextual because it draws upon not only the generic conventions of literary representation but the larger sociohistorical and cultural texts that create the full portrait of a life narrated. The literacy narrative becomes more than just a story about acquiring language and education, more than a nostalgic remembrance or recounting of social and political struggles. The literacy narrative is a re/vision of those dominant narratives from the perspective of the minor subject, the autoethnographic process that unpacks the tensions between competing representations of literacy, race, and citizenship.

Becoming Minor

> I'm twelve and I'm stuck on the mainland without anything to do and no one to hang out with. My own family is holding me hostage. This family vacation has lasted too long I think to myself. We started two weeks ago in Seattle and made our way across Canada, down the East Coast, and now New Orleans. Why can't we just go home, to my comic books and friends?
>
> "Hey, look over here," my sister Genny calls to me.
>
> I drag myself over to a table she's standing next to. I'm expecting to see some New Orleans thing—voodoo dolls, pralines, or some such junk. I look down at the table and there are stacks and stacks of comic books. Not just newer comics, but lots of old ones too. Maybe I can find some X-Men or Legion of Superheroes, those really old ones that cost $2.00 at the collector's store. I'm excited as I start to rifle through the

stacks. No I have that one. What's with all of these old Super-
mans? Isn't there anything good here?
   "Hey boy!"
   I don't look up.
   "Hey boy! What'cha doing there?"
   I slowly raise my head and look over to where the voice
is coming from.
   "Hey! Can't cha read English? Don't cha know English?"
   A finger wags in my face as I follow where it points to:
"No Reading Comic Books" warns the sign.
   I look back at the man behind the finger. He's staring at
me with contempt. His plaid shirt is pulled over a big belly
and he leans toward me as he squints. I pull back, not sure
how to respond. "Of course I know English," I think to myself,
"Why do you think I'm looking at the comic books?" But I re-
main silent, unable to speak, unable to prove that I know En-
glish. I turn my back and walk away, feeling a little frightened
and a little indignant. Who is he to ask if I know English?

In New Orleans, at that comic book stand, was perhaps the first
time I understood myself as racially other. It's not that I didn't know
that I was of Asian ancestry. In fact in Hawai'i it was "normal." Most
of my friends were either Japanese or Chinese or Filipino (the American was assumed), and those *haole* (white) kids were the ones who
were probably going to stand out in my neighborhood. Racial othering had a different dynamic when I was growing up since it was
more likely that my friends and I would be placing those others not
like us on the margins. So when I found myself disempowered and
othered by that man in New Orleans, I felt both shame and confusion. Shame, because it was the color of my skin that seemed to
indict me. Confusion because this was perhaps the first time I experienced blatant racism. Race became a reality for me.

   What I found lacking was the ability to articulate the shame
and confusion. Outside of Hawai'i I had become a minority and did
not understand the ways language and dominant culture functioned

in this particular situation. I could have offered a retort in my "best" English to the comic book seller, but would this have made a difference? I could have said something in Hawai'i Pidgin but this may have only reinforced his perception of me as "illiterate." Or I could say nothing, which is what I did, as I searched for a way to process this experience, to understand what action I could have taken to assert my citizenship and to intervene in the dominant discourse of race that this man employed.

The possibilities of minority discourse provide a way to counter dominant discourses of race. Just as dominant discourses of race act to organize subjects into relations that will function in the maintenance of dominant culture, minority discourse acts to create alternative practices as well as to interact with and disrupt dominant discursive formations. In asking "what is a minor literature," Gilles Deleuze and Felix Guattari argue that "a minor literature doesn't come from a minor language; it is rather that which a minority constructs within a major language" (16). In particular they examine how Kafka, as a German Jew, staked out a minor position within the dominant culture of German language and literature, transforming dominant discourse to his own purposes. Minor literature works to deterritorialize language, connect the individual to political action, and provide a collective assemblage of enunciation (Deleuze and Guattari 18). Minor literature moves beyond the specific identification with a class of writer and toward the understanding of "revolutionary conditions for every literature within the heart of what it called great (or established) literature" (18).

Abdul JanMohamed and David Lloyd extend this theory of minor literature by Deleuze and Guattari and argue for a theory of minority discourse:

> However, an emergent theory of minority discourse must not be merely negative in its implications. Rather, the critique of the apparatus of universalist humanism entails a second theoretical task permitted by the recovery of excluded or marginalized practices. The positive theoretical work involves critical-discursive articulation of alternative

practices and values that are embedded in the often-dam-
aged, -fragmentary, -hampered, or -occluded works of minorities. This is not to reassert the exclusive claim of the
dominant culture that objective grounds for marginaliza-
tion can be read in the inadequacy or underdevelopment of
"minority" work. On the contrary, it is to assert that even
the very differences that have always been read as symp-
toms of inadequacy can be reread transformatively as the
indications and figurations of values radically opposed to
those of the dominant culture. A theory of minority discourse is essential precisely for the purposes of such re-
interpretation, for, in practice, the blindness of dominant
theory and culture towards the positive values of minority
culture can easily engulf us. (8)

Like Pratt's strategy of autoethnography, minority discourse, then,
can act to re/vision the dominant discourse of literacy and to transform it for the projects of minor subjects. As JanMohamed and
Lloyd point out, minority discourse is not "merely negative," not
simply the construction of an oppositional discourse or position to
the dominant. Rather, like autoethnography, minority discourses interact with dominant discourse because minor subjects understand
the material conditions under which they operate and must account
for their positions within dominant culture in order to critique it.
Raymond Williams's discussion of hegemony provides another important theoretical foundation for "minority discourse." In particular, Williams's use of the term "emergent" is critical in thinking
about the minor: "By 'emergent' I mean, first, that new meanings
and values, new practices, new relationships and kinds of relationships are continually being created" (*Marxism* 123). Williams's use
of "emergent" is useful because it describes the continual creation
of voices, of experiences, of stories despite attempts by dominant
culture to regulate these practices. As Williams argues, the emergent is "never only a matter of immediate practice; indeed it depends crucially on finding new forms or adaptations of form. . . .
active and pressing but not yet fully articulated" (*Marxism* 126). It

is this development of a minor position, something analogous to emergent culture, and its own use of dominant discourse that leads to the deterritorialization of dominant discourse.

In fact, JanMohamed and Lloyd argue that in order to be "minor," subject-position cannot help but be foregrounded. A "minor" subject cannot rely upon an authentic or essential position; this is how dominant culture constructs "minor" subjects. Rather, to assume a "minor" position is to understand how to articulate that position:

> "Becoming minor" is not a question of essence (as the stereotypes of minorities in dominant ideology would want us to believe) but a question of position: a subject-position that in the final analysis can be defined only on "political" terms—that is, in terms of the effects of economic exploitation, political disenfranchisement, social manipulation, and ideological domination on the cultural formation of minority subjects and discourses. The project of systematically articulating the implications of that subject-position —a project of exploring strengths and weaknesses, the affirmations and negations that are inherent in the position —must be defined as *the* central task of the theory of minority discourse. (9)

Their emphasis on subject-position is key, I think, as they suggest a strategy of understanding fully the implications of any move before making a move. "Becoming minor," then, is a conscious choice (as opposed to being simply an assigned position) that creates the possibility to respond to hegemonic culture without being subject to its construction alone of how someone from "minority" culture should act. By examining the implications of a minor subject-position, by realizing how a lack of political, economic, educational, and cultural capital can have material consequences, minor subjects can understand how they are being exploited and begin to develop strategies to address their oppression. This is the move to connect individuals to political action.

While the minor are subject to being constructed as a "generic" minority, this strategy of the dominant can give rise to a broad "coalition" response to hegemonic culture:

> However, more importantly, the collective nature of all minority discourse also derives from the fact that minority individuals are always treated and forced to experience themselves generically. Coerced into a negative, generic subject-position, the oppressed individual responds by transforming that position into a positive, collective one. Therein lies the basis of a broad minority coalition: in spite of the enormous differences among various minority cultures, which must be preserved, all of them occupy the same oppressed and "inferior" cultural, political, economic, and material subject-position in relation to Western hegemony. (10)

The construction of a broad minority coalition to respond to the discourse of literacy as the defining condition of American citizenship seems to me to be an important move that both allows for the re/vision of literacy and avoids any attempt by dominant culture to dismiss "nonliterate" or "illiterate" subjects. Rather than believe that "English-Only" policies are directed primarily at Spanish-speaking Latinos, or that Ebonics is an African American "problem," or that immigrant Asians keep to themselves in ethnic enclaves, there is a need to understand that coalition politics are an important act by a wide range of peoples in the interests of social justice. This is the collective, even revolutionary, assemblage of enunciation that complicates American dominant culture.

While Asian American subjects need to participate in these broad minority coalitions, I also believe that Asian Americans face their own specific difficulties when they participate in dominant discourses of literacy, race, and citizenship. Even when coalitions can function effectively as a political entity, there remains a necessity for specificity in understanding how particular cultural groups interact with dominant American culture, as well as acknowledging heterogeneity within these groups, which complicates expectations for generic representative experiences. In their study *Racial Formation in the United States*, Michael Omi and Howard Winant offer the following definition of "racial formation":

> We use the term *racial formation* to refer to the process by which social, economic and political forces determine the content and importance of racial categories, and by which they are in turn shaped by racial meanings. Crucial to this formulation is the treatment of race as a *central axis* of social relations which cannot be subsumed under or reduced to some broader category or conception. (61–62)

This definition provides a useful framework to consider the specific "meanings" that result from thinking about Asian American as a racial category. Included in these "meanings" are the ways literacy and citizenship are read through the racial category of Asian American as it operates as the "central axis of social relations." The Asian American subject, then, presents distinct differences (but not exceptions) from other racialized subjects because he or she will produce particular meanings based on the organization of social relations and the status of a specific racial discourse. Literacy and citizenship for Asian American subjects will be configured differently because of different social and cultural experiences as well as engagement with different cultural representations of Asian American literacy and citizenship by dominant culture. However, as part of becoming minor there is also a need to recognize a collective heterogeneity both within and among racialized subjects, acknowledging different histories and experiences but also acknowledging collective experiences of racism, discrimination, or other forms of racial formation imposed by dominant discourse.

Becoming a Citizen

> *"What do you mean you're getting naturalized?" I look intently at my friend, Alan, whom I had known since we both*

started middle school. "You're not a citizen?" "Do you have a green card?" I was puzzled (both then and now as I try to sort through this new awareness of something different between us).

"My parents," he began to explain, "are becoming citizens, and since I'm a minor I'm becoming one too."

Alan was Filipino but it never occurred to me that this meant he actually was a Filipino citizen. In Hawai'i you were Japanese or Chinese or Filipino or Samoan and the American was assumed. I knew that Alan had visited the Philippines, even for extended periods to visit family, though it never seemed like he was "from there." Alan had a slight accent of some sort but mostly talked like I did. He didn't dress like those FOB/FOP kids (Fresh Off the Boat/Fresh Off the Plane) we knew were newly arrived in Hawai'i from the Philippines or Laos or Samoa or some other non-American place. We had similar interests in sports and music; he seemed as "local" as any of the other kids I knew. But now he was different.

Even in a place like Hawai'i, where racial and ethnic difference was the norm and the immigrant generation often stretched back no further than your parents or grandparents, it seemed strange to me that a peer whom I had always assumed was like me was, in fact, not. Alan was not the last of my friends to be naturalized and to become a U.S. citizen. While Alan met the requirements to be naturalized as a minor because his parents were naturalized, I had other friends who did not become U.S. citizens until they reached their eighteenth birthday because their parents chose to remain U.S. resident aliens rather than give up their status as citizens in their home country. As I reflect on this common experience growing up in Hawai'i—not even being aware of a person's citizenship—I begin to understand how the concept of citizenship begins to shape our understanding of culture and the way we act within this culture. In becoming aware that Alan was not a citizen like I was a citizen, I began to read him differently, trying to detect any sign that would mark him as "foreign." And while I could perhaps hear more of an accent now, or see that he really wasn't dressing like the rest of us, these are differences that are more the result of the generic expectations I placed upon him as a noncitizen. What I did not understand was that Alan, though only now becoming a citizen in the legal sense, had already begun his own process of citizenship, where he was already making meaning through his interaction with American culture. Henry Giroux describes this process and correctly emphasizes its pedagogical aspects:

> The concept of citizenship must also be understood partly in pedagogical terms as a political process of meaning-making, as a process of moral regulation and cultural production, in which particular subjectivities are constructed around what it means to be a member of a nation state. (7)

Renato Rosaldo suggests a term, the "polyglot citizen," which is extended by Mary Louise Pratt to describe the "changing realities in the U.S., notably the arrival of large, new immigrant populations," but to also account for the realities of a polyglot history of the United States ("Daring" 6). The polyglot citizen, in Pratt's construction, is "a point of intersection of multiple threads that weave in and out to make the dense fabric of society" ("Daring" 8).

In these definitions of citizenship we see the tensions between dominant and minor emerge as claims on who can participate and in what way become central questions. Does legal status alone determine "citizenship?" Is legal status as a citizen enough to protect a minor subject from being constructed as Other? How do we re/vision citizenship into a productive critical process that creates and allows for mixed and multiple subjectivities and not the binary categories of citizen and alien?

P. Joy Rouse suggests a process for this re/vision, a rhetoric of citizenship, which I find compelling because it does not seek to define legal or strict criteria for what it means to be a citizen despite its reference to citizenship. Rather, it creates a space to consider the possibilities of what citizenship should be and how this meaning can be expanded to include those who have often been perceived as illegitimate or potentially illegitimate: "Located within the polis of America, rhetorics of citizenship work toward the common good of the country; within early nineteenth-century university practices, this meant that learning was for public use rather than for individual gain" (116). A rhetoric of citizenship works toward reexamining membership, looking at the needs and common good of an unrestricted public. Rouse develops this concept of a rhetoric of citizenship based on the writings of Margaret Fuller about the nineteenth-century conditions for women in America and their push to be included in the public life of the nation:

> My focus on alternative sites of and examples of rhetorics of citizenship demands a revised definition of the citizen. I use the term here to denote individuals' relationships to a number of contexts. Although Fuller, her students, and the women she addressed were not legally considered citizens by the United States government, I am more concerned with Fuller's vision of their possible roles as citizens in their immediate communities. I interpret Fuller's practice as a rhetoric of citizenship because she was engaged in issues of immediate concern to local communities. Using her as a "test case," I hope to indicate enriching possibilities for future work that will attend to the teaching, speaking, and writing practices of marginalized Americans without assimilating them into unchanged, traditional categories, work that will change these categories and create new ones. (116)

Like the concerns of nineteenth-century American women, the concerns of present day racialized writers demand a revised definition of citizenship. Just as Rouse does not focus as much on addressing the specific legal status of citizenship for women, I do not focus on legal definitions of citizenship except to consider some of the social contexts that provided for laws and policies that constructed racialized subjects as ineligible for citizenship. Rather, like Rouse, I want to emphasize the strategy of "cultural citizenship," a term suggested by Rosaldo to describe those subjects attending "not only to dominant exclusions and marginalizations, but also to subordinate aspirations for and definitions of enfranchisement" (37). Cultural citizenship describes the constructed relations between individuals and the larger culture that dictate the ways these writers participate in these communities, how these communities construct them, and how these writers locate themselves in America. Rouse suggests that engagement in local communities in and through local narratives will reconfigure the ways we think about citizenship and the nation. Rosaldo notes that "cultural citizenship" operates in "an uneven field of structural inequalities where the dominant claims of universal citizenship assume a propertied white male subject and usually blind themselves to their exclusions and marginalizations of people who differ in gender, race, sexuality, and age" (37). I find Rouse and Rosaldo useful in moving toward a strategy for minor subjects to re/vision citizenship and the Nation and to negotiate resistance put forth by dominant American culture.

As Lisa Lowe argues in her study *Immigrant Acts,* Asian American subjects, despite their native standing in the United States, are often constructed as Asian immigrant subjects:

> In the last century and a half, the American *citizen* has been defined over against the Asian *immigrant,* legally, economically, and culturally. These definitions have cast Asian immigrants both as persons and populations to be integrated into the national political sphere and as the contradictory, confusing, unintelligible elements to be marginalized and returned to their alien origins. "Asia" has been always a complex site on which the manifold anxieties of the U.S. nation-state have been figured: such anxieties have figured Asian countries as exotic, barbaric, and alien, and Asian laborers immigrating to the United States from the nineteenth century onward as a "yellow peril" threatening to displace white European immigrants. (4)

Because of the manifold anxieties about the meanings of U.S. citizenship, Asian bodies must be classified as alien despite both birthright and legal standing in the United States as citizens. America can maintain its cohesion as a "Nation" only if it can organize its subjects in ways that account for their difference but also subsume those differences, either by minimizing (assimilating) difference or maximizing (exposing) difference. This act of imagining becomes problematic as not only Asian bodies but all racialized bodies then become subject to the disciplining power of the state in order to maintain classifications for understanding "National" culture. As Lowe points out, national memory acts to account for the Asian American, linking this racialized subject to both historical and current social and geopolitical relations to Asia:

> Yet the project of imagining the nation as homogeneous requires the orientalist construction of cultures and geographies from which Asian immigrants come as fundamentally "foreign" origins antipathetic to the modern American society that "discovers," "welcomes," and "domesticates" them. A national memory haunts the conception of the Asian American, persisting beyond the repeal of actual laws prohibiting Asians from citizenship and sustained by the wars in Asia, in which Asian is always seen as an immigrant, as the "foreigner-within," even when born in the United States and the descendent of generations born here before. (5–6)

Asian American citizenship becomes problematic, then, if dominant culture always constructs Asian Americans as alien or assimilated alien. The narratives that Asian Americans produce, then, must problematize the construction of citizenship and engage those discourses that have narrated different histories for them if they are to operate constructively in the sense of minority discourse articulated by JanMohamed and Lloyd. Minor subjects must invert and expand the meaning of citizenship so that all subjects must rethink what it means to be a citizen:

Thus, "becoming a national citizen" cannot be the exclusive narrative of emancipation for the Asian American subject. Rather, the current social formation entails a subject less narrated by the modern discourse of citizenship and more narrated by the histories of wars in Asia, immigration, and the dynamics of the current global economy. These new conditions displace a former conception of culture and the formation of the citizen it upheld, generating the need for an alternative understanding of cultural production. These discussions consider Asian American culture as one terrain on which the subject formerly narrated by the discourse of citizenship is superseded by a differently located political subject. (33)

While I agree with Lowe's formulation of the Asian American subject on a new discursive field, I do want to question her replacement of the discourse of citizenship. As Sau-ling Wong also points out, there is a need to rethink the Asian American subject because of the changing demographics that make newly immigrated Asians the largest population among Asian and Asian American subjects in the United States ("Denationalization" 1). Wong suggests the need for denationalization, a strategy that blurs the boundaries between the Asian and Asian American subjects in order to develop more appropriate cultural criticism in a changing transnational sphere ("Denationalization" 5). Lowe is making a similar point by articulating the need to engage current histories and configurations of Asian and Asian American subjectivity. While I agree and understand this move by both Wong and Lowe, I find it difficult to move away from the discourse of citizenship partly because it is so ideologically infused. That is, while I understand the critique of citizenship and I agree that it is more useful to theorize Asian American subjectivity to account for an ever expanding field of play, I think it is still necessary to engage the discourse of citizenship in order to reconfigure it. This need for reconfiguration is like the process of autoethnography as minor subjects engage in dominant discourse to both participate in and critique dominant culture.

Thus rather than assuming a simply oppositional stance or

moving beyond "citizenship," it is the process of "minor re/vision" that intervenes into existing discourses of power, that both acknowledges and rewrites the American Story. I choose the term "minor re/vision" carefully, knowing that it may suggest that only "minor" changes need to occur. However, I invoke "minor" as a subject position, to suggest that those in "minor" positions need to both revise existing narratives about America to include themselves and offer a re-vision of what America is and can be.

While I have been attempting to theorize the position of minority discourse in dominant discourses of literacy, race, and citizenship, I think it is important to remember the implications and consequences when we engage these discourses. In many ways we are talking about culture and how culture uses discussions about literacy and citizenship to often talk about race. Geoffrey Nunberg's summary of the ideological implications of the English-Only movement has applications to my discussion about literacy, race, and citizenship:

> Even if the official-language movement is really an "official-culture movement," it could not have been formulated in such terms. We could not very well entertain a constitutional amendment that read, "The United States shall henceforth be officially constituted around such-and-such a conception of American culture." It is only when the issues are cast in terms of language that they become amenable to direct political action, and that culture can be made an official component of American identity. The great debate is in reading the debate as literally concerned with language alone—all the more because these are relatively new themes in the American political discourse, and we have no history of Language Questions to refer to. Of course, there are real questions of language at stake in all this, but they are not *merely* questions of language; they never are. (494)

Language, or for my purposes, literacy, becomes a guise under which issues of culture and citizenship can be discussed. And while

Nunberg points out that culture can never be explicitly referred to (although E. D. Hirsch does so couched in cultural literacy), constructions of American culture remain present in dominant discourses about language and literacy. The challenge is to present alternate constructions of culture that will not act to replace other constructions, but rather to provide appropriate forms for a polyglot citizenry.

Lowe articulates her own formulation of Asian American culture. I see this formulation of culture as an opportunity to read dominant discourses of literacy, race, and citizenship and to read the literacy narratives of Asian Americans as the cultural work that re/visions America:

> Asian American culture is the medium through which alternatives to liberal citizenship in the political sphere are narrated, where critical subjects and collectivities can be produced in new configurations, with new coherences. To consider testimony and testimonial as constituting a "genre" of cultural production is significant for Asian immigrant women, for it extends the scope of what constitutes legitimate knowledges to include other forms and practices that have been traditionally excluded from both empirical and aesthetic modes of evaluation. (156)

This "genre" of Asian American cultural production begins the work of using narrative to re/vision the ways Asian American subjects engage American culture. For Asian Americans to narrate their lives is to narrate their citizenship in American culture and to both challenge and re/vision the discourses of literacy, race, and citizenship in order to create socially responsible and just action.

As I have tried to lay out in this chapter, the process of minor re/vision is a complicated one that requires people who find themselves on the margins of American culture to engage with dominant discourses of literacy, race, and citizenship; to imagine themselves as minor; and to argue for a cultural citizenship that inserts them into and rewrites the American Story. It is the emergence and production of literacy narratives that facilitates this process. Through their stories about becoming and being literate and developing a sense of self in relationship to the community, minor and minority writers use language and literacy to insert themselves into American culture. The literacy narrative provides these writers with both a form and function that inserts them into a common cultural script of American individualism and achievement through hard work and education but also subverts this story through their use of minority discourse. These writers who become minor use the literacy narrative to deterritorialize dominant discourses that have constructed them in specific ways, to move toward political action by recognizing their sociopolitical conditions, and to provide a collective assemblage of experiences which precludes the essentializing of identities. In starting to narrate literacy and citizenship, we initiate a process where we begin to understand the contexts for our literacy, to re/vision how and why we are literate, and to transform literacy for use in our own projects.

2 / Reading Literacy Narratives
Connecting Literacy, Race, and Citizenship
Through the Stories of Others

In chapter 1, I described the process of minor re/vision, a strategy for minor and minority subjects to use to confront and intervene in dominant cultural practices through the use of literacy narratives. In this chapter, I want to explore literacy narratives that also illustrate the process of minor re/vision as a means for coming to awareness of the work at stake in such interventions. The readings in this chapter examine the narrating of literacy and citizenship in Richard Rodriguez's *Hunger of Memory,* Victor Villanueva Jr.'s *Bootstraps: From an American Academic of Color,* Carlos Bulosan's *America Is in the Heart,* and Maxine Hong Kingston's "Song of a Barbarian Reed Pipe" from *The Woman Warrior.*

In his moving and controversial autobiography, *Hunger of Memory,* Richard Rodriguez describes his journey toward literacy, moving from a native Spanish-speaking home to doing graduate work in English Renaissance literature and finally to living his life as a professional writer. Rodriguez seemingly embodies the American Dream, and the appropriation of his story by both conservatives and liberals who seek to reform American public education is a strong illustration of the transformative power our culture attributes to literacy. However, Rodriguez himself warns his readers that his story is his own and his life does not stand as a model for others—"But I write of one life only. My own" (7). He also recognizes, though, that the telling of his story, the disclosing of his life, becomes an important act of displaying how language and life are intertwined—"If my story is true, I trust it will resonate with significance for other lives" (7). In his view, he discloses his life, not to hurt his family (a concern of his mother), but to share a life that may hold lessons for others.[1]

In an equally moving and highly complex mixed-genre narrative, *Bootstraps: From an American Academic of Color,* Victor Villanueva weaves fragments from a journey through a complicated acquisition of schooled literacy that led to his becoming a highly regarded literacy educator. In his narrative, Villanueva describes a life of struggle and low expectations interrupted by unexpected opportunities and the power of ideas. Rather than limit his story to a narrative of individual achievement, Villanueva enacts social analysis and cultural critique in order to develop an understanding of the larger structural forces that played a role in shaping his life: "This is an autobiography with political, theoretical, pedagogical considerations" (xviii). Like Rodriguez, Villanueva does not necessarily hold himself up as a model, but he is also certainly aware of the lessons that his life may offer.

Carlos Bulosan's writing weaves together fragments of personal experience and social and political commentary often within the metaphor of writing. In his many essays and perhaps his best known work, *America Is in the Heart,* Bulosan provides scenes of literacy to represent both a personal and political struggle against racism and other forms of oppression. In Bulosan's mind, writing provides the means not just for personal change but also for social change, and we see in his work a call for the writer to be a citizen: "the writer must participate with his fellow man in the struggle to protect, to brighten, to fulfill life. Otherwise he has no meaning—a nothing" ("Writer" 143).

Maxine Hong Kingston's *The Woman Warrior* has occupied an important and vexed position in Asian American writing. Kingston has been both admired for bringing voice to Asian Americans and condemned for reinforcing orientalist stereotypes of the Chinese. Her strategy of mixing memoir, memory, and imagined fictive stories is important in expressing an identity that is in continual creation, but the desire to rely on easily understood categories creates tension in the ways people want to read her work. For Kingston, telling stories is a way for "those of us in the first American generations. . . . to figure out how the invisible world the emigrants built around our childhoods fits in solid America" (*Woman* 5).

While it may seem odd to include Rodriguez and Villanueva in

a book about Asian American literacy narratives, I do so strategically for two reasons. First, I turn to Rodriguez and Villanueva because *Hunger of Memory* and *Bootstraps: From an American Academic of Color* are often read as exemplary literacy narratives: Each
author describes his own acquisition of English and literacy, his position in American culture as a Latino (Rodriguez as a Mexican
American; Villanueva as a Puerto Rican), and his move toward participation as a full citizen. *Hunger of Memory* performs one type of
cultural work as it relies on a dominant cultural narrative of development and assimilation in the construction of citizenship. *Bootstraps* performs a different type of cultural work as it writes a minor
cultural narrative through its deterritorialization of language (in
form and practice), its move toward political action in its critique
of American culture, and its complicating of identity, contributing
to a collective assemblage of experiences that challenge expectations of a representative or exceptional life. I then turn to Bulosan
as an exemplary narrative because *America Is in the Heart* functions
both as a conventional literacy narrative (like *Hunger of Memory*)
and as a minor narrative (like *Bootstraps*), complicating a reader's
understanding of the cultural work of literacy. Bulosan's position as
an Asian American writer and his use of writing for political purposes illustrates the connection between literacy, race, and citizenship for those in minor positions. In Maxine Hong Kingston's "Song
for a Barbarian Reed Pipe," we see the dominant narrative of silence
and literacy imposed on minor subjects as they are instructed about
American citizenship. But a re/vision of this narrative takes place
as the narrator, Maxine, in first accepting this narrative begins to
transform the pain and shame into new understanding about her
position in American culture.

I connect Rodriguez, Villanueva, Bulosan, and Kingston to provide my second purpose in including these two Latino literacy narratives in this book: to draw an analogy between Rodriguez and Villanueva, as Latinos, and Bulosan and Kingston, as Asian Americans,
in order to complicate the American racial landscape beyond Black
and White. In my reading of American culture, Latinos and Asians
are more susceptible to overdetermined representations as "foreign-

ers" or "aliens" and not as full citizens. The question of language is also key in drawing this analogy since stereotypes of Latinos and Asians often construct them as non-English speaking or of limited English proficiency and literacy. While African Americans must engage stereotypical representations of Ebonics and "street" language constructed by dominant culture, their position in American culture as citizens is seemingly less problematic and less disputed despite continuing pressures of racism and other difficulties in participating in American culture. That is, African Americans appear more firmly located in American culture as citizens because there is a better awareness of the political and legal history that has argued for full recognition of African Americans as citizens.

In this chapter I also discuss *Hunger of Memory* and *Bootstraps* as narratives that have played a significant role in my own conceptualization of the relationship that people of color have to literacy. What I hope to offer here is not a close theoretical reading of these two texts alone, but rather a discussion about how moments from these texts have had an effect on my own emerging literacy narrative. From Rodriguez and Villanueva I turn to read Bulosan's and Kingston's Asian American literacy narratives, to build upon my experience of reading race in literacy narratives to connecting race and literacy in my own emerging consciousness about Asian American citizenship. It is also important to remember that both Rodriguez and Villanueva write under the legacy of both Spanish and U.S. colonialism, a position that Bulosan is also subject to because of the history of colonialism in the Philippines. Writing under these conditions despite historical distance still informs their relationship to dominant culture and how they assume minor positions to explore their own lives in America.

Reading Lessons: Literacy, Race, and Citizenship

My first encounter with Richard Rodriguez was through an excerpt from *Hunger of Memory*. I was an undergraduate (I think) English major at the University of Hawai'i, and I was doing an independent reading in rhetoric and composition theory—unusual for an undergraduate, but I had already discovered composition as a field through my work as a peer tutor and I hoped to go on to graduate school to study composition and rhetoric. This was in 1989 (I think), and the discipline of composition was in a transitional phase— moving away from the large scale empirical and protocol studies towards a blending of literary, critical, and rhetorical theory into praxis. In my independent study, I was focusing on a project about theorizing peer-tutoring. I was experimenting with narrative a little bit as I kept a tutor log about my tutoring experiences, but in many ways I remained absent in the writing. I could write about the students whom I tutored—I could not write about myself.

On one occasion, the professor with whom I was doing the independent study gave me a handout, "An Education in Language," by Richard Rodriguez. I read the piece with interest and obligation but no real connection to the story being told. I did not learn English as a second language. I did not feel distanced from my parents or family. And in Hawai'i, I did not feel like I lived in *gringo* (or in Hawai'i, *haole*) society—most of the people I knew looked like me, came from working- and middle-class families, and attended the university. I filed that essay away and went on to the next thing.

My next encounter with Richard Rodriguez was in graduate school. I was taking an interdisciplinary seminar in literacy, and after some introductory theoretical readings that included work by Jack Goody and Ian Watt, Brian Street, and Ruth Finnegan, we turned to narrative. Among the narratives we read were Jamaica Kincaid's *Annie John,* Mike Rose's *Lives on the Boundary,* Frederick Douglass's *Narrative of the Life of Frederick Douglass, An American Slave,* and Rodriguez's *Hunger of Memory.* This time I read Rodriguez with a passion. Perhaps it was that I was now displaced both physically and psychologically from Hawai'i as I found myself in Ann Arbor, Michigan, which while relatively diverse was certainly not Honolulu. Or perhaps it was that I was more conscious about language and its uses as I took more course work in literacy studies and composition and rhetoric. Or perhaps I began to become aware of the ways literacy and race interact in the construction of identity and citizenship. While I did not necessarily agree with Rodriguez and his positions on bilingual education or affirmative action, there was something about what I saw as real pain in his expressions of identity that kept me connected to his writing.

Rodriguez constructs his autobiography explicitly as a literacy narrative, a term he does not use though he identifies his text as a "book about language." Not only does he look at the practices of reading and writing, but he also theorizes the role language plays in the formation of his identity. Though he may eschew considerations of race for discussions of class, they are both present in his connections to language. Language, both the anxieties it causes and the nostalgia it can evoke, takes center stage:

> This autobiography, moreover, is a book about language. I write about poetry; the new Roman Catholic liturgy; learning to read; writing; political terminology. Language has been the great subject of my life. In college and graduate school, I was registered as an "English major." But well before then, from my first day of school, I was a student of language. Obsessed by the way it determined my public identity. The way it permits me here to describe myself, writing . . . (7)

Through the writing of his text, Rodriguez is involved in the construction of his identity through language. His use of narrative is both authorizing and limiting at the same time: his personal voice provides a sense of "authenticity" and "authority" to this story; because he uses a "personal" voice (despite his claim of public citizenship) he may be reduced to being made representative of an entire race or to being the exception to his race. To Rodriguez, language becomes essential, the most important force in the making of his identity. Rodriguez theorizes language as an act of naming and defining a location outside of history, reaching across time and place in order to represent public identities unaffected by the personal or the local. Ramon Saldivar describes this as an "ideology of the self," where Rodriguez's essentialist impulse undermines the potential power of his narrative:

Rodriguez's autobiography, however, speaks to us from a position beyond history, as if the dynamic forces of historical change could no longer touch him.

In other words, the story Rodriguez tells us lacks the verisimilitude of autobiography's second demand: philosophical self-analysis. He fails to consider, as autobiography might induce him to, that the author lives, moves, and has his being in historical projections that constitute him as a subject. And an author cannot simply tell us the "truth" about himself, a truth that will "resonate with significance for other lives" [7], without undertaking some kind of philosophical reflection on the place of his private life in public history. I wish to emphasize this point in particular because Rodriguez seems so certain about the innocence of the split he makes between the "private" and "public" self. The desire to extract ourselves from the world, either to conceive it or to command it, only anchors us more deeply in it. (161)

Saldivar is right to emphasize the difficulty in separating the public and private selves. While Rodriguez appears to make this split and assumes that it can be done so unproblematically, he apparently ignores the autoethnographic tension that still exists in the narrative. While there is a resistance on his part to engage those representations of him (or of Latinos) constructed by dominant culture except to dismiss them and to prove his own proficiency in Standard English and legitimacy as a citizen, there remains a tension in the text and *in the context* that I believe does function autoethnographically. While Rodriguez is free to choose any position he wishes on issues that get attached to his racial condition (bilingual policy, education policy, etc.), he cannot escape the need to critically engage the representations about race and identity that will get constructed no matter what he says or does.

While Rodriguez himself may resist a conscious autoethnography on his part, I still find that his concepts of public and private languages and the perceived conflict that exists between them acts as an interesting analogy for autoethnography, where the minor language can deterritorialize the major language. I also want to acknowledge that *Hunger of Memory* draws together for discussion questions about the pressures of race and ethnicity, language, and citizenship within dominant culture. And Rodriguez addresses the conflict quite eloquently, describing the complex relationships between discourse communities—family, school, neighborhood, ethnicity, class—and how we are each members within any number of these communities. He recounts the painful transition from speaking Spanish (his intimate family language) to speaking English (the language of school and authority). And yet as he remembers the pain he is also forceful in asserting that his learning of English, what he calls public language, has allowed him to participate in society:

> Without question, it would have pleased me to hear my teachers address me in Spanish when I entered the classroom. I would have felt much less afraid. I would have trusted them and responded with ease. But it would have delayed—for how long postponed?—having to learn the language of public society. I would have evaded—and for how long could I have afforded to delay?—learning the great lesson of school, that I had a public identity. (19)

Rodriguez makes the point that if he had not learned English or at least was delayed further in learning English he would have continued to be a disadvantaged student. But more telling in his comments is his belief that English, that this public language, is necessary if he is to participate in culture as a citizen. Rodriguez is caught in a very difficult situation: on one hand, he acknowledges an identity, that comfort and trust exist for him in Spanish; on the other hand, he recognizes that English is the language of the larger public culture in which he lives. There is a sense, then, that Rodriguez believes he must choose one identity over the other, that he must move away from the intimacy of the family to be a part of the larger society, that he must give up his private identity and language in order to become a citizen.[2] Here is where Rodriguez fails to see how his private language acts to deterritorialize public language, where the purpose and potential of one language can inform and expand the purpose and potential of the other language.

However, the problem is not that citizenship is created simply through the acquisition and use of a public language. The problem is Rodriguez's placement of so much value in being constructed by the language and by the public instead of presenting himself as an already active participant in the community as a *minor* subject. That is, Rodriguez does not enter into the public conversation with his own identity, one informed by the intimacy and connections created by his family and Mexican American culture. But rather, he enters the public conversation with the expectation of being defined, of being identified, of becoming a part of American culture. And like the privileging of the individual that has become so important in the construction of America, Rodriguez believes he has achieved "full individuality":

> In public, by contrast, full individuality is achieved, paradoxically, by those who are able to consider themselves members of the crowd. Thus it happened for me: Only when I was able to think of myself as an American, no longer an alien in *gringo* society, could I seek the rights and opportunities necessary for full public identity. (27)

Rodriguez appropriately recognizes the paradox of his construct: the individual cannot exist away from the society; the individual can only be within society. And yet if this is the case, Rodriguez is assuming a social totality that does not allow for the re/vision of citizenship and institutions in American culture; but rather, forces people into meeting the requirements for membership and into fitting already existing definitions of America. Thus when Rodriguez makes the important move to reconceptualize himself as American —"no longer an alien in *gringo* society"—he does not consider why his present location in culture as a Mexican American does not already position him as American. He seemingly avoids being completely appropriated by American culture by recognizing that with his public identification as American he can now seek the "rights and opportunities" attendant to that identity. Perhaps his move can then be thought of as subversive since his acquisition and mastery of both his public "American" language and identity can be an opportunity to dismantle the structures that have oppressed him, the act of becoming minor. However, his emphasis again on "public identity" reveals his acquiescence to the hegemony of American culture. Certainly, his reconceptualization of himself as an American is important, but how is he defining what it is to be American? How does he negotiate the many competing factors that contribute to an "American" identity? Is he creating an essential American who is largely constructed through language and public membership as suggested? But perhaps the most important question never asked by Rodriguez is "Why am I not *already* American?"

Part of this need to identify himself as American through the most important signifier that he can imagine, Standard English, is due to the anxieties he feels about his racial condition and status as citizen. Certainly, Rodriguez, even as a child, understands that he is an American citizen. He was born in the United States and his parents did everything on their part to help their children grow up in the land of their birth. However, despite his legal status as citizen, Rodriguez still feels like an outsider. He seeks citizenship and does everything possible to attain it through education:

> Always successful, I was always unconfident. Exhilarated by my progress. Sad. I became the prized student—anxious and eager to learn. Too eager, too anxious—an imitative and unoriginal pupil. My brother and two sisters enjoyed the advantages I did, and they grew to be as successful as I, but none of them ever seemed so anxious about their schooling. A second grade student, I was the one who came home and corrected the 'simple' grammatical mistakes of our parents. ('Two negatives make a positive.')

Proudly I announced—to my family's startled silence—
that a teacher had said I was losing all trace of my Spanish
accent. (44)

Rodriguez exhibits his anxiety about citizenship by working extra
hard to fit in, taking advantage of schooling, and demonstrating his
language proficiency (even expertise) to his family. His greatest
achievement and surest marker of his becoming more American is
his loss of his Spanish accent. Anxiety is created because Rodriguez's
understanding of language and Standard English is built upon the
specific representations of usage and legitimacy privileged in American culture.

In an interesting move, Rodriguez turns to another literacy narrative hoping to find some explanation and comfort for the anxiety
he feels. His use of Richard Hoggart's *The Uses of Literacy* and Hoggart's parable about the "scholarship boy" is both appealing and disappointing. The use of Hoggart's narrative is appealing because it
provides an analysis of class that takes into account the desire that
is cultivated for bourgeois existence. And in turning to another literacy narrative, Rodriguez illustrates the way culture uses these
narratives in the writing of other narratives, the focus of my own
project. However, I find Rodriguez's use of Hoggart to be disappointing because he does not seek to perform his own analysis of
his situation but rather simply fits his life into the template provided by the "scholarship boy" narrative. In an even more disturbing move, Rodriguez attributes a nostalgic representation of language and schooling to Hoggart that drives his own desire and
remembrance:

But Hoggart's calm prose only makes me recall the urgency
with which I came to idolize my grammar school teachers.
I began by imitating their accents, using their diction,
trusting their every direction. The very first facts they dis-
pensed, I grasped with awe. Any book they told me to
read, I read—then waited for them to tell me which books
I enjoyed. Their every casual opinion I came to adopt and

to trumpet when I returned home. I stayed after school 'to help'—to get my teacher's undivided attention. It was the nun's encouragement that mattered most to me. (She understood exactly what—my parents never seemed to appraise so well—all my achievements entailed.) Memory gently caressed each word of praise bestowed in the classroom so that compliments teachers paid me years ago come quickly to mind today. (49–50)

It is difficult to read not only this passage but Rodriguez's entire text and not wonder why he does not interrogate his desire beyond acknowledging it. This is one of the most frustrating things about reading this narrative because Rodriguez often seems on the cusp of making an important theoretical point and yet will back away as if such a move will undermine his narrative strategy. And perhaps his narrative strategy is to resolve his anxiety through the nostalgia that he weaves throughout the text. I must admit that I am often moved by his writing and yet cannot help but wonder if I am being manipulated by the nostalgia and pain.

In the final section of his narrative, Rodriguez examines how his private and public lives again conflict. Just as his childhood and early education were filled with conflict in trying to maintain the boundaries between the intimacy of private language and the requirements of public language, his life as a writer has seen those same conflicts. As he continues his construction of public identity, he finds that in many ways he has lost the intimacy, the connection that language, either private or public, once provided:

> The loneliness I have felt many mornings, however, has not made me forget that I am engaged in a highly public activity. I sit here in silence writing this small volume of words, and it seems to me the most public thing I have ever done. My mother's letter has served to remind me: I am making my personal life public. Probably I will never try to explain my motives to my mother and father. My mother's question will go unanswered to her face. Like everything else on

these pages, my reasons for writing will be revealed instead to public readers I expect never to meet. (176–77)

By writing his autobiography, Rodriguez probably has done the
most public thing he may ever do. And yet this public revelation has
in part isolated him further because he has reified himself within
the text. He claims a citizenship, but it is a citizenship that does not
consider how he already existed and acted in ways that made him
part of the culture. Rodriguez argues the point eloquently that only
after he learned English could he participate in the public and be
recognized. However, despite his native language being Spanish, he
did exist and did have cultural citizenship, a position that acknowledges both his place in dominant culture and the important work of
being minor. What Rodriguez fails to recognize is that the separation between the public and private he describes is false. What he
has conceived of as the private is a romanticized notion of the family
and modes of communication that never acknowledge that the construction of his cultural citizenship occurs in a locus populated by
others (though family members) and active in engaging dominant
culture through a minor position. And what he conceives of as the
public is simply a notion of assimilation (a term he uses himself) to
the larger dominant culture and its requirements and expectations.
Tomas Rivera, while recognizing the pain and the potential of *Hunger of Memory*, views it as ultimately denying the humanist identity
that Rodriguez claims to seek:

> *Hunger of Memory* is thus a humanistic antithesis for sev-
> eral reasons. First, because its breadth and dimension is
> so narrow, unaware as it is of the traditions that should in-
> form it. Second, it is ultimately an aggregation of cultural
> negations. Richard Rodriguez prizes as authentic only that
> which he learns in classrooms. Third, he underlines the si-
> lence of culture as negative. Finally, Richard Rodriguez be-
> lieves that it is only through English that he can elaborate
> what is correct and not correct for the community as a
> whole. (13)

Rivera sums up nicely the points that have been elaborated on. What remains to be asked is what is at stake for Rodriguez when he transforms his private stories into public texts? Is he simply transforming the local into larger cultural moments? Does he do the work necessary to challenge the boundaries between public and private conceptions of language?

The move that Rodriguez does not make is to consider how his private language (and thus his potential as a minor subject) informs the public language (and citizenship) that he values so much. Instead of deterritorializing the dominant discourse of public life and citizenship, he believes that the only thing he can do is to choose one identity over the other. But I believe that deterritorialization can take place and that even the presence of his private language has already begun the work of re/vision of the public.

Rodriguez calls his *Hunger of Memory* an "American story." I agree with him and have tried to flesh out the connections between this "book about language" and the American Story. But I also see *Hunger of Memory* as an American story because it reveals the anxieties and pain that minor subjects often face when narrating their experiences in American culture. Rodriguez's story about education is a story about pain:

> This is what matters to me: the story of the scholarship boy who returns one summer from college to discover bewildering silence, facing his parents. This is my story. An American story. (5)

Often the irony or critique in Rodriguez's narrative is overshadowed by the political and ideological rhetoric that often accompanies readings of his text. His American story is one of conflict and complexity, not the easy story of citizenship or assimilation that it is often reduced to by various audiences. Rather, it is perhaps the most American story possible because it reveals confusion, desire, ideology, and rhetoric. Antonio Marquez describes *Hunger of Memory* as part of a national experience, entering the text into the complicated tapestry of narratives that make up America:

> Indeed, Rodriguez's autobiography is part of a national experience. But his credo must not be seen as a joyous celebration of birthright; *Hunger of Memory* makes it amply evident that it is a sensibility that garners the confusion, ambivalences, and paradoxes that accompany the problematic task of "making it in America." (246)

To read Rodriguez, then, is to read one particular story but it is also to read a national narrative that is complicated by literacy, race, and citizenship. Instead of the Nation emerging as a complete whole story, we must begin to see the many stories that create the "minor" narratives of America. We must see how private language can transform public language. We must be willing to become minor in order to re/vision citizenship and not accept the dominant cultural narrative of easy and required transition from one self to another, from private to public, from alien to citizen.

While my encounters with Rodriguez have touched that part of me that seeks to rethink my own personal history of literacy, my encounters with Victor Villanueva have touched both that desire for personal history as well as a need to critically reflect on my emerging professional identity as a teacher and scholar of color. As Hephzibah Roskelly comments in her review of *Bootstraps,* the shifting narrative and juxtaposition of memory, theory, and critique results in an effect that is "sometimes a little jarring, but self-conscious. And its self-consciousness promotes similar awareness in readers" (719). What I will narrate here is my developing awareness of my life in composition through fragments of Villanueva's narrative.

Villanueva opens *Bootstraps* with "Good Debts: Words of Indebtedness," a moving and revealing acknowledgement of those who have helped him get where he is. He begins by musing, "I think of how it would be if the numbers of academics of color actually reflected the demographics of the country" (vii). And then he describes his meetings at NCTE headquarters with other scholars of color:

I am glad to be among other professionals of color for those few days. In those few days, we laugh, and we swap stories which tell of our ways, ways which tell of our particular cultures, ways we have in common as people of color. And we work. And our work reflects the things we have in common with many of our fellow professionals, and our work reflects the things we see and hear and feel, aggravating things sometimes, painful things. (vii)

When I first read this as a graduate student, I felt a sense of solidarity with Villanueva. As a faculty member now, I understand the importance of such meetings even more profoundly. As a graduate student, what I had seen up to then in my short professional life as filtered through my graduate program and the conferences I attended made it clear that people of color, despite the sensitivities of an institution or organization, were still struggling to be heard, still fighting for a place beyond the perception of tokenism. But I also remained a bit naive as I felt that perhaps I was exempt from anger and some of these anxieties because I grew up in a multicultural setting and had every expectation of returning home to Hawai'i to teach and live. I did not read race as part of the condition of my everyday existence or professional life.

I did have friends and colleagues who read race as part of their experience, and I often was a bit confused by what I saw as a self-created burden. I heard stories about racial slurs shouted from cars, or slights by salespeople, or students complaining about the difficult accents of their Asian teachers (when their instructors were native-born Americans). But I had not yet experienced any of these acts of bigotry—maybe they were just too sensitive. Faculty of color would ask me how I was doing. "Are you adjusting to the mainland?" they would inquire. "Have you had any problems?" "Let me know if I can help." "No," I would respond, "everything seems to be going well." Perhaps I was overwhelmed by this new experience on the "mainland." I was attending an elite university, working with leading scholars in my fields of interest, living on my own for the first time, and the university was paying me for all of this in the form of a fellowship. I was Hoggart's "scholarship boy."

Though in many ways I was not a "scholarship" boy. I was from the middle class though I grew up in a working-class neighborhood. My father was a white-collar government employee, my mom a homemaker, though at various times she worked outside the home as a clerk or teacher's aide. My siblings all attended the university, and three of us already had advanced degrees. I did not feel out of place—in fact, I felt as if I had made the right choice to pursue a Ph.D. at an elite university, and I was fortunate to have many graduate students of color and many faculty of color to provide a sense of belonging. But despite these seemingly positive conditions, I struggled with my own developing sense of racial consciousness. For the first time in my life I was a "minority."

In *Bootstraps*, Villanueva reveals many moments of self-doubt, even as a professional who has seemingly "made it." It's in these moments that I value Villanueva's text the most as he provides a lens to examine the experience of education, the life of an academic, and the many interruptions that occur in everyday life as a person of color. For example, just reading that Villanueva himself had to come to his own racial consciousness helps me start to unpack my own complicated feelings about race. Villanueva writes:

> I didn't always see myself as a person of color. Nor did I question my competence back then, though the more the awareness of color, the greater the insecurity as I grew older. But in those early years I was *el blancito,* after all. I could see myself as poor, the working class. And there is a connection between class and color, some overlap, matters to be discussed later in this book. But "color," back then, meant shades of brown and black. It hadn't occurred to me that the Puerto Rican would somehow not be white, no matter what the pigment. (xii)

As an Asian American, I often receive conflicting messages from our larger culture, from my institution, and from my profession and discipline. Like Villanueva, I often understood "color" to refer to African Americans and Latinos, to those groups who asserted a pan-ethnic racial category as both a cultural and political necessity. In Hawai'i I was not Asian American. My father was ethnically Chinese, my mom was ethnically Okinawan, and like many in Hawai'i, I was just one of those kids who grew up in a multi-ethnic home and neighborhood. We did not identify ourselves as Asian American. Perhaps more importantly, you were "local" (born and raised in Hawai'i) or a "mainlander" (from the continental United States). I did not become Asian American until I left Hawai'i and entered a situation as a "minority," where those kinds of pan-ethnic coalitions are important political categories. In American culture, Asian Americans are often seen as having already "made it." Asian Americans are the "model minority," a term coined to suggest that minorities could succeed in the U.S. through hard work and belief in the value of education. In my professional life, Asian Americans are the invisible presence, part of the landscape and yet often not part of the larger discourse on diversity as our culture still struggles to address appropriately the educational inequities faced by "underrepresented" minorities.

For Villanueva, achieving his goal of a Ph.D. is not the end of the journey. Rather, it is the beginning of being critically conscious and still facing the many "problems" that the romantic narrative of education was supposed to resolve neatly. To Villanueva, it is a life of contradiction:

> Containing contradictions is difficult, sometimes crazy making—a mutual affirmation and denial. American academic of color. Fully an academic. I imagine what I would do were I among the truly wealthy: lottery fantasies. I imagine that after seeing the world I would settle down to reading and to writing, learning and teaching, likely about politics and language—academics. Yet fellow academics are foreign to me in many ways, and I think they will always be, that I will always somehow be an outlander. I am of color, now fully aware of the color, and I am of poverty

(not just "from" poverty), never (not even now, economically) of the middle class, not even quite the colored middle class (who are not equal with the white middle class). So I often feel alone professionally. But I just as often feel a member of a professional community—a community that extends beyond the university that employs me, community that includes all English-language teachers. Contradictions. (xv)

But these contradictions are not the public/private dichotomy set up by Rodriguez. The contradictions are overlapping, the layering of one experience over another, the layering of one language over another. Cultural literacy and critical literacy, Villanueva argues, are "necessarily important to the American of color, the colonized, the one who is American and yet other" (xv). This is where Villanueva makes a move that Rodriguez seems to be unwilling to make. In narrating his life, Villanueva plays out the tension between the public and private rather than accepting that the public and private must remain separate—he begins to deterritorialize language. Even though his mother makes her own plea to keep things private (just as Rodriguez's mother did), Villanueva uses his life to read the systems of culture, to provide an argument grounded in his own experience to explain his views on literacy, race, and citizenship.

Another feature of *Bootstraps* that I find important is Villanueva's attention to his own writing process. When Villanueva describes his own struggles to acquire academic discourse in his community college, university, and graduate school courses, he invites the reader into an intimate and important space: He shares his anxiety about writing. What Villanueva describes is process, "discovering what to write while writing, no prior thesis statement, no outline, just a vague notion that would materialize, magically, while writing" (68). In seeking to use the discourse of literary studies, Villanueva discovers a pattern, a genre: "an introduction that said something about what others had said, what he was going to be writing about, in what order, and what this would prove" (70). Writing becomes more than a single task, it becomes a series of drafts, as "papers are written over days, weeks, paragraphs literally cut and laid out on the floor to be pasted" (73). We see in Villanueva those ideas about writing that we use in our own classes, which inform our theory, that help our own writing: process, audience, and revision. Here is the sense of re/vision that Nancy Sommers describes, where it is the work that happens between the drafts that matters. Not only is Villanueva engaged in the literal re/vision of his writing, he is engaged in a metaphorical re/vision of his identity.

When Villanueva discovers rhetoric in a seminar, "Theories of Invention," taught by Anne Ruggles Gere, there is a sense that he has begun the process of his own rhetorical invention, and he begins to imagine himself as a writer and a teacher:

> Not all at once, not just in that first class on rhetoric. I discover some things about writing, my own, and about the teaching of writing. I find some of modern composition's insights are modern hindsights. I don't mind the repetition. Some things bear repeating. The repetitions take on new significance and are elaborated upon in a new context, a new time. Besides not everyone who teaches writing knows rhetoric, though I believe everyone should. (74)

For Villanueva, writing becomes a way to discover, learn, and think (74). Rhetoric is the conscious use of language, the understanding of the power of language, and a way to understand people (77). What writing and rhetoric provide Villanueva is a way to understand his place in the academy and in American culture—writing becomes a means for citizenship. Much like Villanueva, it was when I turned to my own writing that I began to understand issues of race, class, gender, and culture. I needed to think about why I wrote about what I did, and why I write the way I do, and why I write. I was the missing subject in my writing. I could theorize others and their writing, but I did not theorize myself as I was placed outside of culture and writing, somehow exempt from my own uses of literacy.

I began to engage my own writing and my own history of literacy as I read Rodriguez and Villanueva and taught a service-learning course set in literacy tutoring programs.[3] I asked students to reflect on their personal literacy experiences, to analyze the literacy work they were doing at the tutoring programs, and to combine all of this with the theory we were reading. To appreciate and understand the work the students were doing, I needed to reflect on my own literacy experiences. In order to understand the way literacy worked in the communities where we worked, I needed to understand how literacy worked in the community in which I grew up. In order to understand the many ways race, gender, and class worked in these communities, I needed to understand how race, gender, and class shaped my life. I needed to write.

And I still need to write as I struggle to figure out now this professional life of mine. Despite being credentialed, despite being relatively successful in my teaching and research, I continue to seek a place in the profession, to know that there are others who look like me, who share my questions and concerns, who have had similar experiences to mine. I need to understand how the profession sees my work and sees me. Am I paranoid? Am I too concerned about race? Do I see slights where there are none? Do I need to be wary of even those "friends" and supporters of my concerns? Here is another lesson from Villanueva:

A long dinner table at a fancy Italian restaurant in New York. Some of Victor's fellow graduate students are seated there. Some of his heroes are seated there too, those he had read. One of his heroes tells of the need for more work on basic writers. Then some glasses of wine later, the same hero tells of being bilked by a portorican boy during the most recent New York blackout: "Clever, the things the portoricans will do for a buck." The hero seems genuinely charmed by the incident. The comment is completely innocuous. The hero seems not to hear his own stereotyping, seems not to understand, or be troubled by, the economic and racial conditions that make for clever portorican hustlers. And, in this stereotyping, the hero had not seen Victor as a portorican, wouldn't have thought about it, likely, since portoricans are not rhetoricians or compositionists. In the fifteen years since Victor first entered the University, the seven years active as a professional, he has yet to meet another Puerto Rican Professor of Rhetoric and Composition. (119)

A few years ago, I attended a reception for "Scholars for the Dream," a program to support people of color new to the profession. The reception is an annual event and is a wonderful gathering to encourage the mentoring and continued support of underrepresented groups in the profession. What made this reception stand out to me though was its location at Trader Vic's, a pseudo-Polynesian tiki lounge filled with stereotypical artifacts like grass shack walls, tiki gods, and tiki torch lamps. I was not particularly offended, though I wondered if the organizers had thought about what were clearly problematic representations of race and culture in this location. The figurines of Polynesian children on the buffet table with their requisite brown skin, round tummies, flower lei, and island attire did not seem to strike the crowd as exploitative. The idea of the tiki lounge did not seem to remind anyone of a history of Western colonialism in the Pacific, a fact that continues to have a lasting legacy as Native Hawaiians among other Pacific peoples struggle for their sovereignty rights as indigenous cultures. I point to this experience not to place blame on the organizers or to cry about a lack of awareness both in the larger organization and among people I count as friends. Like Villanueva's experience, I see this as an example of the need for vigilance on my part and of continued self-examination by the profession of its role in addressing the everyday struggles of diverse groups of people. Here is where we need to have a collective assemblage of enunciation, to see collective experiences of minor subjects and the need for political awareness, instead of replacing one form of hegemony with another.

In 1990, NCTE passed a resolution entitled "On the Critical Shortage of Minority Educators." In this resolution, NCTE made a commitment to

> Expand its efforts to recruit, guide, and retain ethnically and culturally diverse group members, for example, Hispanic, African American, Asian American, and American Indian, who might enter the English languages arts teaching profession.

This resolution closed by stating that NCTE will "encourage and support its affiliates in their efforts to recruit ethnically and culturally diverse educators for membership and leadership roles."

This was in 1990. At the 1999 convention, (the one with the tiki lounge reception), Villanueva reported some discouraging figures in his Chair's Address:

> If CCCC membership demographics can tell us much, though, the numbers aren't encouraging, with a 92% white membership, 5% African American, 1.4% Chicanos or Latino, 1% Asian American, and 0.5% Native American/ American Indian. ("On" 651)

A cursory review of CCCC convention programs confirms these numbers for Asian Americans. As I examined the listing of conference participants for each year beginning in 1990, I relied on my familiarity (or lack of familiarity) with Asian surnames and used the broadest definition of Asian Pacific American, for example including South Asians as well as Pacific Islanders. The numbers I collected were approximate and not precise. In any case, they are disappointing. For example, for 1990 I identified fifteen Asian Pacific American participants. For 1995, I identified thirty. For 2001, about thirty-five. While we could say that in eleven years we more than doubled our participation, the fact that we went from fifteen to thirty-five, that we added twenty people in eleven years is not good.

Again, in his address in 1999, Villanueva made a call for action:

. . . people of color writing frankly, sympathetically about matters concerning racism, and all of us writing about what matters to those students of color. That's what will attract people of color in sufficient numbers to affect racism. We can do better than 7% among our teachers and scholars of color, better than a representation that is statistically insignificant in our journals. ("On" 652)

Here was another contradiction. At the convention where I experienced the energy of Villanueva's call to action, his recognition of people of color and their contributions and importance to the profession, I also experienced the disappointment of the tiki lounge reception, where people of color gathered in celebration and solidarity within the context of a colonial legacy that continues to exploit Pacific peoples. Perhaps I was not being too sensitive. To affect racism, as Villanueva says, we must work to move beyond needing to acknowledge a presence of people of color (because there are so few), to having the numbers of academics of color actually reflect the demographics of the country.

What Villanueva has taught me is a type of politics of the professional, that there is a need for scholars of color to make their presence felt if we are to transform education and the profession to meet the needs of all people. What reading *Bootstraps* has meant to me is both personal and political. I have seen the life of an academic of color in my profession narrated in a way that reflects the struggles and the pleasure, that reveals the anxiety and nostalgia, that teaches me that it is okay to have doubt and that there is much work to be done. Villanueva closes his narrative with another contradiction between the individual and the collective:

And each group does have historical, cultural, political, and economic conditions peculiar to that group. I can only really know and tell about one man of color's conditions. There are experiences that I no doubt have in common with others of color, experiences those not of color will never be able to understand fully. By the same token, I can never know, not fully, the experiences of the white middle class. Yet we all have our commonalities. We are—all of us—affected by the hegemonic and by its fragmenting ideology of individualism. With every man for himself only a few will win out. We are individuals, but that doesn't mean we must dive headlong into individualism. We need to cling to our various collectivities—Puerto Rican, Latino, of color, academic, American—and they need not be mutually exclusive if we consider them critically, and if we accept that we carry contradictions. We all stand to gain by developing a critical consciousness. (142–43)

Reading Rodriguez and Villanueva together creates a contradiction that has moved me toward critical consciousness. It becomes clear, as Villanueva says, that these are individual stories, that there are things we will not fully understand about each other's experiences. But we also have responsibilities to our multiple communities, our peoples, our students and teachers, our nation. What we need to work toward is creating dialogues of critical consciousness, having interactions that will create awareness beyond simple faith in democracy, diversity, and literacy.

Reading Asian American Citizenship

If you want to know what we are, look upon the farms or upon the hard pavements of the city. You usually see us working or waiting for work, and you think you know us, but our outward guise is more deceptive than our history.
                        —Carlos Bulosan, "Freedom from Want"

These opening lines from Carlos Bulosan's short essay, "Freedom from Want," appeared in the 6 March 1943 issue of the *Saturday Evening Post*. The essay, inspired by Franklin Delano Roosevelt's 1941 State of the Union address, "The Four Freedoms," describes the struggles of the laborer in America and the importance of democracy in achieving freedom from poverty, as well as the inverse, conquering poverty to achieve democracy. On the page opposite Bulosan's essay was a Norman Rockwell illustration, the third in a series of four paintings by Rockwell that depicted Roosevelt's "The Four Freedoms." The painting portrays a large family dinner (perhaps Thanksgiving) with formal setting—white linen tablecloth, good china, silverware. The grandmother presents the roast turkey; grandfather prepares to carve. Around the table happy family members chat and admire the food. In *Norman Rockwell's America,* Christopher Finch describes the scene as "beautifully articulated" because Rockwell succeeds in "compressing his theme into a single, concrete image. Nothing is overstated, and this gives the composition a force of authenticity which I find missing from *Freedom of Speech*" (172).[4]

While I agree with Finch's judgment of the power and meaning of the painting, I find that the juxtaposition of Bulosan's essay with the painting problematizes the articulation of the idea "freedom from want," and of "The Four Freedoms" and American democracy in general. In the May/June 1995 issue of the *Saturday Evening Post,* remembering World War II, Maynard Good Stoddard recognizes the ideological power of the *Saturday Evening Post* and the important role Rockwell's *The Four Freedoms* played during the war:

> In 1943, with its enormous circulation, the *Post* earned abundant publicity and goodwill not only by publishing the Four Freedoms but by using Rockwell's paintings to promote the nationwide war-bond campaign. Thus, the *Post* became part of the great media propaganda machine that helped raise hundreds of millions from the private sector to pay for, and ultimately to win the war. (60)

Thus, while the appearance of Bulosan's essay in the *Saturday Evening Post* alone raises interesting questions about the construction and reception of Bulosan and his writing in specific, its pairing with the Norman Rockwell painting also raises questions about the construction and reception of Asian Americans and their writings in general and reveals what seems to be a larger ideological project at hand. While Bulosan never specifically refers to his Filipino background and employs a mild socialist rhetoric, the undertones of race and citizenship are clear in his essay.[5] His opening lines cajole, "If you want to know what we are, look upon the farms or upon the hard pavement of the city," recalling images of migrant workers waiting for jobs. Later in the essay, he questions his place in America:

> But sometimes we wonder if we really are a part of America. We recognize the mainsprings of American democracy in our right to form unions and bargain through them collectively, our opportunity to sell our products at reasonable prices, and the privilege of our children to attend schools where they learn the truth about the world in which they live. We also recognize the forces which have been trying to falsify American history—the forces which drive many Americans to a corner of compromise with those who would distort the ideals of men that died for freedom. (12)

There is a disjunction between Bulosan's words and the image presented by Norman Rockwell and the *Saturday Evening Post*. While the promise of democracy is certainly an ideal captured in both text and image, the "realities" presented by Bulosan and Rockwell could not be more dissimilar. Bulosan's text acts to critique America (albeit subversively) while Rockwell's painting acts to co-opt Bulosan and to assimilate the "good" Asian during the tensions of World War II by presenting an idealized American portrait, the dream of life, liberty, and happiness in America that in theory is available to all.[6]

This tension between Bulosan's essay and the Rockwell painting illustrates the pressures created in the cultural acts of reading and writing that operate in the formation of a cohesive narrative. The acts of reading and writing by Asian American writers often employ a different rhetoric as their subject matter and the interpretation of these subjects may vary from other racial or cultural groups and vary even among various Asian ethnic groups. These differences exist not because of some cultural tie to an imagined native "homeland" (i.e., Japan, China, the Philippines, etc.); but rather these differences exist because of the very different experiences in America which are shaped by the myths (or the myth-making) about race, culture, and language. The narrative imagined by dominant culture in America, however, operates to assimilate subjects by employing a rhetoric of American democratic ideals and opportunity. How this rhetoric works, though, is determined by those racial markings that construct a subject as Other, and in the case of Bulosan specifically, as Asian Other. American dominant culture acts to cultivate a desire for America and yet maintains a tight hold on who can enter into it. It is striking that while Bulosan writes about the struggle of workers (and implies nonwhite workers), Rockwell portrays a prosperous white family who, not surprisingly, has achieved the American Dream. Rockwell's portrait in effect acts to maintain Otherness by keeping it absent and by equating American assimilation with white middle-class existence.

In this section I will discuss the tensions in these competing narratives by focusing on what seem to be central strategies by Asian American writers in their responses to how dominant American culture constructs them. In particular, I will discuss how language and literacy are used as a way of constructing the Asian or Asian American Other, and how Asian American writers challenge these constructions by writing subversive narratives of (Asian) American citizenship. The deterritorialization of dominant discourse reveals dominant structures that have naturalized language and literacy and the way they are used to organize and discipline subjects. I build upon my reading of Rodriguez and Villanueva and move to Bulosan and Maxine Hong Kingston as a way to trace my reading process and my developing narrative about the ways literacy and race interact in the construction of citizenship. Rodriguez and Villanueva were starting points, creating a framework for examining dominant discourses about literacy and race. In order to understand constructions of literacy and race particular to Asian Americans, I turn first to a well-known Asian American text, *America Is in the Heart* by Carlos Bulosan, and then to Maxine Hong

Kingston's "Song of a Barbarian Reed Pipe" from *The Woman Warrior.*

Despite growing up in Hawai'i, with its significant Filipino and Filipino American population and growing awareness of ethnic and cultural identity in its multi-ethnic community, I had not heard of Carlos Bulosan until I reached Ann Arbor for graduate school. This was not particularly surprising since Asian American literature was not a course offered when I was an undergraduate. And those Filipino or Filipino American writers I was familiar with were writers from my own community—people like Michelle Cruz Skinner and R. Zamora Linmark, who were actually English majors around the same time I was and who eventually had their work published.[7]

But when I arrived in Ann Arbor and began reading Asian American literature, I soon became aware of how much I did not know about Asian America, its history, its diversity of peoples, and its literatures. When I read *America Is in the Heart* for the first time, I was amazed at the story being told, of the difficult journey both to America and in America. And reading Carlos Bulosan's work, I was stunned to learn of the long history of Asian American writing, of writing that moved beyond stereotypical travel narratives and personal accounts of a new life in America, of writing and literature that was more than sociological study of being Asian or Asian American. I saw in Bulosan someone who was writing political tracts, arguing for social justice, and doing so in a variety of forms —fiction, poetry, and essays—mostly in the 1930s and 1940s. I began to appreciate and to understand that Asian Americans have always been writing and have used their writing and literacy to record their experiences, to express themselves, and to challenge social injustice in its myriad forms.

But just as Asian Americans have always written, they have also been subject to being constructed by a dominant culture that tries to assign specific meanings to their work in order to account for their presence. As the following positive review of Bulosan's *America Is in the Heart* by William S. Lynch in the *Saturday Review of Literature* suggests, Bulosan is the exceptional Oriental who will translate the Orient for America:

> To the vast and still growing stack of tracts on intercultural relations "America Is in the Heart" is a valuable addition. As a treatise on a very special phase of the problem, a phase which has not had the literary treatment it deserves, it is particularly important. More than that it is a promise from one who by his unusual background in American letters should bring to us something lacking today in our literature. There is unquestionably a new vigor in the Orient. *We need Carlos Bulosan to translate it for us and to help us assimilate the attitudes and persons it sends to our shores.* (8, emphasis added)

When Carlos Bulosan's narrative *America Is in the Heart* was published in 1946, it received much critical attention. In his review, Lynch also describes what he sees as the undying loyalty of Bulosan to America in spite of the hardship and violence he experiences. Lynch is certainly admiring of Bulosan, but this is what is problematic as Lynch constructs *America Is in the Heart* as a narrative of assimilation and American success. While Lynch recognizes the faults of America, and is in fact angry and embarrassed over America's treatment of "Orientals" and other minority groups, his attitude is also patronizing. However, it is his suggestion that Bulosan act as "translator" so that Americans may understand the Orient in order to "assimilate the attitudes and persons it sends to our shores" that is even more problematic. While Lynch may see Bulosan as a valuable cultural informant, his expectations that America would listen to such a voice and accept "Oriental" views during an era of heightened racism verge on the naive. Lynch's liberal guilt does not dismantle the "necessity" of translation but rather reinforces the assumption of foreignness that keeps Bulosan marginalized.

Other reviews offered similar reactions, recoiling at the horror of Bulosan's experiences and admiring his resolve in his pursuit of the real America. *Look* magazine (5 August 1947) even declared *America Is in the Heart* one of the "Fifty Best Books" for 1946. Like Lynch's review, these other reviews read the text as a narrative of assimilation, about the courageous "foreigner" whose desire to be a part of America is so strong that he will endure the pain and humiliation of homelessness, racism, and physical and mental abuse. While these reviews also acknowledge the failings of America, their construction of Bulosan as a "cultural translator," as someone who can act as native informant about his Filipino culture, changes the focus from Bulosan's critique of America to Bulosan's description of and insight to Filipino life. It is not surprising that reviews often noted the appeal of the first part of *America Is in the Heart,* which details the narrator's life in the Philippines.

The role of the "cultural translator" raises complicated questions in the reading of texts written by people of color. While it may be appropriate, even necessary, to provide the kind of cultural information that allows for a richer reading of a text, the notion that a "native informant" is necessary to make such a reading available is problematic. Bonnie TuSmith argues:

> When we teach ethnic literatures, therefore, we necessarily must serve as "cultural translators" if we expect the material to be understood on its own terms. The task of the instructor is twofold: (1) we must make it possible for monocultural students to *access* other cultures in meaningful ways, and (2) in dealing with the formidable task of bridging cultures while simultaneously addressing gender issues, we must not lose sight of our primary objective: that of teaching the creative literary productions of serious writers. (20)

While I agree with the impulse to encourage the best informed reading possible by discussing a text in relationship to larger historical and cultural contexts, I believe that the role of the "cultural translator" is limited at best and can actually act to perpetuate the perceptions of and expectations for the "foreign" and "exotic."[8] A belief is created that Asian American texts (as well as other texts by people of color) remain inaccessible without a "translator." This is further complicated when questions about the legitimacy of language ("literary" or "literate" language) is a subtext in the reception of Asian American texts because of concerns about foreignness: An expectation is created that not only must culture be translated, but literally language must be translated.

However, while Bulosan has been constructed as a "cultural translator" in order to make the Philippines and Filipino life available to America, he can also be seen as a "cultural translator" of America. I see this partly in those reviews that acknowledge the horrible experiences in America described in *America Is in the Heart*; Bulosan reveals the violence of America through this narrative. However, Bulosan's "translation" of America is seen even more clearly if *America Is in the Heart* is read in its full ironic meaning, as Marilyn Alquizola suggests:

> I propose that reading *America Is in the Heart* as a subversive text is more tenable than reading it as a narrative which works toward the conclusion that assimilation in America is a viable and desirable goal. Applying an assimilationist interpretation would generate more problematic contradictions, both within the pages of the text and outside it, from its immediate sociohistorical context to its global implications. ("Subversion" 200)

Alquizola develops her argument based primarily in questioning the status of the narrator of *America Is in the Heart*. Her suggestion that the narrator, Carlos, is "fictive," a construction of Bulosan that brings together elements of his own life and the collective lives of other Filipinos he knew, challenges the reading of the work as a narrative of assimilation ("Fictive" 211). By questioning the "authenticity" of the narrator (i.e., the authenticity of this "real" life story), Alquizola points out that the optimism and naivete of the "fictive" narrator acts as a device to critique America. Her argument also exposes the orientalist impulse by an American audience to accept and believe this immigration narrative, as well as the impulse to view Asian American writing as confessional and autobiographical.[9] Ironically, Elaine Kim, in her important study *Asian American Literature: An Introduction to the Writings and Their Social Context*, also reads *America Is in the Heart* as an example of an immigration/assimilation narrative, seeing Bulosan as one of the "Asian goodwill ambassador writers" who seek American acceptance (57).[10]

While I agree with Alquizola's ironic reading of *America Is in the Heart* and what she sees as Bulosan's political subtext in the book, I also think that there are additional tensions created by the various narrative themes found in *America Is in the Heart*. Certainly the tension between an assimilation narrative and social critique is apparent though the social meaning of such readings depends greatly on sociohistorical context and audience. As Alquizola points out (and I have discussed briefly), the reception of Bulosan was mediated in large part by America's involvement in World War II and the political alliance between the United States and the Philippines during the war ("Subversion" 202). The travel motif is another important narrative theme that again sets up a tension between an American sensibility and an Asian American sensibility. That is, while travel in American literature often operates as exploration and adventure, as the discovery of new lands and opportunities (reenacting the colonial impulse), travel in Asian American literature is often constructed in terms of immigration (once again) and restriction. Travel or the inability to travel because of exclusion laws, internment, and so on operates in very different ways in Asian American literature. Sau-ling Wong describes the difference in mobility in terms of "Extravagance" and "Necessity":

> One striking difference presents itself upon the most cursory comparison between mainstream and Asian American discourses on mobility. In the former, horizontal movement across the North American continent regularly connotes independence, freedom, an opportunity for individual actualization and/or societal renewal—in short Extravagance. In the latter, however, it is usually associated with

subjugation, coercion, impossibility of fulfillment for self
or community—in short, Necessity. (*Reading* 121)

The differences in discourses on mobility adds to the ways in
which different meanings are found in Bulosan's text. An ironic
reading of *America Is in the Heart* changes the text from a narrative
of assimilation to a sociocultural critique of America. Accordingly,
the meaning of citizenship in the text also changes. While the narrative of assimilation sets up the journey to citizenship by plotting
the narrator's course from the Philippines to America and across the
American West in search of the American Dream, the sociocultural
critique brings into question notions of citizenship by pointing out
the contradictions in American policies about citizenship. That the
narrator still believes in America when it denies him citizenship
(though the Philippines was a United States territory) and exploits
his labor certainly is an indictment of America.[11] The narrator's
travels across the American West are not a metaphorical journey to
citizenship but rather a frustrating journey in which the citizenship
he seeks, by believing and living American ideals, eludes him. As
Wong points out, Bulosan writes a mobility narrative that in essence
keeps the narrator, Carlos, moving in place without achieving his
goals:

> The place names crowding the pages, on the other hand,
> threaten to undermine this reassurance by contrasting with
> its insubstantiality: if America is in the heart, doesn't it
> mean that it is nowhere, that its rallying aspirations have
> not been realized in any of these actual places? If they had
> been realized the narrative would have shown a meaning-
> ful arrangement of place names, a trajectory of struggle
> and triumph. Yet there is no blazed trail, only chaos, a
> senseless jumble of brutalities. (*Reading* 133–34)

The frustration of immobility, or rather the emptiness of mobility,
creates a situation for Bulosan and the narrator, Carlos, to translate.
If the promise of America is not fulfilled on Carlos's journey, he

must make sense of it somehow. The "chaos" and "senseless jumble of brutalities," as Wong describes it, needs to be translated by Carlos and by Bulosan in order to give meaning to his journey to America and journeys within America. That is, translation, an act of colonial violence, is inverted to dismantle the violence that Carlos has experienced.

This need for translation is part of another narrative theme, and the one I want to focus on most closely: the literacy narrative. Reading *America Is in the Heart* as a literacy narrative draws together the central themes in this text with what I have been describing as key issues in the construction of Asian American identity and production of Asian American texts. Though I will be discussing translation as a symbolic act—not the literal translation from one language to another—the importance of acquiring English in *America Is in the Heart* cannot be overstated because of the ideological meaning infused in English. Oscar V. Campomanes and Todd S. Gernes suggest that Bulosan's "The Story of a Letter" acts as a sketch for *America Is in the Heart*. In this story, a father in the Philippines receives a letter written in English from his son in America. The letter remains unread until the narrator—the youngest son—can journey to America and acquire the language he needs to read and understand the letter. Once the narrator has the language to read the letter, this is what he learns:

> Dear father. . . . America is a great country. Tall buildings. Wide good land. The people walking. But I feel sad. I am writing to you this hour of my sentimental. Your son.— Berto (44)

Not only does the narrator perform an act of translation, but his brother Berto does as well as he tries to make his experiences in America available to his family. However, why Berto chooses to write in English is not clear when he knows his family would not be able to read his letter and would need to find a translator. The ideological power of America has begun to assimilate Berto as he perhaps unconsciously performs an act of colonialism, replicating the relationship between the United States and Philippines. In this sketch we begin to see the first hints at the importance placed on literacy and writing that will become central themes in *America Is in the Heart*.

In *America Is in the Heart*, there is a similar moment of translation when Carlos realizes he is able to use English:

> I bought a bottle of wine when I arrived in San Luis Obispo. I rented a room in a Japanese hotel and started a letter to my brother Macario, whose address had been given to me by a friend. Then it came to me, like a revelation, that I could actually write understandable English. I was seized by happiness. I wrote slowly and boldly, drinking the wine when I stopped, laughing silently and crying. When the long letter was finished, a letter which was actually a story of my life, I jumped to my feet and shouted through my tears:
>
> "They can't silence me any more! I'll tell the world what they have done to me!" (180)

Unlike "The Story of a Letter," where there is a certain sadness when the narrator finally reads the letter, translates it for his father back in the Philippines, only to find out that his father died before he could read the letter, Carlos is ecstatic over his newfound ability. Carlos declares that he will use his skill in English to reveal the violence he has experienced in America. That he makes this pronouncement while he has been drinking is interesting since it suggests that in some way this behavior deviates from his usual affirmation of America. Carlos's rants can be dismissed because of his drunkenness, but he could also be more "truthful" at this point as he sees beyond the dream of America.

While acquisition of English is an important moment in Carlos's literacy narrative, his acts of writing are infused with social meaning as they act not only to create an identity but also to translate his experiences in America for an audience that is confused by the contradictions they themselves have experienced in America.

Campomanes and Gernes see writing in Bulosan's work as an important social act as well as personal act:

> The act of writing for Bulosan is a revelation, an expression of kinship and community, a gesture of autobiography, and an act of breaking silence, of bearing witness to the struggles not merely of the Filipinos but of all oppressed peoples in America striving for liberty, autonomy, wholeness, and self-worth. (24)

For Bulosan, writing moves beyond a sphere of institutionalized and sanctioned discourse. This is perhaps best seen as he critiques constructions of education early on in *America Is in the Heart*. While education is often a larger theme in the literacy narrative, constructions of oppressive and rigid educational institutions are often juxtaposed against more liberal expressions of literacy acquisition. The faith that Carlos and his family put in education and what they believe will be the material benefits of that education are heartbreaking. Rather, education, or the educational institution, is what ultimately causes the collapse of the family farm and forces Carlos and his brothers to go to America in search of work and, ironically, a better life. This first indication of education as a commodity becomes the backdrop for Carlos's quite opposite desire for education and literacy because he sees them as liberating practices. His self-education and discovery of the pleasure of writing re/vision literacy as a means for creativity:

> Every day the words poured out of my pen. I began to cultivate a taste for words, not so much their meanings as their sounds and shapes, so that afterward I tried to depend on the music of my words to express my ideas. This procedure, of course, was destructive to my grammar, but I can say that writing fumbling, vehement letters to Eileen was actually my course in English. What came after this apprenticeship—the structural presentation of ideas in pertinence to the composition and the anarchy between man's

experience and ideals—was merely my formal search. (235)

Even though Carlos worries that his grammar is poor, he is not limited by the conception of literacy as cultural discipline. Rather, he writes and fumbles but after this period of his "apprenticeship," becomes engaged in "literate" practice. Carlos recognizes, however, that this practice is merely his "formal search," the use of convention in order to present his ideas and experiences.

As the narrative progresses, Carlos finds himself more immobile, due partly to his increasingly poor health, but perhaps symbolic of his growing literacy and interest in writing; he becomes settled in order to translate his experiences into written text. This also creates a dichotomy as body and mind are posed against each other: The failing body can no longer travel; the growing mind becomes the means for exploration. But Carlos still feels the frustration as well, unsure of his ability as a writer though still strong in his desire to tell a story if not to write:

I felt that I was nearing the end, and every day created a havoc in me. I wanted to do something but I did not know where to begin. I had a vague desire to write, my mind was teeming with ideas, but I was not sure of myself. I yearned to know someone who was a successful writer, but the men around me were violent and crude. I needed some kind of order to guide me in the confusion that reigned over my life. (265)

The confusion and chaos that Carlos feels exists partly because he has not yet begun his translation of his experiences. Though he feels compelled to write because writing would help him begin to bring order to his life, he also resists writing because he questions the value and legitimacy of his own life's experiences. As a Filipino and Asian American, Carlos worries that his story, as important as it may be, is not important to others. His search in the library for writers who would validate his own experiences is painful:

> I had only one escape—the Los Angeles Public Library. I
> planned to read ten thousand books on all subjects, but
> reading only made me live the acute pain of the past. When
> I came upon a scene that recalled my own experiences I
> could not go on. But mostly I felt that other writers lied
> about life, that they were afraid to depict it as it really was
> in their environment. (265)

Or perhaps his search in the library and not finding others like himself is valuable. Carlos begins to appreciate the complexity of his
own experiences and the difficulty in writing them. He sees other
writers as not being able to create these meaningful experiences,
perhaps relying on stereotype, cliché, and genre in order to tell a
story. For Bulosan to include this comment through Carlos is in-
triguing. Such a comment supports the ironic reading of *America Is
in the Heart* and is even tongue-in-cheek as Carlos condemns those
"other writers that lied about life" while Bulosan himself may have
fictionalized his own life story.

Or perhaps Carlos could not identify with those writers that
"lied about life" because their experiences were very different from
his own. While I will not raise a question about the "authenticity"
and "legitimacy" of a person's life experience here, I will speculate
that Carlos does privilege race and class in his search for "true" stories. He finds inspiration in the Korean writer Younghill Kang's
autobiography, *The Grass Roof* (265). And then he finds his ideal:

> Was there an Oriental without education who had become
> a writer in America? If there was one, maybe I could do it
> too! I ransacked the library, read biographies omnivo-
> rously, tried to study other languages. Then I came upon
> the very man—Yone Noguchi! A Japanese houseboy in the
> home of Joaquin Miller, the poet, who became the first
> poet of his race to write in the English language.
>   Here at last was an ideal. (265)

While Carlos identifies with Kang to a degree because he is an
immigrant and writes about the Korean revolutionary movement,

Carlos also feels some class anxiety since Kang came from a family of scholars and had attended an American university. Carlos identifies much more with Yone Noguchi because of his apparent humble beginnings as a houseboy for the poet Joaquin Miller. But Carlos also feels a kinship with Noguchi because he is "the first poet of his race to write in the English language," a position in which Carlos finds himself and seeks comfort.

Though Carlos continues to write articles and poems for the various Filipino and labor newspapers and bulletins, it is the publication of his first book of poetry that brings this literacy narrative to a symbolic climax. However, the circumstances under which Carlos's book of poetry is published raise questions about how the book is being constructed and marketed by the publisher:

> A week after the fall of Bataan a letter came from a small publisher. He wanted to publish an edition of my poems. Was it possible that I would have a book at last? Not quite sure if it was time for me to assemble my poems, I arranged and revised them in restaurants at night. (320)

Carlos appears to put aside the possible exploitation by this publisher who takes advantage of the Philippines's situation during the war to sell books. What matters to him is that his book, his poetry, will be published and entered into a public that will hear his stories about class and race oppression. Again his naivete acts to signify and reveal the exploitative practices of the publisher who uses World War II and the campaign in the Philippines to sell a Filipino writer. Carlos's "success" in America is tempered by the war in the Philippines, which perhaps is the harshest reminder of the very hard journey he has experienced. The journey toward literacy and the translation of America still does not allow Carlos to escape the violence of his life:

> When the manuscript was finished, I sent it to the publisher. I began another assignment, a small anthology of contemporary Philippine poetry. My anxiety about my relatives in the Philippines dampened the excitement I would

have felt at this notice of my literary work. Here was something that I had been working for with great sacrifice, but the war had come to frustrate all feelings of fulfillment. (320)

While Carlos cannot escape the frustration of his life with the publication of his book, he still recognizes his achievement. While the ironic reading of *America Is in the Heart* delivers a scathing critique of America, it is still hard to ignore the moving achievement of Carlos, who has suffered and worked hard to be a writer. When Carlos holds the book in his hands, he is holding more than just poems; he holds the story of his life and the translations of his experiences in America for a larger public:

> When the bound copies of my first book of poems, *Letter From America,* arrived, I felt like shouting to the world. How long ago had it been that I had drunk a bottle of wine because I discovered that I could write English?
>
> The book was a rush job and the binding was simple, but it was something that had grown out of my heart. I knew that I would not write the same way again. I had put certain things of myself in it: the days of pain and anguish, of starvation and fear; my hopes, desires, aspirations. All of myself in this little volume of poems—and I would never be like that self again. (320)

Carlos recalls his journey to literacy. And yet what he values in the book is not anything of material value, just of personal value and a recognition of his own change. Carlos does not extol the virtues of literacy, does not attempt to convert others. He instead understands that his acquisition of literacy was more than just the learning of discourse conventions or acquiring the ability and means to produce his own book. Literacy, his own conception of what it was and what it could do for him, becomes a liberating practice that in the end gives him the means for cultural criticism.

While the above scene is hopeful and in many ways suggests that personal fulfillment may be enough, Bulosan explodes the "literacy myth" and any promise of significant political and material change by destroying Carlos's book. Carlos looks for his brother, Amado, to show him his book and finds him drinking with two women. He tries to share his book with them, but one of the women laughs at him and tears the pages from the book. Carlos is distraught and Amado strikes the woman, who sobs,

> "I just felt bad, that's all," she said. "I just felt bad. If you stay on in this lousy street you'll be ruined. See what happened to me? I wanted to be an actress. I came from a nice family, a nice family in Baltimore. . . . " (321)

A contrast is drawn between Carlos, whose literacy has given him a symbolic measure of success, and the woman, who has not been able to succeed despite being of the "right" background in her mind. Her anxiety about Carlos's "success" is revealing. For a Filipino to produce a book of poetry flies in the face of her expectation that her race and class standing will be enough to succeed. But the violent reaction by Amado is also problematic because it reproduces the oppression that has employed literacy in the creation of gender and race hierarchies. Literacy or literate culture has been privileged and Amado's violent response acts to reinforce the status of literacy by disciplining the woman who destroys the book. Carlos is left to pick up the pieces and to think about what the value of literacy really is: "I put the remnants of the book under my coat and walked to the door. Amado got up to say something, but stopped and looked down in defeat" (322). The symbolic climax of this literacy narrative is overtaken by another symbolic moment. When Carlos picks up the remnants of his book, the value of literacy is still ambiguous. For Carlos, there seems to be no social or material gain, partly because of his race and political views.

And yet the remnants represent a fragmented life that holds much personal and social meaning. The difficulty for Carlos has been creating a cohesive narrative of his life. Such a narrative might ring false since it is generated more by the desires of an audience than by the purpose of the writer. The fragments of his book can be seen as fragments of writing, or acts of writing that each hold their own meaning. Campomanes and Gernes suggest that Bulosan's act of writing is an attempt to weave together the fragments:

> Although directed against oppression, his act of writing bore the impulse to build intersocial and cross-cultural bridges of communication, meshing the personal and the social, his life story and the story of Pinoys, into a complex and enriching synthesis. (30)

I do not think that the weaving together of these fragments constitutes a cohesive master narrative. But I do find Bulosan's multiple acts of writing in *America Is in the Heart* to be an attempt to translate and critique America in order to keep the idea and ideals of America alive. It is through these various acts of writing that seem to disrupt rather than narrate an ideal America that important work occurs. Only through these disruptions and then re/visions of how literacy, race, citizenship are operating in *America Is in the Heart* can a new narrative be written that invites multiple readings around these terms.

> Sometimes I hated the ghosts for not letting us talk . . .
> —Maxine Hong Kingston, *The Woman Warrior*

> Basic English skills are at the very core of what these public schools teach. Imposition of a requirement that, before a child can effectively participate in the educational program, he must already have acquired those basic skills is to make a mockery of public education. *We know that those who do not understand English are certain to find their classroom experiences wholly incomprehensible and in no way meaningful.* (emphasis added)
> —United States Supreme Court, *Lau v. Nichols*

On 21 January 1974, the United States Supreme Court handed down a decision in *Lau v. Nichols* that was to become recognized as the major precedent in the protection of educational rights for language minorities.[12] The original suit was filed by Kinney Kinmon Lau and twelve non–English-speaking Chinese American students in Federal District Court in San Francisco against Alan Nichols, the president of the San Francisco Board of Education. The suit alleged that Chinese-speaking students were denied equal educational opportunities because the schools did not provide the necessary means to facilitate their learning of English. Without the remedy of a mandatory bilingual education policy to support non–English speakers, schools often placed these students in classrooms where English was the language of instruction but with no means to teach the students English or to translate subject material. The San Francisco Board of Education argued that they provided the same educational environment and instruction for all students and should not be compelled to provide special instruction for students who happen to enter school with a deficiency. Both the Federal District Court and the Ninth Circuit Court of Appeals agreed with the San Francisco Board of Education. However, the United States Supreme Court unanimously overturned those lower court decisions in favor of Lau and ordered the lower court to develop a plan to remedy the discrimination. Significantly, the Supreme Court based its decision on Section 601 of the Civil Rights Act of 1964 rather than on the Equal Protection Clause of the Fourteenth Amendment, which would have provided the force and authority of constitutional guarantee.[13]

Not only did the Lau v. Nichols decision make an important statement about the right of equal educational opportunity for all, it was also a symbolic act of lifting the silence from a group that had been silenced by institutional policy and practice, silence that was in some ways sanctioned by the larger culture. While I agree with the Supreme Court decision and recognize the significance of Lau v. Nichols in the development of policies and practices to help language minority students, I want to suggest that even in this lifting of silence, there is a type of silence that still exists. That is, despite attempts to create equal opportunity in education, whether it be the protection of language minority students or racial minorities, an act of silencing still occurs as students contend with the pressures of American culture, which still places them on the margins.[14]

What was at issue in *Lau v. Nichols* was the educational disadvantage non–English speakers faced and the responsibility of the schools in addressing this disadvantage. As the Supreme Court stated: "We know that those who do not understand English are certain to find their classroom experiences wholly incomprehensible and in no way meaningful." This is certainly true on one level since not being able to understand what was going on in a classroom would not be meaningful in terms of acquiring the skills and content being taught. However, on another level, this situation would be significantly meaningful as those students in not "comprehending" would be faced with shame and confusion over their place in the class. Even those students who do know English are not immune to the pressures and anxieties created by the "requirement" of English to participate in public life. Even if students do have a command of English, their experiences can be "wholly incomprehensible and in no way meaningful" if they find themselves in a situation that silences them in other ways. This silence is created out of the anxiety that they will not meet the expectations and requirements of public life; that those whose citizenship in the community is never questioned will see them as illegitimate subjects. The silence of Asian Americans protects them from being confirmed as alien; their silence also prevents them from participating in public life and being confirmed as citizens. They are caught in-between.

The construction and operation of silence becomes key in discussing the role of literacy *in English* as not only a legal requirement but also a symbolic requirement of citizenship in America. Literacy in English is often seen as a public vocal performance that declares an individual's ability to participate in American culture: Public speaking without an accent confers "legitimacy." In her study of silence in Asian American women writers, King-Kok Cheung describes the power and anxiety of silence in Maxine Hong Kingston's *The Woman Warrior:*

> Maxine, the narrator of Kingston's *Woman Warrior,* is gagged
> by misogynist proverbs while growing up in a Chinese

immigrant community. But her silence becomes "thickest" when she enters an "American" school, where she is branded as retarded because she is unable to speak English. Having internalized the norms of her schoolteachers, Maxine later tries to torture another mute Chinese girl into speech.

This last episode enacts the Asian American psychological trauma of trying to live up to a dominant norm and points to the dangers of excessive emphasis on vocalization. Monocultural criteria of competence and even feminist antipathy toward silence may run roughshod over the sensibilities of some ethnic groups. While the importance of voice is indisputable, pronouncing silence as the converse of speech or as its subordinate can also be oppressively univocal. *The Woman Warrior* does undoubtedly chart the narrator's progression from tonguelessness to expression, yet young Maxine's acceptance of the dominant culture's equation of "talk" with "brain" and "personality" is no less disturbing than the black girl Pecola's pathetic desire for the "bluest eye" in Toni Morrison's novel. (6)

The lifting of silence by *Lau v. Nichols* becomes even more interesting in light of Cheung's assessment of the "pathetic desire" for English by Asian American subjects and the psychological effects on them. Both *Lau v. Nichols* and Cheung identify the site where this desire and anxiety is cultivated and produced, the "American" school. However, where *Lau v. Nichols* assumes the remedy to the complexities of Asian American identity is the acquisition of English (which would make them more American), Cheung suggests that English becomes a complication in the construction of Asian American identity because of the ideological and psychological implications of English.

In this section I want to focus on Kingston's "Song for a Barbarian Reed Pipe," the last story in *The Woman Warrior,* as a scene of re/vision as well as an expression of anxiety about literacy and citizenship. Within this section, Kingston includes a scene in an "American" school where, as Cheung remarks, "her silence becomes thickest." Though I focus on this school scene to discuss various acts of instruction, I read *The Woman Warrior* as a whole as a narrative about teaching and learning. The telling of stories by the narrator and her mother performs a pedagogical purpose: What is real? What is make-believe? As the narrator, Maxine, learns throughout the book, she must decide what is useful, what her mother's lessons are, and what stories she will tell. The text, *The Woman Warrior,* is the result, and its readers are then faced with the same choices Maxine faces. What is real? What is make-believe? What do we learn?

If there was an Asian American writer whom I was familiar with (beyond the local Asian American writers of Hawai'i), it was Maxine Hong Kingston. It was difficult not to be aware of *The Woman Warrior* and *China Men* since they both received national acclaim and were probably the Asian American texts that would most likely be taught in the classroom. But Kingston's presence was even more strongly felt because of the time she spent in Hawai'i, teaching at one of the local private schools while she wrote *The Woman Warrior* and *China Men,* and returning for readings and lectures after the success of her books. Though I did not read either *The Woman Warrior* or *China Men* until I began graduate school and began to focus on Asian American literature, I do recall an early memory of *The Woman Warrior* from my childhood. It was probably the mid 1970s (*The Woman Warrior* was first published in 1976) and I remember my eldest sister reading from *The Woman Warrior* to my sister Genny. I was a little puzzled since I thought Genny was too old to be read to—she would have just started college—but then I was fascinated by the scene as one sister read to another, as if they were passing on their own stories. And each time I read *The Woman Warrior* these many years later, I begin to understand both the "talk story" that occurs in the text and the type of "talk story" I saw being acted out between my sisters.

As I began to unpack both the story of *The Woman Warrior* and the historical contexts for Asian American literacy, I was amazed at another coincidence surrounding these issues: the decision for *Lau v. Nichols* was handed down on my birthday, 21 January. It was almost as if I was destined to cross paths with these issues of Asian American literacy, to encounter these texts, which would help me understand what I was trying to learn about these writers and their projects.

In "A Song for a Barbarian Reed Pipe," we are presented with one of the most powerful and painful scenes in the book as a young Maxine confronts and torments another Chinese American girl because she will not speak. The status of this girl is ambiguous. Is she really another girl, though a reminder to Maxine about her own "illegitimate" status? Is she the psychological manifestation of Maxine, her twin, her double who represents to Maxine those things she hates the most about herself? Is she a "racial shadow," as Sau-ling Wong argues, representing the tension between Maxine's desire for an unquestioned American identity and those characteristics she believes deny her that identity (*Reading* 78)?

Before this confrontation, though, there are numerous hints at how much importance is placed on language and the anxiety language and the required performance of it can create. Maxine's mother recognizes the emphasis placed on *oral* language in America and does what she thinks will be best for Maxine:

> "I cut [your frenum] so that you would not be tongue-tied. Your tongue would be able to move in any language. You'll be able to speak languages that are completely different from one another. You'll be able to pronounce anything. Your frenum looked too tight to do those things, so I cut it."
>
> "But isn't 'a ready tongue an evil?'"
>
> "Things are different in this ghost country." (164)

An orientalist reading of the exoticness and cruelty of this act of mutilation would construct this as Chinese, and yet Maxine's mother claims to do it because of the demands of America. What is ironic, however, is that it is not the tongue that needs to be freed but rather Maxine's mind which, when faced with the pressure of public display, tightens up:

> When I went to kindergarten and had to speak English for the first time, I became silent. A dumbness—a shame—still cracks my voice in two, even when I want to say "hello" casually, or ask an easy question in front of the check-out counter, or ask directions of a bus driver. I stand frozen, or I hold up the line with the complete, grammatical sentence that comes squeaking out at impossible length. (165)

The legacy of her schooling still haunts the adult Maxine. Her discomfort with English, or rather the performance she must enact, is clear. While she fumbles with language, she also takes painstaking care to be hyper-literate—the "complete, grammatical sentence that comes squeaking out at impossible length"—so that her legitimacy and citizenship will not be questioned though such unease will mark her nonetheless.

Though it is unclear whether Maxine could speak English or not when she entered kindergarten, the effects of the silencing that *Lau v. Nichols* was supposed to correct are portrayed in Maxine's early educational experience. In silence, Maxine finds comfort, though she does communicate with others when it suits her:

> During the first silent year I spoke to no one at school, did not ask before going to the lavatory, and flunked kindergarten. My sister also said nothing for three years, silent in the playground and silent at lunch. There were other quiet Chinese girls not of our family, but most of them got over it sooner than we did. I enjoyed the silence. At first it did not occur to me I was supposed to talk to pass kindergarten. I talked at home and to one or two of the Chinese kids in class. I made motions and even made some jokes. I drank out of a toy saucer when the water spilled out of the cup, and everybody laughed, pointing at me, so I did it some more. I didn't know that Americans don't drink out of saucers. (165–66)

The purpose of kindergarten is a mystery to her, so much so that she "flunks." But if kindergarten and schooling are mysterious to Maxine, it is due partly to the mystification of school and the way achievement is constructed by American culture. The young Maxine is unaware that she needs to talk in order to "pass" kindergarten. The young Maxine does not understand that a test in the first grade where the teacher read aloud the questions while she covered her answer sheet in black would result in a zero IQ. When she makes her classmates laugh by doing what she thinks is reasonable solution to having spilled some water, she does not understand she is being seen as the "Oriental" and as un-American.

However, when Maxine develops an awareness of the expectations of schooling, she begins to feel the pressures of performance. She now understands the consequences of not talking and this creates even more anxiety as she internalizes this "deficiency" and even constructs it as "Chinese":

> *It was when I found out I had to talk that school became a misery, that the silence became a misery.* I did not speak and felt bad each time I did not speak. I read aloud in first grade, though, and heard the barest whisper with little squeaks come out of my throat. "Louder," said the teacher, who scared the voice away again. The other Chinese girls did not talk either, so *I knew the silence had to do with being a Chinese girl.* (166, emphasis added)

Her American schooling seems to emphasize the differences; or at least to Maxine that is what is going on. In contrast, the situation at the Chinese language school was much different. Students did not feel silenced and were able to respond to both teachers and classmates without any anxiety:

> When we had a memorization test, the teacher let each of us come to his desk and say the lesson to him privately, while the rest of the class practiced copying or tracing. Most of

the teachers were men. The boys who were so well behaved
in the American school played tricks on them and talked
back to them. The girls were not mute. They screamed and
yelled during recess, when there were no rules; they had
fistfights. (167)

This marked difference in schools reveals something about pedagogical practice as well as perceived cultural differences. One factor
is the construction of "safe" spaces for the students. Students felt
more comfortable in Chinese school than in American school. It
may be a familiarity with culture—the stereotype of the ethnic enclave—but I would also suggest that it is a familiarity with the expectations of schooling (or lack of) at each place. At the American
school the boys were so "well behaved," perhaps because they were
afraid to act, afraid to be judged by the American school when they
did not even know what they were being judged on. At the Chinese
school the girls did not have to be "mute" because they did not have
to fear being constructed as "dumb" or un-American. The students
perform their identities in order to fulfill the representations expected of them both in Chinese school and American school. What
might be the most important difference, though, are the ways in
which students were able to express their identities in these public
spaces. In the American school, students were made to perform,
made to risk presenting themselves in a public that would already
have expectations and assumptions about who they were. In the
Chinese school, students were still asked to perform, but not in the
same type of public space. They do share their identities with their
teachers, but the pressure and anxiety of such a public display is
lessened because they understand the appropriate social practices
of this classroom and are not the constructed minor subject of
dominant culture.

However, this lesson on pedagogy is lost on the young Maxine,
who finds herself caught in the ideological power of the American
school. When Maxine confronts the "other" Chinese girl in the
lavatory of the American school, she is on a mission to make her
talk. This act of talking is mired in a complex set of expectations

and misplaced beliefs about the political and material rewards that will result. In short, Maxine's project is to "teach" her "student" how to be an American:

> "You're going to talk," I said, my voice steady and normal, as it is when talking to the familiar, the weak, and the small. "I am going to make you talk, you sissy—girl." She stopped backing away and stood fixed. (175)

That Maxine is able to talk with a voice "steady and normal" at this moment is revealing of her new role as teacher and American, confident in this identity with the assurances of belonging to the dominant community. Her comfort is also generated by the "familiar, the weak, and the small," all descriptions that could apply to Maxine and which support interpretations that this encounter is between Maxine and herself.

Again the insistence on declaring a public identity and performing a public self becomes the focal point in Maxine's act of teaching:

> "Say 'Hi,'" I said. "'Hi.' Like that. Say your name. Go ahead. Say it. Or are you stupid? You're so stupid, you don't know your own name, is that it? When I say, 'What's your name?' you just blurt it out, o.k.? What's your name?" Last year the whole class had laughed at a boy who couldn't fill out a form because he didn't know his father's name. The teacher sighed, exasperated, and was very sarcastic, "Don't you notice things? What does your mother call him?" she said. The class laughed at how dumb he was not to notice things. "She calls him father of me," he said. Even we laughed, although we knew that his mother did not call his father by name, and a son does not know his father's name. We laughed and were relieved that our parents had had the foresight to tell us some names we could give the teachers. (177)

Maxine's torment of the girl performs three purposes. First, she insists that the girl declare who she is, to present a public identity that will enter her into the public discourse of culture. Second, Maxine uses this encounter to reify the differences between herself and the girl. Her knowledge, for example, about why children do not know their fathers' names, gives her an authority over the girl since she can claim she is somehow more American by knowing her father's name even though it is an alias provided by her mother to appease Western expectations. And third, Maxine's torture of the girl is symbolic of the torture both of them experience as being constructed as less than American.

The lesson that Maxine is trying to teach is supposed to provide the knowledge that will protect them. However, the results seem less than successful:

> "Why won't you talk?" I started to cry. What if I couldn't stop, and everyone would want to know what happened? "Now look what you've done," I scolded. "You're going to pay for this. I want to know why. And you're going to tell me why. You don't see I'm trying to help you out, do you. Do you want to be like this, dumb (do you know what dumb means?), your whole life? Don't you ever want to be a cheerleader? Or a pompon girl? What are you going to do for a living? Yeah you're going to have to work because you can't be a housewife. Somebody has to marry you before you can be a housewife. And you, you are a plant. Do you know that? That's all you are if you don't talk. If you don't talk, you can't have a personality. You'll have no personality and no hair. You've got to let people know you have a personality and a brain. (180)

Maxine begins to equate talk (and thus English and literacy) with all of those signifiers of American citizenship. Her list of what talk can get you reads like a stereotypical (as well as gendered and now outdated) checklist for the American Dream: cheerleader, pompon girl, housewife. She also makes the equation between talk and personality, and talk and a brain. Maxine lists all the characteristics of being American, and silence is not among them. Silence becomes the marker of Asian American citizenship, or perhaps of being just "oriental." Maxine's act of teaching reflects the extent to which she has bought into the ideological project of Americanization. As King-Kok Cheung observes: "To read this incident simply as reflecting young Maxine's intense desire to explode the stock image of the quiet Oriental damsel obscures the extent of her indoctrination: silence equals a zero IQ" (88).

What Maxine's act of teaching also reflects is the example of teaching to which she has been exposed. Her education in American school has not been about English, social studies, history, mathematics, or other subject areas. What she has learned is that she must practice and reproduce this ideology of Americanization if her racially marked self is to have any hope of being recognized as American. She accentuates the differences, as Sau-ling Wong notes, because any marker of "Asianness" would prevent her claiming of citizenship:

> When Maxine forces the girl to speak up, she is seeking confirmation that her own meager, fragile achievements in assimilation would guarantee a hopeful future. A recent and insecure convert to Americanization, she cannot tolerate counterexamples. A single hopeless case of unassimilability would throw the inevitability of her entire undertaking into doubt, obliging her to seek another redemptive alternative. The violence she discharges onto the girl escalates in proportion to her growing realization that, in a profound sense beyond issues of specifiable, modifiable behavior, they are "the same" to the non-Chinese. Manners can be changed, but not skin color; as the Other, Chinese Americans will always, to some degree, be spurned. In this light, the gorilla held under canvas is not so much any individual's id as American society's potential for institutionalized racist violence, of which the protagonist temporarily becomes a deputy. (90)

Maxine's teaching of American citizenship reproduces the discursive violence that has been enacted upon Asian Americans whether through immigration policy, education policy, or any number of legally sanctioned practices that discriminated against Asian Americans based solely on race. Kingston's telling of this particular story acts as a lesson about the power of lessons and how students can internalize the messages given by various ideological projects. Just as Bulosan turns America into the subject of his project, so does Kingston, who in presenting one story about the teaching of American citizenship, gives us another story about the pain of the most important lessons. Minor re/vision works in complicated ways as we see in each of these narratives. However, there is often a blurring between what is supposed to be Asian American culture and what is supposed to be American culture. Asian American subjects begin to re/vision culture and the ways dominant culture constructs them through the discourses of literacy and citizenship. The blurred distinctions begin to suggest a re/vision of American citizenship.

In reading the literacy narratives of Richard Rodriguez, Victor Villanueva, Carlos Bulosan, and Maxine Hong Kingston, I have described how each narrative functions in specific ways to address issues of literacy and citizenship. While *Hunger of Memory* functions in more conventional ways to provide a developmental narrative of individual achievement, it is still valuable for illustrating the anxiety that emerges when literacy, race, and citizenship converge. *Hunger of Memory* is also valuable because it does touch a part of our lives, which forces us to re/vision our own literacy histories. The narratives by Villanueva, Bulosan, and Kingston also act as conventional narratives of development as we see how subjects within these texts acquire literacy and education in their movement toward participation as citizens. However, these narratives also subvert these conventional stories with their critical examinations of America. *Bootstraps* functions both as a critique of America and as a critique of the profession, reminding us that we must all be critically conscious and vigilant as we make literacy our profession. *America Is in the Heart* and *The Woman Warrior* undercut expectations about what it means to be Asian or Asian American by providing readers with difficult scenes of education and literacy. In these narratives, education and literacy do provide the means for achievement and citizenship, but these things are not gained without both material and psychological pain. While the romantic narrative of America might suggest that these achievements are worth the pain, there is a need to understand fully what is at stake for those in minor positions. Rather than simply accepting risk and loss for the promise of a better future, these narratives re/vision what the American Story can be by challenging dominant discourses about literacy, race, and citizenship, and by offering alternatives that continue to uphold the idea of America.

3 Reading Hawai'i's Asian American Literacy Narratives
Re/Visions of Resistance, Schooling, and Citizenship

> At the University of Michigan, a graduate student has recently passed a language proficiency exam in Pidgin by translating a passage from the Bamboo Ridge *Pake* anthology published by Bamboo Ridge Press. Another graduate student subsequently petitioned to do the same.
>
> —Cristina Bacchilega, "Pro-Vocations: Multivocality and Local Literature"

In the fall of 1993 as I completed my last set of qualifying exams before I became a candidate for the Ph.D., I faced having to fulfill my advanced language requirement. I toyed with the idea of taking the Latin exam, but it had been five years since I had completed my undergraduate foreign language requirement, and though I believed I could successfully pass the reading exam, I wasn't really motivated to revisit Latin. As I thought about the situation, it occurred to me that perhaps I could petition to use Hawai'i Creole—Pidgin—to fulfill the requirement. A precedent had been set when another graduate student successfully petitioned that she be allowed to use Jamaican Creole (though she later passed her exam in a more "conventional" language). As I thought about the implications of "institutionalizing" Pidgin, I felt both anxiety and excitement about the prospect. The anxiety existed because I worried about how this might be perceived. When attempts to study Ebonics or other "nonstandard" discourse forms reached mainstream media, there were often outcries about legitimizing "slang" and "street" language. Even in Hawai'i, where Pidgin is common and for the most part culturally accepted, it still remains on the margins of Standard English and controversial when issues of identity and legitimacy are at stake. For someone who was working toward a Ph.D. in English, Pidgin could be a risk.

But there was also excitement about inserting Pidgin into an institutional setting; for Pidgin to be recognized as a language by an elite university made a statement. As part of my petition, I had to explain that Pidgin was not my primary language despite growing up in a community where Pidgin was used widely. Because my mother attended English Standard schools for her secondary education, I argued that Standard English was the primary home language. This argument plus a review of research on Pidgin and the availability of someone to create, administer, and grade the exam allowed the petition to be approved. I completed my exam by translating a selection from the play "For You a Lei," by Wai Chee Chun Yee, published in the Bamboo Ridge Press anthology *Paké: Writings by Chinese in Hawaii,* and answering an essay question that asked me to discuss the difficulties and subtleties of translating the passage. I was now a footnote in the history of Pidgin and even became a minor celebrity when someone announced at the next Association for Asian American Studies annual meeting that I was the first person ever to pass a language exam in Pidgin. Others even asked about the process and how they might go about petitioning Pidgin for their exams. I had made Pidgin public and "legitimate." However, making Pidgin public in Michigan and in the academy is not the same as making Pidgin public within our larger culture. Can a minority discourse act in the re/vision of public citizenship, especially when faced with a long history of linguistic discrimination?

In this chapter, I explore scenes of re/vision by two of Hawai'i's Asian American writers, Marie Hara and Lois-Ann Yamanaka, and focus on how their literacy narratives act to respond to specific historical and sociocultural contexts for literacy. While chapter 2 focuses on how reading literacy narratives has informed my understanding of the ways literacy, race, and citizenship are connected, this chapter focuses specifically on Hawai'i's Asian American literacy narratives and the way they operate in the re/vision of minor subjects, in the insertion of these minor subjects in culture as citizens, and in the uses of literacy in these processes. In the literacy narratives that I discuss here, we see the effects of imposed standardization on students and how the resultant silence and anxiety can shape their lives. But we also see how minority discourse can be used strategically and how resistance to standardization can lead to critical awareness about the ways literacy, race, and citizenship are often conflated to the detriment of students.

The resistant literacy of Hawai'i's Asian Americans is manifested in the use of Pidgin as seen in the narratives by Marie Hara and Lois-Ann Yamanaka, which focus on the anxieties caused by schooling and the politics of Standard English. While there is much anxiety about language and the "necessity" of Standard English, Pidgin becomes a language that inverts its "lack" into a "presence," a re/vision of literacy and citizenship that binds together a community dealing with a legacy of racism and social injustice. To begin, I provide a brief social history of Hawai'i's literacy context in the twentieth century, looking at the legacy of the plantations and English Standard school. I then turn to the literacy narratives by Hara and Yamanaka, which in a sense build upon the Asian American narratives of Bulosan and Kingston, where we see the position of the minor come into play. In their uses of literacy and language, the characters in the narratives by Hara and Yamanaka deterritorialize dominant discourse, move toward political action, and provide collective experiences that complicate dominant narratives about Asian Americans. To understand the larger implications of these literacy narratives by Hara and Yamanaka, I then examine the public discourse about Pidgin in contemporary Hawai'i and how this affects both the classroom and larger culture. In examining the history, narratives, and public discourse about literacy in Hawai'i, I provide a specific case to illustrate how literacy, race, and citizenship are connected, to show how literacy narratives are a way for those in minor positions to re/vision what citizenship and literacy can mean, to provide alternatives and re/visions to the American Story.

Re/Visions of a Literacy History

Children growing up in Hawaii, coming as they do in their plastic years under the influence of the public school, preparing them for the assumption of the responsibilities which life in Hawaii demands, should come to feel that, in cutting cane on the plantation, in driving a tractor in the fields, in swinging a sledge in a blacksmith shop, in wielding a brush on building or fence or bridge, as well as in sitting at a doctor's or merchant's or manager's or banker's desk, there is opportunity for rendering a necessary as well as intelligent, worthy, and creative service.

> —United States Department of the Interior,
> *A Survey of Education in Hawaii* (1920)

Americans know that their impressionable children, literally surrounded throughout the school-day and at playtime by these swarms of Orientals, will unconsciously pick up and adopt Oriental manners and mannerisms. . . . [T]he American child will be held back to the pace of the Oriental, who is studious indeed but toiling under a terrific weight of lack of English words and word-images to respond to the efforts of the teacher.

> —Anonymous school authority of Hawai'i, quoted by
> Riley H. Allen, "Education and Race Problems in
> Hawaii" (1921)

One of the realities of life is that our kids may have to go out into the world beyond Hawaii, to compete for jobs, and certainly if they can't speak the accepted means of communication well—English—then they're going to have a hard time.

> —Ben Cayetano, Governor of Hawai'i (1995)

In 1920, the United States Bureau of Education published *A Survey of Education in Hawaii*, a study requested by the governor and the

Superintendent of Public Instruction of the Territory of Hawai'i and
funded in part by the territorial legislature. This study was the first
comprehensive examination of the system of public education in
Hawai'i and thus was viewed with much importance, since it not
only evaluated Hawai'i's educational system but also provided the
territorial government some gauge of Hawai'i's status as a United
States territory and its success in meeting the ideals of America.
The American Council of Education in their own study, *Hawaiian
Schools: A Curriculum Survey, 1944–45,* called the 1920 survey a
"significant milestone in the history of education in the Territory of
Hawaii" (16–18). In his historical study *A Century of Public Education in Hawaii: 1840–1940,* Benjamin O. Wist, past dean of the University of Hawai'i's Teachers College, called the 1920 survey a "significant event" with recommendations that were "far-reaching in
influence," especially those recommendations relating to foreign
language schools, to secondary schooling, to vocational education,
to teacher training, and to higher education (158).

Wist's evaluation of the impact of the 1920 survey was indeed
accurate as significant changes in educational policy and legislative
action related to education did occur after the report. However,
the nature of and motivation for these changes during this era are
mired in a complex set of actions and beliefs about race and culture
in Hawai'i that still have lasting effects in contemporary Hawai'i.
These actions and beliefs include attitudes about language (i.e.,
Standard English and other "foreign" and nonstandard languages),
territorial education policies to support the plantation economy, and
constructions of race and social class. This chapter will examine
how these conditions in territorial Hawai'i have shaped the conditions of Hawai'i today, where attitudes about literacy and race have
become institutionalized in Hawai'i's cultural discourse. As part of
understanding the contexts for literacy in Hawai'i today, I will focus
on what I see as the racial and literacy legacy of two significant institutions in Hawai'i's history and culture, the plantation and the
English Standard school. While these two institutions have changed
significantly since territorial Hawai'i—the plantations and mills are
mostly a memory now; the system of English Standard schools no

longer exists—I want to discuss their importance in contemporary Hawai'i as illustrated by the public debates that occur around these issues still, and my own position as a (former) Hawai'i resident and now literacy researcher and teacher.

I opened this section with three passages that reflect the attitudes about the state of education in Hawai'i and its effects on Hawai'i's children. The first two passages point out attitudes about race in territorial Hawai'i that ranged from a paternalism carried over from the plantations to xenophobia, which while not as severe as on the mainland United States at the time still existed to a large degree. Hawai'i's public school students, for the most part Hawai'i's nonwhite students, were often seen as nothing more than future plantation laborers, as the passage from the 1920 survey above suggests. We see this attitude more clearly when the then soon-to-be territorial governor Wallace R. Farrington, who in anticipating the 1920 survey recommendation to shift to a vocational curriculum said, "It is expected that the Federal Survey Commission . . . will recommend in its report that academic and classical courses be thrown overboard and replaced by domestic science, agriculture and manual training. We hope that this recommendation will be made" (Tamura 126). While Farrington does not mention race directly, there is an understanding by him (as well as by the 1920 survey) that those students who will be most affected are the nonwhite majority found in the public schools, primarily the children of immigrants brought in as contract laborers. The construction of race by those in positions of power and by Americans in Hawai'i in general, then, becomes a key factor in understanding the motivation for the territory's educational policies, which on the surface seemed to address very real educational concerns, such as English language education.[1] But often underlying these policies was an anxiety about race and the "oriental" influence, as the second quote above from an anonymous Hawai'i school authority indicates.

Buoyed by the recommendations of the 1920 survey, the mainly white education establishment and territorial government began to institute a series of policies that often discriminated both explicitly and implicitly against the majority nonwhite population, and in particular, against the Japanese immigrant population *(issei)* and their American-born children *(nisei)*. The 1920 survey was used as justification for an English language policy that included the creation of a "select" grammar school (Central Grammar School), which was soon expanded into a system of English Standard schools that existed from 1924 to 1948, serving mostly the white middle class of Honolulu. An attempt to regulate foreign language schools (again aimed primarily at the Japanese community) was also made but was eventually ruled unconstitutional by the United States Supreme Court in 1927.[2] In the aftermath of World War II, the increasing push for statehood, and the changing economy and political scene of Hawai'i, these policies eventually became less "necessary" and the de facto segregation of the English Standard schools and other discriminatory practices were phased out. However, the effects of these early policies and the construction of race that was in operation are still felt today. As the final quote above from a recent governor of Hawai'i indicates, there still exists an anxiety in the community about the use of Standard English and demonstration of literacy and the attendant constructions of race, class, and citizenship. Cayetano's statement reflects both a very old attitude about language in Hawai'i and a very current one as Hawai'i Creole and Pidgin seem to gain more "legitimacy" through the production of various cultural texts that have begun to garner mainstream exposure both in and beyond Hawai'i.

Despite a fading presence in today's Hawai'i, the plantation and English Standard school have become cultural institutions, acting as tropes that invoke certain images and memories for Hawai'i residents. And even for those generations removed from the plantations and English Standard schools, there are still remnants, or perhaps eruptions, of the institutional effects found in contemporary Hawai'i. In my own experience, I have been touched by the legacy of the English Standard school: My mother attended English Standard schools during her intermediate and high school years; my own neighborhood elementary school was once an English Standard school, a fact that some teachers pointed to with pride. The plantations and English Standard schools are not just historical moments, not just memories. They are part of the cultural memory of Hawai'i, where narratives of identity are woven together, often marked by common experiences, shared histories, and perhaps most importantly, by the shared language of people whose lives were also marked by their racialization as Other. In laying out the significance of these institutions, I will provide a brief discussion of the social conditions created by the plantation and then move to an examination of how the English Standard school worked to regulate the society created by these new conditions.

The significance of the plantation in Hawai'i's history cannot be overstated. While sugar plantations began operations in Hawai'i in the mid-nineteenth century, the 1875 Reciprocity Agreement between an independent Hawai'i and the United States, which removed tariffs from Hawai'i's sugar, created an incentive for increased production and export to America (Beechert 48). This required new labor, and the plantations began a process that dramatically changed the makeup of Hawai'i's population. Between 1850 and 1920, over 300,000 Asians (from China, Korea, the Philippines, and with the largest number from Japan) came to Hawai'i to work on the plantations (Takaki, *Strangers* 132). This huge influx of Asian laborers shifted a population that had been 97 percent Native Hawaiian or part-Hawaiian and 2 percent white in 1853 to a population that was 62 percent Asian, 16.3 percent Native Hawaiian or part-Hawaiian, and 7.7 percent white in 1920 (Takaki, *Strangers* 132). In 2000, Hawai'i's population continues to reflect the impact of the plantation era with a makeup that is 41.6 percent Asian, 9.4 percent Native Hawaiian or Pacific Islander, and 24.3 percent white *(United States Census 2000)*.[3]

This dramatic change in the makeup of Hawai'i's population also resulted in another important legacy of the plantation: the development of Hawai'i Pidgin and Hawai'i Creole. Because of the importation of different ethnic groups as labor, including white ethnics (e.g., Portuguese and Puerto Ricans) in addition to the Asian groups described earlier, a pidgin language developed on the plantation as a rudimentary form of communication. The plantation management needed to be able to direct their multi-ethnic and multilingual workers, so they used a simple language system intermixed with vocabulary from Hawaiian, Japanese, Chinese, English, and other languages.[4] As the children of the laborers grew up and participated in both the plantation community and larger community, a creole became the first language of this first American-born generation. This creole, though, continues to be referred to colloquially as Pidgin. However, the development of Pidgin in addition to the "official" standing of English acted to further displace the Native Hawaiian language. English became the language of instruction and government; Pidgin became the language of the (nonwhite) community; and Hawaiian was actively discouraged, even forbidden, to the point that Native Hawaiian children who spoke Hawaiian faced corporal punishment and laws were established that made the use of Hawaiian in school illegal (Schutz 350–53).[5]

As this imported plantation labor settled and started to have families, the plantation and school converged. The plantation now sought to create and maintain a labor pool as the workers made Hawai'i their home and their children began school. However, according to historian Ronald Takaki, many plantation owners did not want to see the children of laborers educated beyond sixth or eighth grade, fearing that the more educated these children became, the less likely they were to continue to work on the plantation when they became adults (Takaki, *Strangers* 172). Even the 1920 federal survey seemed to support this idea of preparing students to enter agriculture:

Nevertheless, outside of teaching, the islands offer comparatively few opportunities in the professions; therefore, the great mass of the children and young people now in the schools, if they are to become stable, self-supporting, worthy members of society must find their opportunities either in agriculture itself or in occupations directly related to agricultural enterprises. Aside, then, from the core work of running throughout the entire system from the kindergarten to the university which should properly make for literacy, for culture, for general information, for catholicity of view and of interest, the school, at every step of the way, should be laying a foundation for occupational success. (35)

And while the federal survey suggested that the public schools prepare students to work in the islands, most likely in agriculture, the children of the white privileged class who attended elite private institutions like Punahou School also knew their place well:

"What do we care about these vocational discussions?" one of them snapped. "Yes," agreed another. And referring to the school attended by mainly Asian students, he added: "It's all settled; we, the Punahou boys, will be the lunas [managers] and the McKinley fellows will carry the cane." (Takaki, *Strangers* 172)

This statement about race relations and the structures of social class and race become even more clear as the school becomes a site for maintaining these culturally scripted roles. On the plantation, race, social class, and language organized the system of relations; at the school, where race, social class, and language should have not limited the opportunities provided by education, we see how language and literacy, inflected by race, becomes a system that reinforces the plantation social structure.

In 1920, as territorial officials examined the results of the federal survey, the Superintendent of Public Instruction, Vaughan Mac-Caughey, received a petition signed by parents of four hundred children from English-speaking homes in Honolulu requesting the establishment of a public school exclusively for those who spoke Standard English (Stueber 242). These families were part of the growing white middle class that began to migrate to Hawai'i after it had been annexed but who could not afford to send their children to the private schools attended by the children of wealthy plantation owners, industrialists, and Hawai'i's elite.

As it turned out, the 1920 survey recommended that "the pupils who speak English fluently be separated from the others and that the latter be given a different type of English study," dividing students of each grade and subject into three sections (246–47). However, the survey never explicitly recommended the creation of *separate* schools, and MacCaughey took it upon himself to read into the survey the necessary justification to make the following proposals:

1. That the children of those parents who have known no other allegiance than to America have as much right to an education at public expense as have the children of parents of other origins and

2. That such children have a right to such an education under conditions which will insure them and their parents that it can be had without endangering those standards and character quality which are distinctly American and which must be preserved and kept inviolate and are a part of them because of their parentage. (MacCaughey 7)

Thus, the planning for the English Standard school system began, and the schools were instituted in 1924. In 1927, the territorial legislature made official provision for English Standard schools (Act 103 of 1927) by substituting the phrase "standard schools" for "select schools" in section 312 of the Revised Laws of 1925 (Meller 4).

The proponents of English Standard schools took care to point out that this was not a segregated system of schooling based on race or national origin. Part of this concern was due to the territorial status of Hawai'i. When Hawai'i became an incorporated territory of the United States in 1900 after annexation in 1898, its citizens enjoyed the benefits and privileges of American citizenship for the most part. However, these "citizens" did not elect the territorial governor and representatives to Congress, who were rather appointed by the president. Officials and residents also saw the granting of territorial status as an implied promise of eventual statehood, and public education took on the new responsibility of teaching American democracy and citizenship (Wist 140). Thus any policy by the territorial government that would seem to contradict the ideals of American democracy would prove embarrassing to the territory and perhaps hurt Hawai'i's chances of statehood. In developing his policy on English Standard schools, Superintendent MacCaughey offered the following caveat:

> We especially desire that the race of nationality of an applicant be allowed no weight what ever in this test; in other words we desire that the sole consideration, aside from ordinary scholastic requirements for the grade, be the quality of the applicant's oral English. (Stueber 243)

When statehood hearings took place in 1936, then Superintendent of Public Instruction, Oren E. Long, was asked by the committee whether he thought the English Standard system "conforms to the ideal of the American public school system" (Stueber 253). Long replied that it did not and also admitted that "the standard schools created feelings of snobbishness among their students and that, in principle, they were un-American" (Stueber 253).

However, despite the "official" position that English Standard schools did not segregate by race, de facto segregation was very real, and examples of discrimination and bigotry existed. For example, when a group of Japanese immigrant families organized a kindergarten that emphasized Standard English so that their children could pass the oral examination to attend Central Grammar School, American parents (i.e., white parents) were upset because the Japanese children (though usually American born) "easily passed the tests for entrance into the school which it had hoped would, by an exclusion of little Orientals, meet the demand for an 'American school'" (Allen 617).

This attitude did not exist among parents alone, and even the education "experts" were not beyond a "nativist" ideology. Frank F. Bunker, director of the *Survey of Education,* himself saw the value of separating the children based on a perceived cultural difference and threat to the education of American children:

> The fact is, they are different and because they are fundamentally different they are not American and because they

are not American those parents who have known no other allegiance than to America hesitate, and rightly hesitate, when it comes to the education of their own children. (Bunker 1)

Bunker and other supporters of the English Standard school employed the rhetoric of Americanization, often appealing to those very ideals of democracy and American citizenship that their policies and practices often seemed to violate. Despite the fact that many of the children who did attend Hawaiʻi's public schools were American born, and thus American citizens, Americans did not see these children as full citizens because of their different races and cultures. While the Americans suffered from their own anxiety about having their children unduly influenced by "little Orientals," the "little Orientals," the children, also could not escape the anxiety and pressure of being constructed as less than American and as less worthy than other children of receiving a good education.

Re/Visions of Resistance and Schooling

Just as Carlos Bulosan and Maxine Hong Kingston reveal the intersections between literacy, race, and citizenship in their literacy narratives, narratives by two of Hawaiʻi's Asian American writers, Marie Hara and Lois-Ann Yamanaka, reveal these intersections in their own stories about schooling in Hawaiʻi. Though the English Standard school system has not existed for close to fifty years, this two-tiered schooling continues to fuel the anxieties of Hawaiʻi's people who have either grown up under the conditions discussed earlier or in the shadow of this institution.

In her short story "Fourth Grade Ukus," Marie Hara explores the anxiety of Hawaiʻi's Asian American population created by the English Standard school system. In this story, the narrator, Lei, reveals to us many of the pressures and attitudes felt by the nonwhite community, and in this particular case, by the Japanese American community. As the story opens, we learn that Lei's mother has made plans to enroll her at Lincoln School, formerly the Central

Grammar School, which was the model for the English Standard school system:

> Mama made plans all the time. She had figured out what to do. Soon after we settled into a small rental house, we walked over to Lincoln School, a gracious stone building with many trees. None of the students there had to do any manual labor. They used the newest books. They were always featured in newspaper articles and photos that she pointed out to me. Mama had heard that the best Lincoln graduates were sometimes accepted into the private high schools, which was how they "got ahead." (47)

Mama's desire to enroll her daughter in Lincoln School illustrates the pressures and contradictions felt by many in the Japanese American community. While aware of the discrimination and segregation of the English Standard school, many Japanese (both the immigrant generation and the growing American-born generation) still sought to have their children attend these schools. They valued education and the status associated with attending such a school. However, these values are also what many Americans saw as the race characteristics that made the Japanese unassimilable. Pride in cultural heritage, the creation of Japanese language schools, and close-knit communities were cited as evidence of Japanese unassimilability and Japanese nationalism. And yet American-born Japanese children often felt more American than Japanese, seeing the public schools as providing them more of a future in *their* home, Hawai'i, than the Japanese language schools they attended at the insistence of their parents.

The use of an oral examination to determine whether or not a student was admitted to an English Standard school is perhaps the best example of the problematic nature of the English Standard school. This test almost exclusively used pronunciation as the sole means of evaluation. Children were engaged in informal conversation, asked to identify objects, and to describe pictures. Examiners were prompted to note errors in the *TH* sound, lip movement and word endings, expression and phrasing. Evaluations were made based on "pronunciation" and "grammar and fluency" and students were rated as "excellent," "satisfactory," or "unsatisfactory."[6] As the following scene illustrates, the child is easily lost in the process, as Lei questions the logic of the examination but is ultimately judged "unsatisfactory" based on her accent and non–Standard English:

> By the time we were back in the office for the part called The Interview, which was really a test to see if I could speak perfect Standard English, I knew something was funny. I could smell it.
>
> The woman tester was young and Japanese and smiley. I relaxed, thought for sure I wouldn't have to act "put on" with her. But she kept after me to say the printed words on the picture cards that she, now unsmiling, held before my eyes.
>
> "Da bolocano," I repeated politely at the cone-shaped mountain where a spiral of smoke signaled into the crayon-shaded air. She must have drawn it.
>
> She shook her head. "Again."
>
> "Da BO-LO-CA-NO," I repeated loudly. Maybe like O-Jiji with the stink ear on his left side, she couldn't hear. "We wen' go 'n see da bolocano," I explained confidentially to her. And what a big flat *puka* it was, I thought, ready to tell her the picture made a clear mistake.
>
> "It's the vol-cano," she enunciated clearly, forcing me to watch her mouth move aggressively. She continued with downcast eyes. "'We went to see the vol-cano.' You can go and wait outside, okay?"
>
> Outside I wondered why—if she had seen it for real— she drew it all wrong.
>
> Mama shrugged it off as we trudged home.
>
> "Neva' mind. Get too many stuck shet ladies ova dea. People no need act, Lei. You wait. You gon' get one good education, not like me."

That was how I ended up at Ka'ahumanu School which
was non–English Standard. (48)

"The Interview," as Lei understands it, has nothing to do with her
ability to succeed in school. To begin with, she is already aware that
there was "something funny" about the interview. Her feelings are
confirmed when the tester, somewhat ironically a young Japanese
woman, is in Lei's view not qualified to administer the test since
she obviously has never seen a *real* volcano and keeps insisting that
Lei repeat herself as if she could not understand her. While the
interview achieves its purpose of excluding non–Standard English
speakers from the school, it also reveals the very subjective nature
of the test and the very narrow view of what constitutes student
achievement. Standard English seemingly is equated with a cogni-
tive ability to formulate a clear and understandable narrative, which
indicates intelligence. When Lei is evaluated as lacking this ability,
she is sent away to the non–English Standard school to be with
the other nonstandard students. What is never questioned is the
logic of this test and its far-reaching conclusions and consequences.
While Lei does speak with an accent and does use Hawai'i Creole
English, her ability to create a meaningful narrative is ignored because of form rather than content. Perhaps it is better then for Lei
to attend a school where she will be able to engage in meaningful
educational experiences and not be judged solely on the character
of her spoken English.

However, even at a non–English Standard school, Lei cannot
escape the Standard English ideology as she encounters a teacher
in her school, Mrs. Vicente, who is strict in her belief in "proper"
usage. But it is not just proper usage alone that drives Mrs. Vicente.
Throughout the discussion of the English Standard school, there
has been a recurring concern for what constitutes American culture. American culture was constructed as being from the mainland
and being white. And while much of the Americanization campaign was directed at the Japanese in Hawai'i or other immigrant
populations, even the culture of those people native to Hawai'i

could not escape the effects of Americanization. What underlies Mrs. Vicente's concern for language is a concern about the un-American culture(s) of her students:

> Passing outside by Room 103, I overheard her passionate argument with another teacher who wanted to introduce the hula in our PE exercises. Mrs. V.'s reasoning escaped me, but I knew she was against it unconditionally. I stayed hidden in the *ti* leaves under her window just to hear the rush of her escaping emotions as she grew angrier and pronounced words more distinctly.
>
> Mrs. Vicente's face was averted from the horrors she saw represented in the existence of our whole class. To her, we were not by any means brought up well, didn't know our p's and q's, often acted in an un-American fashion as evidenced by our smelly home lunches, dressed in an uncivilized manner, and refused moreover to speak properly or respectfully as soon as her back was turned. Her standards were in constant jeopardy. (55–56)

Lei's assessment of Mrs. Vicente is revealing and insightful. Not only is Mrs. Vicente against those things she sees threatening the order and purpose of school—for example, hula—she is against those things she sees in her students that threaten an American standard of living, and *her* standard of living. But her concerns about the un-American status of her students reveals an anxiety about her own status in Hawai'i. Her surname suggests she is Portuguese (a white ethnic also subject to Hawai'i's racial hierarchy), but she also reveals her family is related to the neighborhood grocers who are Native Hawaiian. What is most interesting though is that while she sees so much fault with her students, she also attempts to identify with them, something that Lei finds suspicious:

> Mrs. Vicente was one of us, she claimed, because she herself had grown up in our "very neighborhood." Her school,

too, she once let out, had been non–English Standard. We were surprised to hear her say that her family was related to the Kahanus who owned the corner grocery store. We knew them, the ones who used to have money. (57)

Mrs. Vicente's very rigid views of her students are driven by her own anxiety about her background and how she is perceived in the community at present. She finds herself, as her students do, in a liminal space, which often creates confusion between the experiences that have shaped her life and the pressures that force her to question the legitimacy of those experiences. She claims the neighborhood in order to claim a "local" identity, which makes her part of the community. But in her attempts at disciplining her students through "schooling" their bodies, she is caught denying her own identity, transferring this anxiety onto her own students.

While Lei remains suspicious and even fearful of Mrs. Vicente, she also begins to seek her approval and the legitimacy she can confer onto her:

To win Mrs. Vicente over, I saw that I would have to be able to speak properly, a complicated undertaking demanding control over all my body parts, including my eyes and hands, which wandered away when my mouth opened up. Therefore, in a compromise with my desire to shine, I resolved to keep absolutely quiet, stand up with the stupid row and ignore the one I wanted to impress. (56–57)

The effects of Mrs. Vicente's discipline are powerful. Lei is compelled to control her own body in order to be the good student, an act that reminds us of the discipline the plantation exercised over its workers. However, in an act that illustrates the psychological effects that schooling had on students, we see Lei convince herself to remain silent, to present herself as "stupid" in order to avoid the humiliation of being publicly corrected and disciplined by Mrs. Vicente. Lei has internalized the ideology of Standard English, and despite her "desire to shine," and a belief that she can "shine," she is willing to keep quiet rather than expose herself as a Pidgin speaker and suffer the implications and consequences of that label.

While the English Standard school system was abolished in 1948 and the last of the students admitted under the system graduated in 1960, the effects of the system continued to exist in the consciousness of Hawai'i's people. Marie Hara's story is set during the time of the English Standard school. This next writer, Lois-Ann Yamanaka, has created a narrative that takes place in the 1970s. While seemingly distant enough from the English Standard school, Yamanaka's work echoes many of the feelings and anxieties discussed in "Fourth Grade Ukus." As she does with her collection of poetry *Saturday Night at the Pahala Theatre*, Yamanaka writes her novel *Wild Meat and the Bully Burgers* as a first-person narrative in Pidgin. The novel follows the adolescent struggles of Lovey Nariyoshi, a young girl caught in the powerful social structures of her community and school, where race and ethnicity, class, and gender dictate social status and action.

While the entire novel is a complex discussion of how social relationships are constructed and negotiated in Hawai'i, often playing upon nostalgia for things past, or exposing things hurtful and familiar in the present, I want to focus on Yamanaka's critique of Standard English. In a chapter titled "Obituary," Yamanaka has created a scene that seems similar to Marie Hara's classroom and reminds us of the rhetoric employed by supporters of English Standard schools. The setting is an English class, where Lovey and her friend Jerome (Jerry) face the daily incantations of the teacher, Mr. Harvey, who espouses the ideology of Standard English:

"No one will want to give you a job. You sound uneducated. You will be looked down upon. You're speaking a low-class form of good Standard English. Continue, and you'll go nowhere in life. Listen, students, I'm telling you the truth like no one else will. Because they don't know how to say it to you. I do. Speak Standard English. DO NOT speak Pidgin. You will only be hurting yourselves." (9)

While Jerry is less convinced by Mr. Harvey's rants and makes a hidden hand gesture to show his disapproval, Lovey does believe in the message. She does not accept it grudgingly, does not simply recognize the practicality and utility of Standard English as a form of communication in a larger community beyond her hometown of Hilo and beyond Hawai'i. Rather, like Lei, Lovey has internalized the Standard English ideology and the status attached to Standard English. Unlike Lei, Lovey has begun to accept the construction of the Pidgin speaker as ignorant and all of the class and race stereotypes attached to Pidgin:

> I don't tell anyone, not even Jerry, how ashamed I am of Pidgin English. Ashamed of my mother and father, the food we eat, chicken luau with can spinach and tripe stew. The place we live, down the house lots in the Hicks Homes that all look alike except for the angle of the house from the street. The car we drive, my father's brown Land Rover without the back window. The clothes we wear, sometimes we have to wear the same pants in the same week and the same shoes until it breaks. Don't have no choice.
>
> Ashamed of my aunties and uncles at baby luaus, yakudoshis, and mochi pounding parties. "Eh, bradda Larry, bring me one nada Primo, brah. One cold one fo' real kine. I rey-dey, I rey-dey, no worry, brah. Uncap that sucka and come home to Uncle Stevie." I love my Uncle Steven, though, and the Cracker Jacks he brings for me every time he visits my mother. One for me and one for my sister, Calhoon. But I'm so shame. (9–10)

The shame that Lovey feels is generated by her expectations of what typical American family life should be. Though she seems to condense all of her anxiety into the shame she feels about Pidgin, she expands the meaning of Pidgin to include all of those things she sees as being represented by Pidgin. Her concerns about her working-class background are so intertwined with concerns about race and culture (as represented by various cultural activities: the baby luau, yakudoshis, and mochi-pounding parties) that they begin to be reminiscent of the construction of the nonwhite population of Hawai'i in the 1920s.[7] Lovey reproduces the construction of the non–Standard English speaker even though the social structure of Hawai'i had changed much since the 1920s and many Asian Americans were able to achieve middle-class status.

However, Lovey does not aspire to the Asian American middle class of Hawai'i. Instead, her shame of all that is represented by Pidgin is also fueled by her desire to be part of the white middle class and to somehow be *more* American. What begins as an anxiety about language becomes an anxiety about identity, deeply influenced by race and the desire for what is accepted as "normal," or perhaps, even American:

> Sometimes I secretly wish to be haole. That my name could be Betty Smith or Annie Anderson or Debbie Cole, wife of Dennis Cole who lives at 2222 Maple Street with a white station wagon with wood panel on the side, a dog named Spot, a cat named Kitty, and I wear white gloves. Dennis wears a hat to work. There's a coatrack as soon as you open the front door and we all wear our shoes inside the house. (10)

Lovey does not simply want to speak Standard English, then, but seeks to change her identity because of what she believes to be the success and comfort of white middle-class life. She buys into the American Dream, which does not necessarily take into account Hawai'i and the very different experiences and lives of its residents. Or that is how Lovey understands what it means to be American. If she cannot be "haole," if she cannot live in middle-class suburbia with all of the signifiers of white middle-class existence, she can at least use Standard English in her attempt to change her identity.

However, Lovey's attempt at creating a white middle-class identity through language is challenged by the very person who is cultivating her desire for it, Mr. Harvey. When Mr. Harvey begins the lesson for the day—to practice Standard English—he not only imposes his ideological agenda but also requires the students to identify themselves, an act that puts the students at risk:

> "Now let's all practice our Standard English," Mr. Harvey says. "You will all stand up and tell me your name, and what you would like to be when you grow up. Please use complete sentences." (10–11)

One by one students stand and identify themselves, unconsciously using Pidgin and not Standard English, which is proof to Mr. Harvey of the hopelessness of the situation. When Mr. Harvey gets to Lovey, she hesitates, perhaps not wanting to reveal herself as a Pidgin speaker. Mr. Harvey does not sympathize and instead becomes impatient:

> "Cut the crap," Mr. Harvey spits. "Stop playing these goddamn plantation games. Now c'mon. We've got our outlines to finish today." Mr. Harvey's ears get red, his whole face like fire with his red hair and red face.
> "My name Lovey. When I grow up pretty soon, I going be what I like be and nobody better say nothing about it or I kill um."
> "OH REALLY," he says. "Not the way you talk. You see, that was terrible. All of you were terrible and we will have to practice and practice our Standard English until we are perfect little Americans. And I'll tell you something, you can keep your heads on your desks for the rest of the year for all I care. You see, you need me more than I need you. And do you know what the worst part is, class? We're not only going to have to work on your usage, but your pronunciations and inflections too. Jee-zus Christ! For the life of me, it'll take us a goddamn lifetime." (12)

In a painful moment, Lovey's aspirations and dreams are lost as Mr. Harvey condemns her as a Pidgin speaker and as less than American. While Lovey's construction of herself and her desire for what she saw as the American Dream is clearly problematic, Mr. Harvey's reduction of his students to plantation subjects is even more so. Lovey and her classmates are subjected to the pressures of race and class in a situation—schooling and education—that is held up as the promise and premise of American democracy. We see the plantation and school converge and the students reduced to their racially marked bodies. Mr. Harvey becomes the arbiter of culture, and his message to his students is that they do not measure up, especially if they want to be "perfect little Americans."

However, Lovey's statement perhaps begins the important work of liberating her from the ideology of Standard English. Facing the pressure of Mr. Harvey and the pressure of using Standard English in order to represent herself, she blurts out: "My name Lovey. When I grow up pretty soon, I going be what I like be and nobody better say nothing about it or I kill um." While I will not argue that Lovey cannot escape her Pidgin identity, that she is revealing her "authentic" identity when she returns to Pidgin, I will suggest that Lovey begins to understand the false premise often set up in advocating Standard English: political and material change is not guaranteed by the use of Standard English. Lovey is forced to identify herself, and when this happens she does assert her right to choose this identity instead of relying upon the promise of Standard English (and of Mr. Harvey) for a better life. This realization allows Lovey to begin to move beyond the very limiting construction of Standard English she has been taught:

> But I can't talk the way he wants me to. I cannot make it sound his way, unless I'm playing pretend-talk-haole. I can make my words straight, that's pretty easy if I concentrate real hard. But the sound, the sound from my mouth, if I let it rip right out the lips, my words will always come out like home. (12–13)

At this point, Lovey seems resigned to being a Pidgin speaker. But she also makes an insightful comment, that Standard English is like "playing pretend-talk-haole." Language becomes a sort of mask that can be useful in our lives, allowing us to enter into conversations and to explore possibilities. But language can also be dangerous if it is used to cover up parts of our lives that play an important role in the shaping of our identities. Lovey understands that her "words will always come out like home." What she is unaware of at this point is that her words can take different forms, her language can change for different audiences, but her words can still remain "like home." And this is what the Standard English ideology overlooks as well. As Mr. Harvey illustrates, those who assert the Standard English ideology often conflate Standard English with citizenship, with intelligence, with being "perfect little Americans." What is often lost is an individual's language and identity, or at least the choice of an individual to transform Standard English for their own uses and not to fulfill some ideological agenda of another who decides what constitutes legitimate public discourse and community membership.

Lovey does not believe she has a choice. Her imagination has been colonized, dictating her use of language and her understanding of culture. It is only when Lovey understands that the words that "sound like home," and the life she lives in Hawai'i, are not illegitimate that she will be able to reclaim her imagination and move beyond the literacy myths that have constructed her life.

We see in the narratives written by Marie Hara and Lois-Ann Yamanaka scenes of resistance despite the overwhelming forces of schooling. Just as we see the narrator Maxine confront her own anxieties and demons in Kingston's *Woman Warrior*, we see Lei and Lovey confront the legacies of a system of schooling that has forced them to question their own literacy. But we also see in these narratives moments of resistance where Lei and Lovey, faced with having their personal histories and experiences overwhelmed by the institutional power of the school and the cultural hegemony of Standard English, speak out and insert themselves into these cultural narratives. Maxine, Lei, and Lovey grapple with the ways they have been constructed through language and literacy but they also use language and literacy to re/vision their own places in their own stories. And these stories become part of the collective experiences that re/vision the American Story.

Re/Visions of Citizenship

In the previous section, I argued that the stories by Marie Hara and Lois-Ann Yamanaka are narrative re/visions of citizenship written in response to the anxieties about race, class, and language generated by attitudes created by the plantation and the English Standard school. While these narratives are set in specific historical moments, and focus on institutions now gone or quickly disappearing from Hawai'i's landscape, their discussions about language and identity remain near the surface in on-going public discussions in contemporary Hawai'i that often polarize the community along racial, ethnic, and class lines. We see in the acceptance of these narratives as literature the legitimizing of the more complex experiences of Hawai'i's peoples. As these complex experiences become the subject of the community's narratives, we see the rising production of various cultural texts in Hawai'i and increased discussions in the community about literacy, race, and citizenship.

The politics of language and public debate about language is certainly not a new phenomenon in Hawai'i, though it has often been a one-sided debate in favor of Standard English. In the late nineteenth century and throughout much of the early twentieth century, the use of Hawaiian was actively discouraged, even made illegal. Pidgin, perceived as a corrupt form of Standard English, was also used as a marker of race and class and proof of the unassimilability of Asians into American life. However, the tide began to change in the 1960s and 1970s, when a renaissance in Hawaiian culture gathered strength and an interest in the Hawaiian language grew. In 1978, Hawai'i's constitutional convention voted to amend the state constitution to recognize both English and Hawaiian as official state languages. In the 1980s and 1990s, the Native Hawaiian sovereignty movement not only created an awareness about the political and social rights of indigenous peoples but also helped to further fuel the interest in and commitment to maintaining the Hawaiian language, an important act of nationbuilding. Also in 1978, the first "Talk Story" conference was held in Honolulu to discuss the emerging production, recognition, and analysis of literature written by Hawai'i residents, resulting in one of the most significant acts in Hawai'i and Asian American literature and literary studies, the creation of Bamboo Ridge Press. Within Hawai'i, then, various acts of "legitimizing" Hawai'i's local culture and local languages gained momentum as an audience was cultivated through making local cultural texts available (i.e., literary texts, but also musical recordings, locally produced television shows, etc.).[8] However, the increasing awareness by a public beyond Hawai'i about Native Hawaiian sovereignty, cultural identity, language politics, and various other social issues has perhaps made Hawai'i residents more self-conscious about how representations of Hawai'i are constructed and how these representations are received by a larger public.[9] A series of events in 1994 and 1995 suggests the power of these representations and also reminds us that the legacy of the plantation and English Standard school still remains strong as Hawai'i residents participated in an extraordinary public discussion about Pidgin that revealed and reinforced many of the same anxieties about race and class that I have discussed to this point.

While the discussion of Pidgin and its place in Hawai'i culture is always close to the surface in the community, it was a letter by Jon Hall that appeared in the morning daily paper, the *Honolulu Advertiser,* on 4 October 1994 that set the tone and began the next round of the "debate":

Your newspaper should print the real reason why Hawaii public schools are among the worst in the nation: students and teachers speak Pidgin garbage, a version of English which is only useful in slums and gang meetings. Is Pidgin widely used in Hawaii's private schools, mainly attended by "upper-caste" Japanese and European Americans? No. Look at their test scores.

Hawaiian public schools will only improve when this

language problem is fixed and the curriculum stops being centered on the Hawaiian sovereignty movement and focuses on the three R's. Case closed.

Hall's letter touched a nerve in the community to say the least. Again, issues of race and class are raised as Hall juxtaposes images of "slums and gang meetings" with Hawai'i's private schools. Hall's construction of culture is also limited as he dismisses the Native Hawaiian sovereignty movement and dismisses Pidgin as a "language problem." What becomes clear in Hall's letter is a very rigid definition of what constitutes "legitimate" cultural practices and texts. In short, it becomes a question about what is "legitimate" culture.

The response to Hall's letter was passionate. A number of letters appeared on consecutive Sundays in the *Honolulu Advertiser* (9 October 1994, 16 October 1994) in the "Focus" (editorial) section. The letters published fell on both sides of the debate and maintained the very divisive rhetoric employed by Hall. The 30 October 1994 Sunday edition of the *Honolulu Advertiser* featured a half page commentary by Honolulu writer Thelma Chang on the front page of the "Focus" section, challenging Jon Hall's characterization of Pidgin as "garbage." Chang also focuses on "legitimacy" and the construction of culture as her commentary points out Hall's denial of history:

[A]nyone who bothers to understand the long and vibrant history of Hawaii and its people would recognize the legitimacy of pidgin and its evolution. Its use was crucial at a time when diverse cultures struggled to survive in the Islands.

Then and now, survival included the necessity of creating a traffic of language to understand each other, to bridge different societies and to create a "comfort zone" within a dominant culture.

As she concludes her piece, Chang makes her most important comment: "Many people who speak Pidgin understand the 'outside' world better than the outside world understands them." The often patronizing racist overtones of those who talk about the disadvantaged Pidgin speaker reproduces the subject positions of plantation Hawai'i. What has changed since plantation Hawai'i though are the class positions and a growing awareness of what constitutes culture in multicultural Hawai'i. What remains the same, sadly, is the anxiety some "locals" still feel about how they sound and talk and the social value they attach to this.

Though Chang's commentary provided a useful and thoughtful sketch of the history of Pidgin and its social and cultural value, the letters that continued appear in the newspapers also continued to reduce discussions about Pidgin to issues of proper usage, "legitimate" culture vs. "illegitimate" culture, and the equation of Standard English with intelligence. Perhaps the most frustrating argument that emerged from the Pidgin debate was a misleading one that suggested that Hawai'i's schools were complicit if not outright responsible for promoting the use of Pidgin in the classroom. In 1985, the Hawai'i State Board of Education sought to mandate the use of Standard English in the classroom but met with widespread resistance from the community. The Board of Education revised the policy in 1987 to simply encourage the use of Standard English. The issue is blurred and becomes not about providing the best methods for literacy education but about simple discipline and the maintenance of a linguistic and social hierarchy.

The argument is made that by not banning Pidgin in the classroom, Standard English is displaced and students unable to move beyond their Pidgin identities will remain uneducable. This argument assumes that unless Standard English is the only language of instruction, students will not be able to learn. This argument also assumes that Standard English is never present in the classroom, that both teachers and students operate in a space of Pidgin accessible only to them. The more likely case is that teachers and students operate in a complicated space where they must understand the rules and practices of various discourse communities. As one twelfth-grade English teacher, Lisa-Anne Lung, wrote in the *Honolulu Advertiser:*

> My students and I are bi-lingual. We speak, write, communicate in different, yet similar languages. Both are equally powerful. My students know when to use "proper" English and pidgin English. I don't agree with "authority" dictating what will or will not be spoken in school. I believe that as long as true learning takes place, no matter what the vehicle, that the student has gained through the experience.

This teacher's response seems to be a reasonable and responsible answer to those who are concerned about a perceived lack of literacy and lack of literacy instruction in the classroom. Though I cannot prove that this teacher's classroom is typical or atypical, I would venture a guess that her views are common among educators who are concerned about reaching students who are at risk rather than alienating them further.

The *Advertiser* again devoted the front page of its Sunday "Focus" section to Pidgin in its 29 January 1995 edition, where three Hawaiʻi residents voiced their opinions (two against Pidgin, one in support of Pidgin). On 4 January 1995, the *Honolulu Weekly,* an alternative newspaper, ran a cover story about Pidgin. Featured on the front page was an illustration that depicted a local television newscast with a translator for the "pidgin impaired." The subject positions in this illustration reflect the subject positions seen in local popular and media culture, which create the tensions in the audience. The news anchor is an Asian American female. The translator is a local male (fashioned after "Bu Laiʻa," ["Bull Liar"] a local comedian/entertainer). The audience is a white couple with confused expressions on their faces. While this illustration is an exaggeration, it does play off both the extent to which Pidgin has entered into popular and mainstream media culture in Hawaiʻi and the anxiety felt by those who object to such "contamination." Like the school, the media are often constructed as a "neutral" or "objective" space that has no place for emergent cultural practices except perhaps as "exotic" artifact or "human interest" story.

In its most extensive coverage, the *Honolulu Advertiser*, over two days in May (14 May 1995, 15 May 1995), featured five stories about various aspects of Pidgin. On the front page of the Sunday, 14 May 1995 *Honolulu Advertiser*, the headline read "Pidgin—happy talk or something unspeakable?" Not only did the stories include an extensive history of Pidgin (with time line included), discussion of the literary and cultural value of Pidgin, and the now expected range of responses from the public, but also a test of Pidgin grammar and editorials recognizing the cultural value of Pidgin but still calling for the exclusive use of Standard English in the classroom. This two-day series seemed to be the culmination of a heated debate that had begun the previous year. For the most part, the feature stories did a good job of presenting a complex picture of Pidgin, a picture that many in Hawai'i may not have been familiar with except for the most negative associations attached to Pidgin. While it appears that there is more vocal support for Standard English over the use of Pidgin, significant movement has been made in recognizing that Pidgin is being transformed into a particular discourse that has important cultural roots and value. Recently more aggressive pro-Pidgin cultural activities have taken place with the publication of *Hybolics*, a magazine about Hawai'i literature and culture with a focus on Pidgin, and *Da Word* by Lee A. Tonouchi, a collection of stories written completely in Pidgin, and stage productions of work by playwright Lisa Matsumoto, who re/visions fairy tales and folk stories through the context of Hawai'i and the exclusive use of Pidgin.

While the debate about Pidgin is far from over, perhaps the increased awareness about Pidgin as more than "broken" English will at least lessen the anxiety of Hawai'i residents who are still concerned about representations of them as less than literate and as less than American. This is the work of minor re/vision, where people of color begin to understand their sociocultural histories, their relationship with dominant culture, and their strategies for transforming literacy to their purposes. In examining the specific history of literacy in Hawai'i, we see how much the issues of literacy, citizenship, and race are contested, ideological, and rhetorical. And perhaps most importantly, we see the materiality of literacy: that literacy is material beyond making people employable or helping them to advance their position in social class. As the case of Hawai'i illustrates, literacy and race become so intertwined that there are material consequences despite rhetoric to the contrary. We also begin to understand more fully the psychological and emotional consequences of literacy when we see characters like Lei and Lovey who are faced with the anxiety and pressures of literacy and race at an early age. But in Lei and Lovey, we also see characters who begin to learn where their language comes from, who confront various forms of discrimination (racial and linguistic) directly, and who move toward both self and cultural understanding about their participation in American culture.

As this historical, literary, and cultural analysis of Hawai'i's literacy situation illustrates, when we examine literacy, we begin the work of reading and writing our culture and moving toward a more complex understanding of literacy and education and what it means to be a citizen in America. What we cannot lose sight of is the long literacy history and legacy of institutions like Hawai'i's English Standard schools, institutions that continue to cause anxiety, feed a discourse of crisis, and teach us many lessons about the ways race, literacy, and culture remain intimately intertwined.

4 / Teaching Literacy Narratives
Reading, Writing, and Re/Vision

First day, first semester, first year, first job: I enter the classroom nervously, surveying the room and trying to maintain some semblance of authority. I am beginning my first full-time teaching position, and my first class is first-year college composition. Twenty-three fresh faces stare back, and I worry about learning all of their names. As I scan down the roll sheet, I notice there are two Kristins, a Kristine, a Kirsten, and two Jeffs. Everyone looks alike to me except for one young African American woman. I take attendance, trying to burn faces and names into my brain. I ask students to introduce themselves: Where are they from, what are their interests, why are they here? I try to assure the class that I'm experienced, have my Ph.D. from a prestigious university, and can identify with them since I've lived in the Midwest for six years. Then I go into my routine about being from Hawai'i, that faraway place that evokes dreams of Paradise—I exploit my "exoticness" to gain some cultural capital in this class. After reading through the syllabus and asking for questions, I dismiss class. Only fifteen more weeks in the term. Only forty-three more class meetings. I hope they like me. No, I hope they respect me. Please, I hope they learn something.

Third week, second semester, first year, first job: I enter the classroom to the strained humming of the *Hawaii Five-0* theme song—dada da da daaaaaaaa da. . . . John, a student from my first semester course, welcomes me with this tune every day. It's become my theme song, a way to prepare me mentally and to signal the start of class. It's the second term, and I'm teaching a composition-and-literature course, the second part of a year sequence writing requirement. I survived the first semester—I enjoyed the first semester.

This week the class is preparing for its first long writing project. Last semester students generated essays around various topics and responded to a wide range of texts: essays, magazines, television, music, lived experience. This term they focus on reading and responding to written texts. As a form of practice and demonstration, I bring in a sample essay for them to work on. I want them to read and respond in productive ways, and I provide something that is similar to the writing assignment I just gave them. The only directions: They should give this essay the same attention they would to a classmate's essay—treat this like a workshop paper. Afterwards, I plan to go over the essay with the class, partly to model a way of responding but also to illustrate how I evaluate writing.

This time the practice essay is something I had written as a sophomore in college. I must admit that when I looked over the essay with the instructor's comments and the final grade of B, I was a little embarrassed to use it in class. Terms weren't defined, the thesis was a little shaky, and I hadn't provided page number citations for the quotes I used from *The Adventures of Huckleberry Finn*. But as I reread the essay, I saw some originality in an underdeveloped idea that actually seemed to have something interesting to say. I saw some rhetorical flourishes, a nicely turned phrase, and even some sophisticated sentence structure. There was something to the essay. I did get a B (revised up from a C+ I think), but the instructor was tough and intelligent and extremely generous as a teacher and person—the kind of teacher I hoped to be. I had felt pretty good about that B and what I felt was a wake-up call from the empty "pretty" writing I had been doing. There were problems with the essay but also some good points as well. A good essay for the class to critique—a piece that needed work but also a piece that had something there.

"The introduction is boring."

"There's no thesis—maybe if the first couple of paragraphs were combined."

"The author seems to have some good ideas but it also seems like he's just trying to sound smart."

"This is at best a C paper."

I stared back at the class, grinning because I was embarrassed about the essay, but perhaps also because I saw myself in these students. The confidence, the assured evaluation of the essay's quality, the real belief that they knew what "good" writing looked like. That was all me as a college freshman and sophomore. Until I did get a C on that essay and everything in my world seemed to fall apart. The skill I had the most confidence in, the ability that I felt was most natural, had let me down. What now? Could I even get a B for the course? I was literate, even intelligent. Why (in my mind) was I failing?

Rereading my sophomore writing and hearing other students respond to it forced me into their place once more. I was not always the "professional" writing teacher. I did not always have the "authority" that I suppose I do now. I was a student trying to write essays I thought were smart and interesting. And perhaps they were smart and interesting—to me—but they were also in need of revision and lots of work.

When I respond to writing now, I cannot help but think of that teacher who dared to give me a C. He was generous, understanding, and tough and taught me to approach writing in a different way. I begin to take risks.

First class, first week, first semester, second year: A new year and a new class. This time, I am another writer in a roomful of writers, cramming the night or morning before class in order to bring a draft to our writing groups. Teacher and student, the lines are blurred as everyone writes, shares, revises, and learns. Another risk.

As a writing teacher, I often ask students to think about the experiences that have brought them to this point in their lives—college—and how these experiences have shaped who they are, how they think, why they believe, and what they write. I also ask them to think about their literacy: What is literacy? What does it mean to them? How do they know they are literate? I do not ask them to write about their personal lives though some choose to do so. And I do not ask them to reveal intimate or private moments though some do because a particular experience is necessary in their making of meaning. What has become apparent to me the more I teach is that our lives are so intertwined in our learning that whatever we do in the classroom both as teachers and students has some refer- ent, no matter how small, to an individual's lived experience. The place of literacy narratives in the classroom makes sense to me as our reading and writing histories cannot help but play a role in our reading and writing of texts. In this chapter, I discuss the use of literacy narratives in the classroom and describe the array of what students write about when asked to examine literacy and culture in texts and in their lives.

In my case, I cannot help but address my lived experience in my teaching every day. As an Asian American who was born and raised in Hawai'i, the difference in and of my life is in front of me as I look at my classes and usually see students who do not look like me. I understand this. Hawai'i is a state where 63.1 percent of its population is Asian or Pacific American and whites are a racial mi- nority at 33.4 percent. Contrast this to Ohio, where I presently live and teach: Here 87 percent of the population is white; 1.1 percent is Asian American. At the university where I teach, 93 percent of the student population is white, and 7 percent nonwhite. In 2000– 2001 among a faculty of 808 there are 95 faculty of color, or 11 per- cent. In 1998 among all higher education institutions, just about 15 percent of the faculty are minorities (National Center). I cite these statistics not to lament the lack of diversity, especially since many places in the United States cannot match Hawai'i for its varied population and nonwhite majority. However, I do raise these figures because of what they have meant for my classroom. In nineteen courses I have taught from 1997 to 2002, I have had twenty-two students of color out of 295, just about the 7 percent minority popu- lation at the university. But when you break down these courses, I have had classes with minority enrollments of one, two, four, and many times none at all. What does it mean for these students to be in a situation where they are often the lone student of color? What does it mean to me when I am the only person of color in the class- room? And what does it mean to both my students and myself when I am perhaps the only teacher of color many of these students may ever have?

It means that the teaching I do is important beyond curricular matters of developing critical reading and writing abilities; that the cultural work of teaching within and beyond the curriculum, in those extracurricular spaces where lives and learning intersect, affect what I teach, how I teach, and whom I teach. While I have never been directly challenged in my classroom about my "agenda" (read "race") or my qualifications (read "Affirmative Action hire"), I still work very hard to not let others assume anything about me. When people ask what I do, I tell them I teach writing and literature, not English, because they may assume that means English as a second language (or is this my own fear?). On the first day of class when we all introduce ourselves, I often say I have lived in the Midwest for a number of years before revealing I was born and raised in Hawai'i. I make it clear I earned my doctorate in English from an elite university. And I assure the students that I have taught many writing classes. Just as I see in front of me a sea of mostly white faces, I am sure they are looking back at me and my dark features, their Asian American (if not only Asian) teacher.

But when I look out at those mostly white faces, I also see "diversity" (a problematic though perhaps necessary term) and work hard not to categorize these students who have been labeled members of J. Crew U (or now, Abercrombie & Fitch U). I have undergone my own re/vision, and I see the minor positions of these students, those who worry that their faith places them on the margins or that their upbringing in a rural community is looked down upon, or even the minor position of those students from the more "cosmopolitan" East or West Coasts who now find themselves in a small Midwestern rural town. When these students write, they bring their lives into their work, analyzing, arguing, or narrating about their culture and their place in it. My work as teacher is to work with these students as they make and shape meaning in their lives. I can only hope that the minor narratives I bring to class (in the form of my life and other texts) are part of this meaning making and shaping even if just a tiny bit; I know these students have made me re/vision the classroom.

Reading Re/Visions and Literacy Narratives

> English 112 is a course about reading and writing criti-
> cally. Our primary subject for investigation this term will
> be the ways reading, writing, literacy, and education are
> represented in our culture. We will be examining these
> representations in many different kinds of texts, primarily
> literature and essays, but also popular culture media such
> as film and television. We will explore our roles as readers
> and writers in our culture and how our positions affect
> the ways we read and write. How do race, class, gender,
> region, faith, sexuality, or other positions shape our inter-
> pretations and analysis? How do these positions shape the
> creation of the texts we will be examining? Or do these
> factors make any difference at all?
>
> —Course description from English 112 syllabus

On the first day of class a few years ago, I read the above course
description to twenty-three first-year students. The makeup of this
first-year writing course was typical of the other courses I had
taught—students mostly from Ohio or Indiana or other parts of the
Midwest with a few from the East Coast. Also like many of my other
courses, there were no students of color, something I had come to
expect, but something that I also found very interesting as I learned
more about these white students from middle-class suburban backgrounds. I proceeded to go over policies for the course, described
our readings, and pointed out important dates on our schedule. After asking for questions about any aspect of the course, and answering the obligatory questions about attendance policy, grading, and
other mundane issues, I let the class out. As I gathered my books
and papers, a young woman who had sat at the back of the room
approached me.

"Mr. Young," she started, "I'm a little worried that I won't do so
well in your class."

"Oh," I responded, "we've just gone over the syllabus—what
are you concerned about?"

"Well, I'm from a tiny town in West Virginia, just across the river from the southern part of Ohio—and it's mostly white."

I nodded my head, not quite sure where this discussion was going, but I tried to be reassuring, to show that I was listening to her concerns even though the issue of race had slipped into this conversation already.

"Well, when you were going over the readings, there's all this multicultural stuff, and I just don't think I'm going to be able to write about these things because I haven't really had any experience with diversity."

I paused a moment before I answered—multicultural stuff—what multicultural stuff did I have on the syllabus? Well, it was partially true. We were reading the *Narrative of the Life of Frederick Douglass, An American Slave,* as well as a novel by Hawai'i writer Lois-Ann Yamanaka, *Wild Meat and the Bully Burger,* and using the collection *The Graywolf Annual Five: Multicultural Literacy.* But we were also reading Scott Russell Sanders's collection, *Writing from the Center,* about growing up in the Midwest and his process of becoming a writer, and Bernard Shaw's *Pygmalion,* which connects literacy, social class, and gender in interesting ways. In my mind we were reading a variety of literacy narratives that explored the acquisition and uses of literacy from a wide array of experiences including race and ethnicity, gender, social class, and region.

"Well," I began to answer, "we're really looking at issues of literacy and education—to explore how writing is represented and used by our culture. So yes, we are reading some multicultural texts, but really we're looking at literacy and how literacy is informed by different experiences."

I looked at the student who did not seem quite convinced, but she nodded and said she just wanted to let me know that she might not always be able to write her best if she didn't understand the material. As she left, I thought about this exchange where race colored her reading of the course; both my race as an Asian American and the ostensible categories of race represented by Frederick Douglass, Lois-Ann Yamanaka, and the vague catch-all of "multicultural." Perhaps examining literacy as a topic in a first-year writing course seemed so unlikely (even pointless since we all "know" what literacy is) that the only other clear signifier of the course was race, especially if the instructor happened to be a person of color. And while I was a little concerned that at least one student had come to the conclusion that there may be some personal political agenda at work, I was also surprisingly pleased by this moment—of course literacy and race, or culture, or however we define "difference" are not mutually exclusive; they continually inform each other and the ways we choose to use writing in our lives. What I needed to do was to work with students to understand how literacy operates in our culture in a variety of ways for a variety of people.

My purpose in the first part of the course is to complicate students' understanding of literacy, to move them beyond thinking about literacy as simply the skills of reading and writing. While students are often aware of the power of literacy to improve a person's life, to create knowledge, and to generally instill Scribner's State of Grace, they are less likely to view literacy as a power used against others to maintain systems of oppression or to construct someone as less than a full person. Literacy needs to become a concept that is no longer inherently "good" or even neutral; rather, it becomes a set of practices (perhaps reading and writing but perhaps much more) used by people for different purposes.

We begin with selections from *Multicultural Literacy:* James Baldwin's "A Talk to Teachers"; Michelle Cliff's "A Journey into Speech" and "If I Could Write This in Fire, I Would Write This in Fire"; and Michelle Wallace's "Invisibility Blues." Each of these essays brings into question our beliefs about literacy and how it has functioned in American culture. Baldwin and Wallace each challenge us to read past the rosy picture often portrayed of American life, especially when it fails to account for many people who do not live the American Dream. Cliff offers her own transformation of literacy as she describes her appropriation and application of new forms of writing to express an identity that has not been represented before. And then we turn to the *Narrative of the Life of Frederick Douglass, An American Slave,* a text that illustrates the material, spiritual, and psychological power of literacy as we see

Douglass narrate his own freedom, construct his own identity, and remove himself from slavery.

In reading the literacy narratives of Richard Rodriguez, Victor Villanueva, and Carlos Bulosan, I focused on the ways literacy functioned for these writers, especially as a means for self-discovery and self-fashioning. I read these narratives not only for "evidence" about the connection between literacy, race, and citizenship but also as a road map in understanding my own relationship to literacy, race, and citizenship. In having my first-year students read literacy narratives, I hope they can begin unpacking the ways that literacy works in the lives of these individual writers. Rather than simply identifying acts of literacy within these texts, I want students to analyze the function of literacy in the person's life, in the text, or in other ways they felt were important. In doing this unpacking, I hope students draw analogies to their own lives, to understand that their own relationship to literacy, race, and citizenship is more complicated than they have imagined thus far in their lives. Thus I ask students to do the following in their first writing project:

> The Function of Literacy (4–5 pages, typed, double-spaced): While the title of this assignment may sound daunting— The Function of Literacy—it is actually pretty clear and straightforward. For this essay I want you to discuss how literacy functions in any of the texts we have read thus far (Baldwin, Cliff, Douglass, Wallace). Think of this project as a cultural critique: you are examining how literacy works and is represented in our culture. The essays and longer works we are reading are the cultural texts to analyze. A larger question to keep in mind is, "What do these texts say about our views on literacy?"
>
> A key in doing this assignment is defining how you are using the term "literacy." Are you examining the ways reading and writing are represented in the text? Do you mean a broad concept of education? Do you mean life skills outside of traditional schooling? Here are some possible approaches:

- Examine representations (acts) of reading and/or writing in a text.
- Discuss the role of education in a text.
- Identify and discuss metaphors connected to literacy (for example, "hunger" for knowledge and freedom, the "journey" toward education and freedom, etc.).
- Discuss the narrative strategies that writers use in their texts (for example, the use of fragmentation by Cliff, the speech by Baldwin, personal narrative by Douglass, etc.).
- Discuss the different concepts/functions of literacy at work in a text (for example, how is literacy used by Douglass and against Douglass; or, how is silence or invisibility connected to literacy?).
- Discuss the connection between literacy and identity. How does literacy shape identity? How does a person become literate? Who decides what literacy is and how does this affect people? What role do race, gender, class, etc. play in the relationship between literacy and identity? What about a connection between literacy and citizenship, or literacy and life?
- Or come up with your own topic related to the function of literacy in a text.

Remember you are doing a *reading* (that is, an interpretation) of a text to support your ideas. I'm not looking for recycling of my ideas or discussion. You should write about something that you find interesting in the text and that you can do a thoughtful analysis of. Think beyond our limited definitions of literacy and explore what literacy means in these texts, texts that often had life-changing effects.

This writing project attempts to lay out a strategy for reading literacy narratives while also providing flexibility for the students in developing their interpretations of the texts. On a conceptual level, I want students to think about how they or others define literacy. If they want to define literacy strictly in terms of reading and writing, that is fine as long as they provide evidence that this is the way literacy is being defined and used in a particular text. If they want to expand their definition of literacy, this also requires that they provide evidence to support this broader meaning of literacy. There is also a language used to describe literacy. In the case of the texts by Baldwin, Cliff, Douglass, and Wallace, terms like "silence" and "invisibility" or metaphors like "hunger" and "journey" are used to describe their experiences with literacy. Why do they use these terms? How are the ways they describe literacy different than the way we might? This conceptual understanding leads them to understand the function of literacy in a particular text, to see literacy in a specific context and to not assume that literacy is always working in a static way, that is, as simply reading and writing skills.

Another goal of this assignment is to have students make connections between literacy and some other aspect of a person's life. For example, if students connect literacy with issues of identity, they can focus on issues of race and ethnicity, gender, region, and social class. In making these connections, does the form of the text work to enhance expressions of identity? For example, does Cliff's strategy of fragmentation make a more poignant point about who she is than a more conventional narrative might? Does Douglass's very personal and detailed narrative account provide a type of order and authority that something less formal might not? How does history play a role in the construction of these narratives? In Cliff's case, a legacy of British colonialism in the Caribbean provides context for her strategy of fragmentation. In the case of Douglass, the context of American slavery and attitudes about the intellectual abilities of and access to literacy for African Americans shape Douglass's narrative strategy. In reading these narratives to identify the function of literacy, students are also reading to understand who these people are and how and why they use literacy. The students must also grapple with how these literacy histories inform their own experiences with literacy. Certainly they cannot fully understand the experience of slavery, but they may begin to become more fully aware of how lack of access to literacy may disproportionately affect urban and poor communities, often made up of people of color.

For this writing project, students often pair Douglass's *Narrative* with another text such as James Baldwin's "A Talk to Teachers." One student, Karla,[1] chose to focus on Douglass and Baldwin and how institutions (i.e., slavery and schooling, respectively) act to limit the uses of literacy and education because of the authors' race and heritage. While she recognizes that literacy becomes a "tool" for Douglass and Baldwin in their personal lives, she also argues that literacy becomes a means for Douglass and Baldwin to lift up their communities by sharing their experiences with a larger audience. Another student, Rick, also examines Douglass and Baldwin but focuses on literacy as key in the development of their identities. In asking how people become literate and how society uses literacy, Rick begins to unpack the ways literacy works in the lives of Douglass and Baldwin and even moves to a point where he challenges the value of the literate/illiterate binary. Another student, Pam, uses the metaphor of "escape" to describe how literacy functions in society and in Douglass's *Narrative*. In her examination of the function of literacy, Pam focuses on both the literal escape from slavery by Douglass and the metaphorical escape from ignorance that Douglas experienced as he acquired literacy in his life. In these explorations of the function of literacy and in other student projects, we see students trying to understand literacy in more complicated ways, as more than reading and writing. But even if students do limit their analysis of literacy to the ways reading and writing are represented or are working, they begin to understand that there are a variety of factors, from race to social class to historical and cultural contexts, that have an impact on the way literacy functions for people.

Once students have begun to conceptualize literacy as more than reading and writing and having some connection to the personal, I try to move them toward grasping the structural and cultural implications of literacy. While asking them to explore the function of literacy moved them toward understanding contexts for literacy, there is still a temptation to locate the responsibility and achievement of literacy in the personal alone. In order to emphasize the structural and cultural contexts for literacy and to focus on reading strategies for literacy narratives, I offer the next writing project to students:

> Critical Approaches to Texts (4–5 pages, typed, double-spaced): For this essay assignment I want you to develop a critical approach to Bernard Shaw's *Pygmalion* and discuss your reading of the "Pygmalion" myth and its place in our culture. By critical approach, I mean that you need to decide on a method for reading the text; for example, you may want to discuss the way gender, class, education, or language and literacy is talked about in the text (like we did in class). Or you may want to focus on issues of teacher-student relationships, the performance of identity (can you make up an entirely new self?), or the desire for middle-class life (can you achieve this just by changing your speech?). Don't do the reading that includes every-thing and the kitchen sink. However, your focus on a main interpretation may still have connections to other issues. For example, if you look at social class you'll probably dis-cuss the way social hierarchy works and is represented (through dialect for example), but you might also discuss social class and gender and how class difference affects the roles of men and women. There are several ways to write this essay but you must use at least one other text in your reading of *Pygmalion*.
>
> Here are some strategies:
>
> - Use Shaw's *Pygmalion* to read other versions of the story (*My Fair Lady, Pretty Woman, Educating Rita,* etc.), or use the other texts to read *Pygmalion*. What are the similarities? Differences? How does the difference in settings and time, etc. affect the story? Does the movie form affect the telling of the story?
> - Use other critical material such as Paula Gunn Allen's "Who Is Your Mother?" or Eldred and Mortensen's

"Reading Literacy Narratives" or other texts we have read (esp. Frederick Douglass, Michelle Cliff, Michelle Wallace) to develop and support your reading of *Pygmalion* (e.g., Compare Douglass and Eliza).

- Or use other material that you have found that seems related and contributes to your interpretation of *Pygmalion*. You may use examples from popular culture (TV, magazines, other movies not mentioned above, etc.). Just make sure that the basics of the "Pygmalion" story are there and that you can make a connection with Shaw's play. Check with me if you need ideas for videos or if you want to borrow a video.

Here are some guidelines for your essay (they may look familiar):

- Remember to define your terms. If you are talking about gender do you mean just women or both men and women? I want you to define and discuss how you are using a term or concept.
- Develop a clear thesis in your introduction. In your essay you need to let the reader know what your main idea is and how you are going to develop and discuss it in your paper. For this essay in particular, you need to let the reader know what your critical approach is. For example: "Bernard Shaw's *Pygmalion* is a critique of social class and the artificial system of manners used to separate people. This is seen in three scenes."
- Focus on specific scenes and passages from the text. If you rely on a general description of something, your analysis and argument will be weak. Also watch a video over again. Don't rely on the short clips we'll view in class or on your memory of *Pretty Woman* from five years ago. If you quote a passage, make sure you include a citation. Use block quotations for longer passages (more than two short sentences).
- Analyze the text. Don't just identify, describe, or sum-

marize. You need to show how and why something supports your idea.

- If you are looking at an issue across texts, make sure
that you are clear about which text you are discussing.
Remember you need to show what the connection is
between texts—you can't assume the reader will make
the same connection.

Remember that this is an interpretation of the text. You
need to support your critical approach with evidence from
the text. If the reader can't see the issue you are focusing
on, then you may have to change your critical approach or
at least find stronger evidence.

There are two important goals that I organize this writing project
around. First, I ask the students to understand the Pygmalion myth
and how it works in our culture as a way for them to work with
metaphor. I also want them to understand the power of metaphor,
to see how stories become so powerful and appealing that they can
often act to blind us to possible dangers. For example, why does a
film like *Pretty Woman* fulfill the desires of such a large portion of
our culture? How does a film like this create uncomplicated portraits of education, social class, and gender? Second, I ask them to
develop and apply a critical method for reading the literacy narrative, specifically, *Pygmalion*. In developing a critical method, I want
the students to learn how to read for patterns, to become critical
readers for ideas that they find interesting, important, and key in
the texts and for themselves. While I do suggest that they read for
social class, gender, or other tropes connected to education and literacy, I also hope that they will develop their own variations on
these readings. However, by asking them explicitly to read for these
ideological positions, I try to move them toward understanding the
structural and cultural implications of literacy beyond the personal.
How is literacy gendered in *Pygmalion, Pretty Woman, Educating
Rita,* and other cultural texts? How is social class working in these
cultural texts? If the students begin to understand that a critical

method for reading can be developed and applied to structural and cultural contexts, they move one step further in their unpacking of literacy as more than simply a personal matter. They begin to understand that there are structural and cultural pressures that inform their own literacy and education.

Students often choose to do a comparison between *Pygmalion* and *Pretty Woman* for this writing project. I think this is due partly to the accessibility of *Pretty Woman,* but I also believe that this film has garnered a particular place in the cultural imagination, providing both a conversion story and a romance that fulfills the desires of an audience that has bought into these cultural scripts. In approaching these two texts, Karla acknowledges up front the appeal of the conversion story and romance and begins to examine why these stories appeal to us. However, she draws a distinction between the realism and pessimism of *Pygmalion* and the fantasy and perfection of *Pretty Woman* and begins to uncover how these two stories function structurally. For Karla, *Pygmalion* acts as a critique of society, unmasking expectations about social class, accent, and gender. *Pretty Woman* acts as fantasy, as a way to reinforce expectations about how someone can be transformed, that love and innate goodness are enough to transcend any obstacle. Pam focuses on constructions of gender and the impact this has on the way education and literacy function in society for women. In looking at the relationships between Higgins and Eliza and Edward and Vivian, Pam examines the way men act as teachers and women act as their students. By unpacking these teacher-student relationships, Pam begins to understand the unequal power structures in the construction of gender and moves toward understanding how literacy and education can also be gendered, and how cultural texts like literature and film can reinforce these power relationships.

These two writing assignments are just a first step in having students undertake the project of reading literacy narratives as a way of unpacking literacy, culture, and citizenship in America. For students to understand and connect this "multicultural stuff" as part of their own experience, they needed to write their own literacy narratives. Reading literacy narratives provides a context in which students can locate personal experiences within a larger framework of literacy history, practices, and concepts. Writing literacy narratives provides students with the opportunity to insert themselves into this framework, to participate in the process of self-discovery and self-fashioning, and to take a critical look at the ways in which they have become literate and use literacy.

Writing Re/Visions and Literacy Narratives

In thinking about the narratives written by Maxine Hong Kingston, Marie Hara, and Lois-Ann Yamanaka, what strikes me is how unfamiliar histories are unpacked. Not only do these narratives provide a discursive space for "minor" voices to tell their stories, but they also require historical contexts that inform these personal expressions about literacy, culture, and identity. In my discussion of Kingston's narrative, I provide a historical context for understanding the legacy of silence within the history of Asian American literacy. In my readings of Hara's and Yamanaka's stories, I lay a foundation for further discussion about the legacy of the English Standard schools and plantations in Hawai'i's literacy history.

What I see in each of these narratives is not only a writing of and about literacy but also a writing of and about history. In writing a literacy narrative, there is a self-discovery about the process of acquiring and using literacy and language, but there is also a process of discovery and critical analysis as one must begin to examine the contexts for his or her literacy. When I ask students to write a literacy narrative, I am not seeking a simple tale of achievement or success. While our culture often encourages us to think about our education in nostalgic ways, this often elides moments of struggle or more complex achievement. There is also a temptation to reduce the literacy narrative to a story of singular personal accomplishment and not to do wider critical cultural analysis of systems of education or literacy contexts.

After asking my first-year students to do an analysis of the function of literacy in a literacy narrative and to develop a critical approach to reading a text, for the next writing project, I ask them to write their own literacy narrative. Before they begin their narrative, we continue to read and analyze narratives from *Multicultural Literacy* and examine the way the narrative constructs the author's identity. For example, Gloria Anzaldua's "The Path of the Red and Black Ink," Carlos Fuente's "How I Started to Write," Eduardo Galeano's "In Defense of the Word," and Guillermo Gomez-Pena's "Documented/Undocumented" each take on a distinctly political project as they connect their acts of literacy and writing with the acknowledgement of a racial/ethnic identity and the development of a political identity, often grounding this identity in geography and cultural location. I have used Rodriguez's *Hunger of Memory* with the essays mentioned above to complicate constructions of and by Latino and Latina writers. I have also used Scott Russell Sanders's *Writing from the Center* as a way for students to connect with a writer from the Midwest. While Sanders's text is less politically focused, it also acts to connect his acts of literacy and writing with his life in the Midwest and the construction of something called a Midwest identity. Using Janet Carey Eldred and Peter Mortensen's essay "Reading Literacy Narratives" to provide a common vocabulary, I ask students to examine their own literacy and life histories through the genre of the literacy narrative:

> Literacy Narrative—Fact and Fiction (4–5 pages, typed, double-spaced): The texts we have read for the last two weeks have focused on the role literacy (and writing in particular) has played in the lives of the authors and their sense of identity. The essays by Anzaldua, Fuentes, Galeano, and Gomez-Pena and the memoir by Scott Russell Sanders all examine how place, language, and cultural identity are connected. This has also been a theme in many of the earlier texts we have read.
>
> For this essay I want you to write a literacy narrative. Remember that Janet Carey Eldred and Peter Mortensen describe the literacy narrative as

those stories, like Bernard Shaw's *Pygmalion,* that foreground issues of language acquisition and literacy. These narratives are structured by learned, internalized "literacy tropes," by "prefigured" ideas and images. Literacy narratives sometimes include explicit images of schooling and teaching; they include texts that both challenge and affirm culturally scripted ideas about literacy.

The literacy narrative you write can be either a personal examination of your own literacy history and the role literacy broadly defined has played in your life, or you can write an imaginative piece (fiction, drama, etc.) that includes the features of the literacy narrative (for example, think about *Pygmalion*). Or you may want to create a mixed-genre piece that includes both fact and fiction, a blend of your own literacy experiences and imaginative elements.

Here are some suggestions:

- Examine a literacy event from your life (like Anzaldua, Fuentes, Sanders). You can talk about your first visit to the library, learning how to write, hating an English class, writing a letter, poem, story, etc. Or you can expand on the in-class piece.
- Create a story (fiction or nonfiction). This story can be about learning language (like *Pygmalion* or Frederick Douglass's *Narrative*). Or you can focus on a specific setting (like growing up in the Midwest or other places as Sanders does).
- Create a blend that brings together your experiences and related stories.

Here are some things to keep in mind:

- Don't just describe. It's important to paint a picture of your experience or the story you're telling, but also provide some self-reflection or analysis. Why is this a meaningful experience? Why are you telling this story?

- Make sure you provide full characters. The reader wants to know whom these characters are and why we should care about what happens to them.
- Think about the connections between literacy (broadly defined) and identity. For example, how do Anzaldua, Fuentes, Galeano, Sanders, etc. connect writing with their lives? Why is writing important to them? What is the connection between literacy and cultural identity for them? How does place influence these literacy experiences?
- Don't try to tell the "Hero" story—I learned how to read and write and the world is now a better place. Also don't worry about being dramatic or traumatic. Sometimes the best stories are in the ordinary everyday things (for example, reading with Mom or Dad, buying your weekly comic book, etc.).

When you write a literacy narrative, whether fact or fiction, you are not just providing simple description. You are examining a specific type of experience and doing a cultural analysis of it. How does this experience fit into your life? How is this experience connected to and influenced by our larger culture? What does this literacy narrative say about you, your identity, and your community?

Perhaps the first noticeable element of this writing project is that students have the option of writing a more conventional literacy narrative where they explore their own literacy histories, or they can write an imaginative literacy narrative where they explore ideas and practices of literacy by creating a story that uses the features that we identify and discuss in our readings of others' texts. Or students could create a mixed-genre piece that would include both "fact" and "fiction" as a way to explore literacy.

This writing project builds upon the students' explorations of "The Function of Literacy" by continuing to ask students to do critical cultural analysis of the ways literacy works in specific contexts. However, by writing their own literacy narratives—either a personal history or creation of narrative where they must create contexts and characters—the students must begin to more fully understand how literacy has both infiltrated and fulfilled their lives. I do warn students against the "Hero" story or conversion narrative where they construct a linear developmental narrative, from preliterate or illiterate to acquiring literacy to becoming an enlightened and successful citizen. While I do not discourage or dismiss the transformative power of literacy in their lives, I do push students to think about the contexts that allow this transformation to take place, whether it is support at home for learning, effective and well-funded schools, or a passion for comic books. What are the things that provide them the opportunity to successfully acquire, develop, and use literacy? This is also an opportunity for students to become "minor," as they can examine their own lives for those moments when they have felt outside the mainstream, when they felt as if no one understood them. While becoming "minor" can be a risk, it also allows students to make connections with an experience that they have narrated in nostalgic ways to overwrite the anxiety. If the students can resolve the tension between the anxiety and nostalgia of their literacy, they have moved closer to re/vision. From this personal understanding of literacy, especially the contexts that support the personal development of literacy, I want students to move toward understanding the public contexts of literacy and how literacy can be both a means of engagement or means of disenfranchisement for people who seek to become public citizens.

Students do tend to construct a dominant cultural narrative about their literacy. One student, Kathy, describes how she could not have escaped literacy even if she had tried because her mother was an English teacher. But along with her mother, others contributed to the immersion in literacy, from an AP English teacher who brought challenging texts to the classroom to a grandfather who shared his stories about growing up and the importance of education. For Kathy, these figures and stories provide a setting for her own tale about literacy as she tries to understand how she has made good on the promise of literacy. Another student, Paula, also writes a dominant cultural narrative as she describes her first memory of reading a book as a preschooler. But what is interesting in Paula's narrative is the way she links her own acquisition of literacy to her mother's life, recalling scenes of watching her mother do "homework." Frustrated at this lack of attention from her mother during these times, Paula turns to doing her own "homework," selecting her own book to "read" even though she did not really know how to read at the time. We see not just Paula's narrative but also the impact her mother's narrative has on her, providing a deeply personal story and connection between mother and daughter. Rick has a different strategy as he writes two contrasting narratives to illustrate how race, social class, and circumstance can have an effect on individual lives. He narrates the life of a fictional character of "typical" intelligence, talents, and attributes but then examines how this person's access and use of literacy may change as he is placed in two very different settings: middle-class suburbia and inner-city working-class neighborhood. While Rick's two-in-one narrative relies on dominant cultural narratives about race and social class among other things, by juxtaposing these two narratives, he uses one to unpack the other, to begin to ask questions about how larger structural and cultural pressures affect the way literacy is acquired and used.

In each of the above writing projects, I focus on a particular component as students work toward understanding the personal and public beliefs about and uses of literacy. We began with defining the uses of literacy, moved to developing a critical approach to reading literacy narrative and then writing literacy narratives, and finally we bring all of these processes together to understand how culture works. In the final writing project for the course, I want students to synthesize the personal and the public, the processes of reading and writing, and examine the concept of culture. This final project asks students to re/vision literacy and citizenship, to think about the ways they have begun to understand their culture in more complicated ways:

Reading and Writing Culture(s) (4–5 pages, typed, double-spaced): For this final essay, I want you to examine the way we read and write culture. That is, how do we participate in making culture(s) through our interpretations, understandings, and critical discussions about culture(s)? Think back over the entire term and the ways we have talked about culture(s). We have looked primarily at the way language and literacy work in our culture and how they are represented in texts. What have we learned about the role language plays in shaping us? How do we use language (in positive or negative ways) to create our culture? What does it mean to you to read a book like *Wild Meat and the Bully Burgers* and to see the way race, class, gender, place, language, etc. all intersect to create a culture?

Find a text from the class that has made you rethink what culture means? It doesn't have to be a text that has changed your mind; but it should be something that has made you think harder and more critically about what the text means and how it affects your view of the way culture works.

Here are some possibilities:

- Examine the ways your view of Hawai'i has been affected by *Wild Meat and the Bully Burgers* or other popular culture texts that we will look at (films, TV, magazine advertisements or stories, etc.)
- Examine the ways a text from our class has affected your understanding of something you experienced previously. For example, how did reading Frederick Douglass's *Narrative* or *Wild Meat and the Bully Burgers* affect your understanding of schooling or what it means to be American? Or how did the collection *Multicultural Literacy* affect your understanding of your own literacy?
- Examine the way one of the social positions we have talked about all term (race, class, gender, etc.) works in multiple texts. That is, how have the texts talked about race, class, gender, etc.? How does this reflect or not reflect the way race, class, or gender is talked about in culture?

- Think about Lovey and the way she participates in the making of culture. She is influenced by the cultural messages she receives from popular culture, family, friends, school, etc. Examine how you participate in making culture. What messages are you receiving or giving? What are you receiving from the texts from class? What messages will you pass on?

Remember:

- Include a text from class in your analysis. Show why this text is key in your rethinking of culture.
- Don't just describe. Analyze and argue. For example, don't say: "My view of culture has been changed forever by this class and I'm a better person now." I want to know how and why you are rethinking your view of culture.
- Using a text to analyze personal experience or vice versa is fine, but make sure you show what the connection is. For example, if you want to discuss the coming-of-age aspect of *Wild Meat and the Bully Burgers* by citing your own experience, fine. But I want you to analyze what the similarities and differences are—you will not have experienced the exact same life as Lovey so you can't say "I know exactly how she feels."

I've been talking about culture(s) in a broad way here. I want you to be aware of the larger issues involved in rethinking culture. However, I also think it's best if you examine and analyze specific examples. Look at specific issues that then have meaning in the ways we talk about culture and its larger ideological force.

While I ask students to reflect on the work they've done for the entire semester and give them the opportunity to engage any of the texts we've read during the term, this final writing project is in a sense organized around Lois-Ann Yamanaka's *Wild Meat and the*

Bully Burgers. This is due in part to its place as the final text we read in class, but I also find it most fully portrays the issues we've been addressing all semester. We see issues of literacy, race, and citizenship at work in this text, but we also must deal with the larger cultural stereotypes that exist about Hawai'i in the American imagination. This is an opportunity for extra-curricular work to occur as I become an important part of how the students engage with this Hawai'i text, functioning as a text myself. Reading *Wild Meat and the Bully Burgers* as a literacy narrative becomes more than an academic exercise, more than simply reading for patterns and symbols, and more than realizing that the experience and value of Lovey Nariyoshi's life is legitimate. Because I am able to provide lived experience as context, students can begin to understand that culture is not simply an abstraction, that the particulars of life in Hawai'i—its language, its politics, its cultural practices—can even have an effect on their life as they interact with their teacher.

This writing project produces a variety of interesting and engaging work as students grapple with the idea of culture and how literacy, language, and writing play a crucial role in the function of culture beyond the typical beliefs that literacy is either simply functional or signifies a State of Grace. Many students begin to unpack Hawai'i as a metaphor, to examine the function of Hawai'i in the American cultural imagination. Paula, for example, begins with an inventory of the images we most often associate with Hawai'i: beautiful beaches, romantic sunsets, tropical drinks, and volcanoes. But she then moves to reconcile these images with the minor story told in *Wild Meat and the Bully Burgers,* and focuses on the anxiety experienced by Lovey over questions of literacy, race, and citizenship. Rick also examines representations of Hawai'i but then moves to unpack larger stereotypes about race, gender, and "minority" cultures and how these function in American culture. What is important in Rick's work is that he begins to understand that culture is not static, that it is always being made, and yet there is often an attempt to create hard and fast stories to satisfy certain desires—that we need recognizable characters, plots, and places in an attempt to understand who we are. Karla also tries to bring the idea of culture into question by drawing a connection between Douglass's *Narrative, Hunger of Memory,* and *Wild Meat and the Bully Burgers.* These texts have helped her ask questions about who has access to literacy, who can obtain education, and what are the consequences for those who are denied or have limited access to literacy and education? She moves toward understanding why these minor narratives are also a part of culture and their value in examining culture. What Karla begins to become aware of is how these minor narratives help her read American culture, help her in locating her own position and how she both constructs and is constructed by culture.

This is the re/vision that I believe is critical in the classroom—that students begin to understand that they are part of culture—not outside of it—and that just as others have an effect on their lives even if in tiny ways, they have effects on the lives of others. Having students read and write literacy narratives provides them with a way of understanding that literacy, race, and citizenship are both personal and public experiences, intertwined intimately and inextricably. Reading literacy narratives allows students to understand that their experiences are tied to the experiences of others though they may occupy different historical, cultural, and social positions. Writing literacy narratives allows students to write themselves into the narrative of culture, to imagine themselves as participants in American culture and not simply as observers. For students to re/vision their own work both literally and figuratively is for them to re/vision their place in American culture, to understand that they are always in the process of narrating their stories.

Classroom Re/Visions

Last week, second semester, fifth year: I sit in a small converted one-room apartment that serves as the meeting site for an after-school program at my university's graduate student housing complex. I'm off to one side observing the undergraduate students from my seminar on literacy and service-learning interacting with the half dozen children there for the program. The kids who attend are the children of graduate students at the university, many of these families from places like Korea, China, Nepal, or other parts of the world. The kids are bright and talkative. For some, English is a second language. They like to draw and write stories and play games. They live in the Manor because it's convenient though on the margins of the university community literally and figuratively. It's become an ethnic enclave just beyond the beautiful new recreational center—the "Asian Invasion," a slur one of my students reported hearing from an acquaintance of hers.

The undergraduates in this seminar are mostly from the Midwest and are English majors (creative writing, journalism, linguistics, and literature), though there's one student in international studies. None of them plans to teach (yet), but they all seem to have an interest in and talent for working with kids. We have been working to create this community literacy program throughout the semester, to understand how literacy is used and what it can mean for a community. We have struggled with definitions and theories of literacy, service, and community. But in the collaboration between the children and undergraduates, there is meaning being made, a re/vision of what literacy is and what our work as literacy teachers can be. One student, Lisa, writes in her journal:

> As a whole, children use literacy to achieve similar ends: maintaining friendships through conversation about similar interests, documenting personal thoughts and events, and questioning ways in which the world works. However, I also realize from working with the children at the Manor that people use literacy in various ways according to what end they want to achieve. Amy seems to use her writing to convey facts to other people. On the other hand, Karen has no problem writing a story, which, even if non-fictional, requires more creativity.

Similarly, it is important to distinguish literacy from intelligence, or more importantly, desire to learn. Amy will not acquiesce to participate in an activity she has no interest in, but she tends to find another activity which will stimulate her literacy skills. In this way, she is demonstrating two positive elements of literacy: the commitment to learning through reading or writing and hesitancy to compromise her desires. The children at the Manor have a desire to express themselves and interact with their surroundings; it is a matter of cultivating this desire so that literacy may become a vehicle for them to successfully do this. Rather than trying to identify why these young people need to empower themselves now, I think we are laying the foundation for methods of empowerment which will become necessary in the future.[2]

In this journal entry, Lisa has begun to re/vision literacy and citizenship and the work she does at the after-school program. Lisa has begun to understand that the children she tutors are already active citizens as they make meaning through their literate acts. In this extracurricular site, the work of re/visioning literacy takes on more meaning as we see children imagining themselves beyond the limits of schooled literacy, of empowering themselves to be active citizens even if they operate on the margins of the university. For Lisa to become aware of this re/vision of literacy by the children is to become aware of her own re/vision of what literacy means in the community, what literacy means in the lives of these children, and how we can re/vision the classroom to include these extra-curricular sites.

I continue to sit and observe, impressed by the children and what they can teach the undergraduates, and impressed by the undergraduates who are willing to take this risk by interacting with the community. I turn to Jason, the six-year-old Chinese boy sitting next to me, and ask him to tell me a story about the picture he has just drawn.

5 / Personal/Public/Professional
Re/Visions of Research, Teaching, and Citizenship

Born today, you are an intellectual by nature. Your head rules your heart almost exclusively and you make all decisions without emotional involvement. Such an approach to life is good when it comes to furthering your career, but it could prove a drawback in your personal relationships. No one likes to feel that he is friends with a machine. You have a great gift for the written word and often do better in your relationships with others if you can communicate by letter rather than face-to-face.

—"Your Birthday—By Stella" (21 January 1967)

As I read this horoscope some thirty-odd years later, clipped and saved by my mother, I am amused by the "accuracy" regarding my interpersonal skills and am amazed by the final sentence's mention of "a great gift for the written word." I had never seen this horoscope until I began rummaging through my mother's file. Now with the kind of predestination indicated by the horoscope, it is no wonder that I have become a writing teacher (though I still find it difficult to call myself a writer) who researches literacy practices and finds himself writing about writing in these pages. Here is some further context for my literacy. I was born in Honolulu in 1967 and raised in Kalihi, living there for twenty-four years before leaving for graduate school. I attended Kapalama Elementary and Kalakaua Intermediate and graduated from Farrington High School in 1985. I then earned a B.A. and an M.A. in English from the University of Hawai'i. I was a "townie" according to my friends from the suburbs, though I never really understood this when these friends were really only twenty minutes or so away from where I lived. And worse than that, I was from Kalihi, a working-class neighborhood known more for the state prison, gangs, and large immigrant population. Though my father had a white-collar management job with

169

the state government, there was never really any thought of moving up the middle-class ladder and relocating. I think this was due partly to both my parents' growing up around downtown Honolulu and their own childhoods in working-class families. So growing up in Kalihi seemed like a very local experience. As my high school's yearbook theme declared my senior year, we were "Made in Kalihi."

Now I recite these facts not to make a claim on my authentic identity. Rather, I find a need to examine my history in Hawai'i because as Hawai'i cultural critic Candace Fujikane has argued, "There are political responsibilities to claiming any identity," especially when "local identity is often used as a means of self-legitimation at the expense of peoples who face ongoing political struggles in Hawai'i" (57–58). And in some ways, my discussion about local identity is even more tenuous as I find myself settled in the Midwest now but often claiming Hawai'i as my subject. But as ordinary as I think my life has been, it is still very complex. Middle-class economic background but working-class environment and aesthetic. Chinese father (that is, Chinese ancestry) and Japanese mother (that is, Japanese ancestry) but not really, because she's Okinawan (that is, Okinawan ancestry). I attend the University of Michigan for graduate school, but I'm not one of the alumni of an elite Hawai'i private school who make up the Hawai'i Club there. So while it often seems I'm firmly located, something acts to undermine this perceived stable position. In fact, there is an element of fiction at work here as I construct a story to connect these facts, to create a cohesion in my life as well as to emphasize those bits of fact that increase the romance of this developmental narrative. From working-class neighborhood to the elite academy, from poor urban setting to the idyllic ivy-covered red brick university—I have begun to participate in these moments of memoir that now are often included in scholarly writing.

As I have begun to write my literacy narrative and have woven parts throughout this book, I have moved toward understanding in more complex ways the issues that have occupied my research, teaching, and professional life. Literacy, race, and citizenship are always central in the cultural work I do as a scholar, teacher, and participant in American culture. Writing my own literacy narrative has inserted a reflective component and has raised the stakes as I become the subject of my own investigation and part of a collective assemblage of minor narratives. Rather than removing a sense of self from these investigations in order to examine distinct acts of literacy and writing, I keep a sense of self present and aware as I seek to understand the emotion, psychology, and politics that are always inflected in our lives. These scenes of re/vision have helped me to understand the contexts for my literacy and for my literacy research and teaching.

In making my literacy narrative public, I offer a personal account of my life as student, teacher, and researcher to suggest the kinds of work we must engage in if we are to act responsibly as a discipline and profession. Whether we are researching the literacy practices of diverse communities, teaching in classrooms that are either widely heterogeneous or narrowly homogeneous, or participating in professional conferences where we make arguments and claims about the work we do, we need to keep in mind our responsibilities to individuals and communities: that in doing research about literacy and in teaching literacy to a variety of people, we are also working to create opportunities, to reveal inequity, and to act in the interests of social justice. Here I offer some of the ways I have had to re/vision research, teaching, and citizenship as I have come to a new understanding of the ways the personal, public, and professional have shaped my life.

Re/Visions of Research

In writing and weaving my personal literacy history throughout this book, I have tried to illustrate a theory for narrating stories about literacy, race, and citizenship. From these literacy narratives emerges a rhetoric of citizenship, a way of understanding how literacy and race work together in the construction of citizenship. In each of my examples, I have considered the personal and public contexts that have informed these narratives. In the tension between the personal and public, the rhetoric of citizenship becomes clear: that in the re/visions of literacy the personal and public cannot be read as discrete narratives but rather must be read together as the parts of a whole story. This is part of the re/vision of research that I have found to be critical in my work: that there is a need to understand the personal and public contexts for literacy as well as a need to understand how the stories that are being written about literacy, race, and citizenship function in our culture. The personal is not simply an individual idiosyncratic story but rather part and parcel of the many stories that inform the larger sociocultural narratives that script America. Thus when we write and include personal narratives in our research, we re/vision our range of data, provide different lenses of analyses, and move toward creating complex portraits of people and their uses of literacy.

For example, in researching one part of the literacy history of Hawai'i, I have turned to inserting myself as a subject in and of this history through my personal memories and a variety of personal artifacts. But my personal narrative converges with the public narrative of literacy in Hawai'i as I examine personal artifacts that also function as public institutional artifacts. For example, the next artifact, my kindergarten report card, provides information not only about my performance as a student but also about how and what was being measured in that performance (see fig. 5.1a–d).

As I read over my report card, I am not so surprised to see that I made satisfactory progress in those areas that could be categorized as "citizenship" skills. "I follow directions" and "I listen when others are speaking." I am also not so surprised that "I enjoy looking at books" and "I try to use acceptable English." I grew up in a middle-class home with parents and siblings who were well educated; I was expected to be a good boy. I do notice that in the second and third quarters I "need[ed] more help" in "speak[ing] clearly and loudly enough" and in "express[ing] my ideas well." This disrupts my own romantic notion that I have always been a good student, that I was verbally gifted and expressive in acceptable ways. What I also find disruptive is that there is an evaluation for the quality of English language usage; disruptive because to me this brings into question how students were being evaluated and

H. E. P. LANGUAGE SKILLS

STUDENT PROGRESS REPORT
K-6

STUDENT   MORRIS YOUNG

TEACHER   Lau, Miyazono, Coronel

SCHOOL   Kapalama

ROOM No.   34/35   YEAR 1972-73

Figure 5.1a

		Quarters			
		1	2	3	4

Has written a series of increasingly complex messages getting another to perform a task:

	1	2	3	4
PW-A 1-30				
31-94				
95-115				
PW-B 1-25				
26-83				
84-115				
116-140				
MC 1-5				
6-10				
11-15				
16-20				
21-30				
31-39				

Typewriting

Typed capital letters of the alphabet and words with correct fingering — Type BL 1 / BL 2

Typed small letters of the alphabet and words with correct fingering — Type SL / Type LW

Typed sentences and paragraphs using shift key and punctuation marks — Type S & Par.

Typed from models: Songs and Poems
Stories
Numerals
Skill Building
Typing Our Language

Types original material — Type a Letter

Communicates with others through typewriting — Type to a Pal

Listening/Speaking

Recognized and named twelve colors and seven shapes — L:CS / S:CS

Recognized and used the prepositions on, to, under, through, and around appropriately — L:Prep / S:Prep

Recognized and used the singular and plural forms appropriately — L:PL / S:PL / L:Det / S:Det

Discriminated among the multiple meanings of selected vocabulary items — MM 1-3 / 4-9

Heard the difference between and produced:
English sounds that may be difficult for children — L:E 1-35 / S:E 1-35

English sounds that are often confused by Island children — L:DM 1-15 / S:DM 1-15

4

		Quarters			
		1	2	3	4
Statement and yes/no question intonation patterns	L:Int				
	S:Int				
Contrastive stress patterns	L:Stress				
	S:Stress				
Distinguished between Hawaiian Dialect and Standard English use of: Verbs 1-4	Grammar 1				
Pronouns					
Questions					
Negatives					
Possessives					
Phrases					
Word Differences					
Discriminated and produced selected Standard English forms: Verbs 1-4	Grammar 2				
	L				
	S				
Pronouns	L				
	S				
Questions	L				
	S				
Negatives	L				
	S				
Possessives	L				
	S				
Phrases	L				
	S				
Word Differences	L				
	S				
Produced several alternative sentences in response to a situational cue	GF 1-12				
Heard the differences between and produced four English dialects	L:DV				
	S:DV				
Heard the differences between and produced formal and informal styles	L:SV				
	S:SV				
Differentiated among the use of selected prefixes and suffixes	Affixes 1-5				
	6-12				
Responded to and gave directions and descriptions using positional concepts, analogies, and attributes:	L:TOC 1-6				X
	S:TOC 1-6				X
	L:TOC 7-15				X
	S:TOC 7-15				
	L:TOC 16-22				
	S:TOC 16-22				
Composed a series of increasingly complex oral messages requiring another to perform a task:	MC 1-5				
	6-10				
	11-15				
	16-20				
	21-30				
	31-39				
Performed a series of tasks through oral discussion as a member of a group:	TOGD 1-9				
	10-18				
	19-27				
	28-36				
	37-45				

5

Figure 5.1c

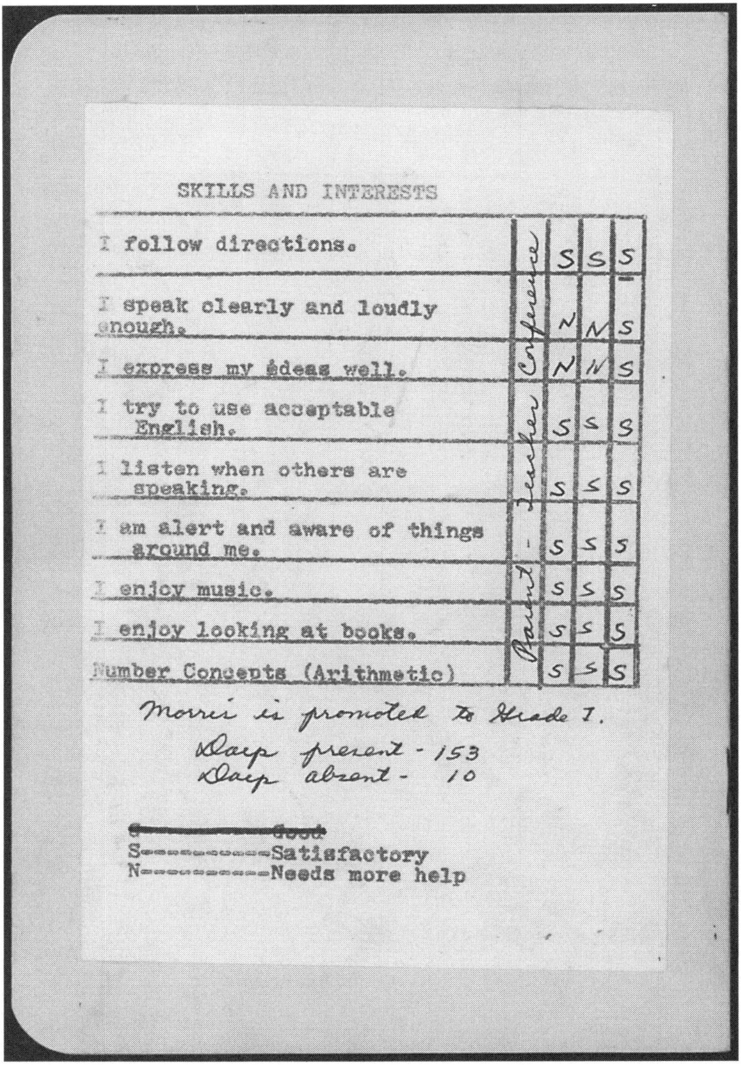

SKILLS AND INTERESTS

I follow directions.		S	S	S
I speak clearly and loudly enough.		N	N	S
I express my ideas well.		N	N	S
I try to use acceptable English.		S	≤	S
I listen when others are speaking.		S	≤	S
I am alert and aware of things around me.		S	≤	S
I enjoy music.		S	≤	S
I enjoy looking at books.		S	≤	S
Number Concepts (Arithmetic)		S	≤	S

Parent - Teacher Conference

Morris is promoted to Grade 1.

Days present - 153
Days absent - 10

G————————Good
S——————————Satisfactory
N——————————Needs more help

Figure 5.1d

what they were being evaluated on. The "Student Progress Report" included here also tells us a partial story of the Hawaii English Program (HEP), a language arts curriculum designed by the State Department of Education and University of Hawai'i and implemented in Hawai'i's public schools. This curriculum was designed to implement more progressive pedagogies that placed the student at the center as learner in a self-directed manner but also to address the legacy of Hawai'i Creole/Pidgin in the community. As we see in the "Student Progress Report," there are sections that ask the teacher to determine a student's ability to distinguish between "Hawaiian Dialect" and "Standard English" as well as to use Standard English forms. While it is common and expected for school literacy to be measured by student skill levels and proficiency, we need to unpack the histories and ideologies that underlie these practices. In the case of my report card, the evaluation of "acceptable English" is mired in the history of public debate about the use and value of Hawai'i Creole described earlier in chapter 3.

While attention to linguistic features played a part in my early education, I was also subject to the more subtle forms of ideology that often inform our culture's faith in literacy and the value of citizenship. Another personal artifact from the file that also acts as a public institutional artifact is a worksheet produced in kindergarten or first grade (see fig. 5.2a–b). This worksheet is an example of my own schooled literacy being reinforced by institutional practices. A familiar literacy ritual found in the American classroom in one form or another is the worksheet. Whether these worksheets are the mimeographed dittos of a past era, mass-produced workbooks that accompany basal readers, or new interactive computer programs, they often operate under the illusion of scientific validity. As Patrick Shannon argues, this type of work "maintains the myths among poor and minority students that they are solely responsible for their difficulty in learning to be literate and among middle-and upper-class students that they are literate simply because they can pass basal tests and other standardized tests" (631). This literacy ritual thus performs a socializing function as students are either made responsible for their own (lack of) social position or are rewarded

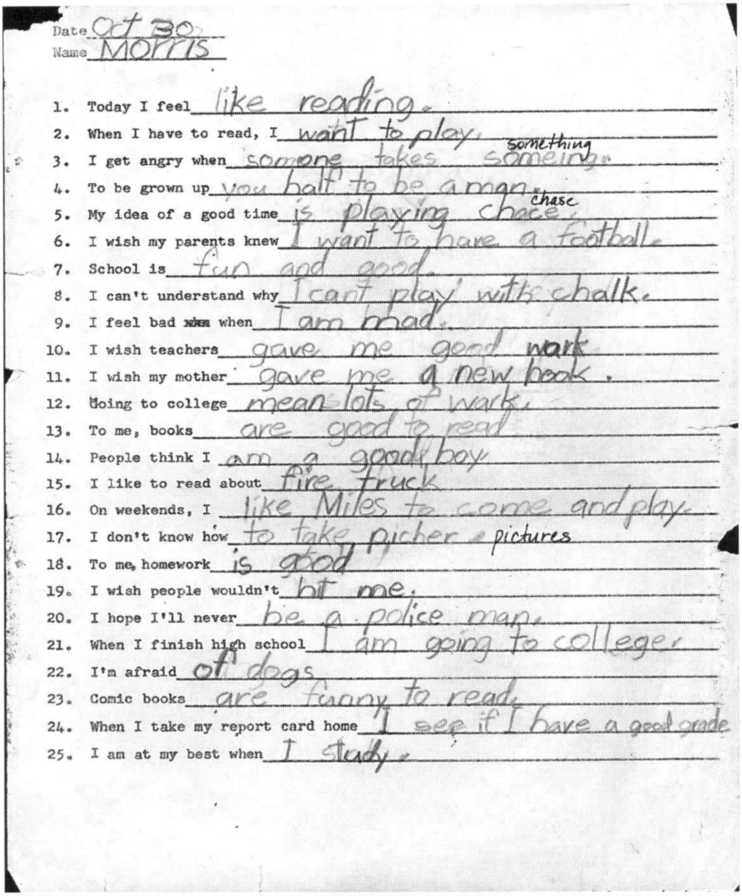

Date _Oct 30_
Name _Morris_

1. Today I feel _like reading._
2. When I have to read, I _want to play something._
3. I get angry when _someone takes someting._
4. To be grown up _you haft to be a man._
5. My idea of a good time _is playing chace chase._
6. I wish my parents knew _I want to have a football._
7. School is _fun and good._
8. I can't understand why _I cant play with chalk._
9. I feel bad when _I am mad._
10. I wish teachers _gave me good work._
11. I wish my mother _gave me a new book._
12. Going to college _mean lots of work._
13. To me, books _are good to read._
14. People think I _am a good boy._
15. I like to read about _fire truck._
16. On weekends, I _like Miles to come and play._
17. I don't know how _to take picher pictures._
18. To me, homework _is good._
19. I wish people wouldn't _hit me._
20. I hope I'll never _be a police man._
21. When I finish high school _I am going to college._
22. I'm afraid _of dogs._
23. Comic books _are funny to read._
24. When I take my report card home _I see if I have a good grade._
25. I am at my best when _I study._

Figure 5.2a

because of their social position. Students learn what it means to be a good citizen by performing the appropriate labor and completing their own individual (though culturally scripted) narrative of progress.

The two-page worksheet is dated 30 October. There is no year, but I suspect it is something I worked on in kindergarten or first

page 2

26. Most brothers and sisters _are good._
27. I'd rather read than _wirte , write_
28. When I read math _I think._
29. The future looks _good._
30. I feel proud when _I am good._
31. I wish my father _makes a playhouse_ [house]
32. I like to read when _it is day._
33. I would like to be _a fire man._
34. For me, studying _good._
35. I often worry about _my fish._
36. I wish I could _. have a boat._
37. Reading science _is fun._
38. I look forward to _going to Miles houses_ [house]
39. I wish someone would help me _catch butterflys_ [flies]
40. I'd read more if _I had a new book._
41. Special help in reading _means teolers_ [tutors]
42. Every single word is _not a conpound word._ [Compound]
43. My eyes _see · good_
44. The last book I read _was in school._
45. My mother helps _in my homework._
46. Reading in junior high school _is hardwork._
47. My father thinks reading _is good_
48. I read better than _Scott._
49. My father helps _me with my reading_
50. I would like to read better than _my brother._

Figure 5.2b

grade. Some of the clues: My written answers are in block print and not cursive, and a classmate I knew only in kindergarten and first grade is named.

On the worksheet there are fifty prompts that are to be completed by the students. There are the standard, "Today I feel . . . " and "I get angry when . . . " But as part of the ideological project of schooling, there are also prompts like "School is . . . ," "I wish teachers . . . ," "Going to college . . . ," "To me, books . . . ," and "I'd rather read than . . . " There are a number of these prompts that act to reinforce schooling in a positive way. And the completion of these prompts often draw glowing portrayals (for a 5–6 year old) of school. Now I admit I was probably well prepared for school. I had much older siblings who did well in school, my Mom had worked as a teacher's aide before I was born, and there were tons of books and magazines around the house. So when I read over these worksheets, I am not surprised at my answers—I was socialized to be a "good boy" (see number 14) and to reproduce the positive attributes of school, literacy, and family. The worksheet acts to write the standard literacy narrative, prompting students to rehearse the "school is good" mantra and perhaps transforming students to believe this.

Patrick Courts argues that the basalization of literacy teaching and learning has diminished literacy by its attention to decontextualized language learning and creation of an artificial performance by the students. As Courts points out, worksheets become an instance of literacy that exists for itself:

> Either you must fill in the blank (or does the blank fill you in?—they have lots of blanks) or you must identify the correct or incorrect answer by circling it, or drawing an X through it. In addition to all of this, students will find that learning to spell involves copying the definition; and learning to write involves writing a sentence or two using the word they copied five times and looked up in a dictionary. . . . In surprisingly few cases does one find kids reading in order to have fun or to learn something because they are too busy reading in order to read. And to the extent that they write at all, they are writing-to-write; they are practicing correct punctuation and usage and business letters—getting ready for the day shift, so to speak. (47–48)

While Courts's description of the classroom critiques our culture's capitalist impulses to prepare workers for an existing labor market, I find that his own belief in education is perhaps overly romantic. Certainly it would be nice to have "fun" or to learn something simply because of curiosity or joy or pleasure. However, the idea that education and learning are unquestioned positive and enlightening experiences has its own ideological underpinnings. As my own experience has shown, I can take such enlightenment ideals for granted because of my middle-class upbringing and my parents' belief in the cultural value of education.

I find my own worksheet actually very clever because of what I see as its ideological project of promoting good schooling. And I hope that students at an early age can have these positive, perhaps less heavy-handed, literacy experiences. But when I read over these questions and prompts, I also wonder about the students who could not comprehend prompts 12 or 21 because going to college seemed like a very remote possibility. Or about those students who could not expect to get a new book as I did in prompts 11 and 40. Or who did not have parents who were available to help with homework (see numbers 45 and 49).

As I reread my "progress report" and unpack my worksheet, I ideally hope to disrupt the legacy of Hawai'i's English Standard schools. As a literacy educator today, I want to see that my own early education was perhaps more progressive than I have remembered it. I want to read the contradictions of my experience and see a more complex life. But in doing so, am I myself creating an artifice from artifacts, returning to the nostalgia of an imagined time? In order to recreate my childhood experiences and give disruptive meaning to those literacy events, I am reading my life through a particular lens. Now I don't discount this reading; in fact I believe that what I have experienced and what these artifacts illustrate create a complex portrait of a life both fulfilled and infiltrated by literacy. But I must read this story like I do any other and apply a critical eye to my own ideological investments in a re/vision of a literate life.

As the report card and worksheet demonstrate—as do my other personal artifacts and the narrative I have written throughout this book—the personal has become the foundation for my research interests in language and literacy politics. Through recuperating these personal experiences alongside an examination of the larger sociocultural histories of literacy, I have come to understand in more complex ways the consequences of our personal, public, and professional narratives and how they are intimately connected and cannot be excluded from one another. I have also come to understand the need to locate myself as both researcher and subject of the research since I cannot escape the ways historical, cultural, institutional, and personal contexts have shaped my approach to and analyses of literacy practices. Drawing on the work of Adrienne Rich and Sandra Harding, Gesa Kirsch and Joy Ritchie argue in their essay "Beyond the Personal" that in addition to acknowledging multiple positions,

> a politics of location must engage us in a rigorous on-going exploration of *how* we do our research: What assumptions underlie our approaches to research and methodologies? And a politics of location must challenge our conception of *who* we are in our work: How are our conflicting positions, histories, and desires for power implicated in our research questions, methodologies, and conclusions? A politics of location allows us to claim legitimacy of our experience, but it must be accompanied by a rigorously reflexive examination of ourselves as researchers that is as careful as our observation of the object of inquiry . . . (9)

In acting as both researcher and object of inquiry, I need to be even more careful as I try to understand how I am located in multiple ways as researcher and research subject. As I have already discussed earlier in this book, it is also necessary to continually challenge those who seek to create representative or exceptional stories about literacy, race, and citizenship, to challenge an essentialist impulse to understand in uncomplicated ways what it means, for example, to be an Asian American or a person of color, or to be literate.

To use the personal to unpack the public is also a way to understand how the ordinary, how daily life, how the minor can disrupt our grand narratives of literacy, race, and citizenship. Part of the project for the use of literacy narratives, I have argued, is that it provides people of color with a means for inserting themselves into American culture, to participate in the cultural work of social change by disrupting dominant structures that act in various forms of oppression. As Ellen Cushman argues in her essay "Rhetorician as Agent of Social Change," there is a need to "take into our accounts of social change the ways in which people use language and literacy to challenge and alter the circumstances of daily life. . . . In other words, social change can take place in daily interactions when the regular flow of events is objectified, reflected upon, and altered" (12). The use of the personal is a way to account for and recognize the change that can occur through our everyday acts of literacy in our lives. The use of the personal also accounts for and recognizes that the minor is part of our everyday acts of literacy in our lives, whether it is in representations of people of color or others in our literature or popular culture, or the Asian American English teacher in the classroom—the minor does interrupt and disrupt dominant narratives every day.

However, there can still be a question about how the personal is used and for what purposes. For example, though I had a negative encounter with a white man in that New Orleans market, I was not abused beyond feeling humiliated and didn't suffer physical harm or other trauma except to point to this event as part of my literacy history. In fact, I expect that this memory will elicit sympathy and understanding as I build a case for using these moments where literacy and race converge and can result in a type of cultural anxiety, a feeling that one is on the margins of culture. Though I am not trading on the real kind of pain and suffering or illicit act that might create a problematic reception of my personal history, I do wonder if I am providing an experience that has enough meaning to be of value in my research about literacy, race, and citizenship? Or am I using the personal merely as a type of ornamentation, or as a type of talisman, or a shield (to use Maxine Hong Kingston's description of the way young women carry *The Woman Warrior*) (Kingston, "Personal" 24)? Do I use the personal to deflect questions about the claims I make about literacy, race, and citizenship? These are some of the difficult questions about my research that I ask myself without any confidence of an answer. But as I grapple with these questions, I begin to understand that I write scenes of personal experience in order to have a text in front of me, to be able to interpret a text rather than simply rely on personal ethos or identity politics to make my case. I write the personal not only for the reader but for myself so that I can engage with the experience and not leave anything to chance. By using the reading and writing of literacy narratives as a methodology for my research, I have been able to examine how literacy functions in culture through both literate acts and dominant discourses about literacy. Asking students and ourselves to use literacy narratives is a way to investigate in more thorough ways our relationship to literacy, how literacy functions in specific contexts, and how literacy functions in larger cultural narratives, which may describe and reproduce values, beliefs, and practices in uncomplicated ways. This is a re/vision of research, a move toward locating more clearly the multiple positions we occupy as researcher and object of inquiry and toward understanding how the personal provides another lens through which we perform our analyses of public culture, using the ordinary, daily, and minor to disrupt dominant narratives about literacy, race, and citizenship.

Re/Visions of Teaching

In chapter 4, I provided scenes from my own classroom to illustrate some of my own anxiety about teaching, about being a teacher of color, and about what I offer in terms of content and practice to address some of these concerns while also meeting the demands of a writing course. When I described that student who expressed her own anxiety about the "multicultural" nature of the course, I also expressed my surprise by her reading of the course. While I

perhaps had seen the multicultural nature of the course as so embedded in issues of literacy that I feigned surprise, I now wonder
why I was not more up front about confronting issues of diversity
head-on. It was partly my anxiety about my presence as a teacher of
color, and perhaps a wariness of having my class become known for
its agenda of "political correctness." But as I become more experienced in the classroom and more invested in the kind of research I
do—especially when I am often my own subject—I am more in-
clined to address diversity head-on as a topic for intellectual discussion and not allow people to assume it's simply a matter of "political
correctness," "identity politics," or "liberal guilt."

Using literacy narratives has allowed me to introduce students
to a wide range of writers, to have students position themselves as
writers, and to see students think about the way they participate in
culture through their literacy. Organizing my courses in this manner has also allowed me to address issues of the minor, to see how
minor narratives interact with dominant narratives about literacy,
race, and citizenship, and to see how students both interact with
minor narratives and even become minor is their own ways. Seeing these interactions in the classroom has moved me toward a
re/vision of my teaching, to see the work I do as having consequences beyond what students learn about writing or appreciate in
their Asian American teacher. While I strategically resist the term
"diversity" because of its overdetermination, I do see this concept
as critical in the re/vision of my teaching as I ask both students and
myself to read and write minor narratives, to examine literacy in
specific contexts, and to think about what culture means in order to
create new meaning for this idea and practice.

The complexities of the classroom and the difficulties for both
teachers and students when "diversity" enters the discussion is a
familiar story. On one hand, "diversity" becomes an opportunity to
explore intersections, to connect the ostensible categories of "difference" (race, gender, class, sexuality) with other social locations and
experiences (e.g., region, faith, language, generation, etc.). It can be
an opportunity to do the difficult work of examining social injustice, systems of inequity, and the complex cultures of a wide array

of groups. On the other hand, there is a real danger that "diversity" has become an empty category often reduced in simplistic ways to *only* mean race, gender, class, and sexuality, and in some cases is distilled further to mean only "feminist" or "Black and White" issues. In this case, we have missed the intersection, and in the classroom, both students and teachers find themselves talking past each other without a way to find meaning together.

As teachers, we need to consider our own role in creating opportunities for productive discussions or in hindering conversations. When we talk about diversity in general, we need to consider the following questions: How do students feel when teachers raise issues of diversity in the classroom? What role can students play and how might they exert influence on these "institutional" discussions about diversity? Does "difference" make a difference? How does "difference" make a difference? How do teachers keep lines of communication open to invite real conversation and avoid charges of "politically correct" programming when students keep to safe and polite responses? Are issues of "diversity" in the classroom being connected to issues of "diversity" in the "real world?" How do we move past the "official" discourse on "diversity" (which is often viewed skeptically) to create new meaning in "diversity?" Does what we *don't* say about "diversity" in our classrooms have a more negative effect than what we do say?

I ask these questions because I think in order to discuss diversity in responsible ways we need to understand our own investments for bringing diversity as a topic into the classroom. We also need to be aware of what our students' investments or resistance to such discussions might be. One semester, I asked my first-year composition class to answer a survey about their experiences with "diversity." The survey was for a presentation I was to help give for the annual symposium "Race, Class, Gender, and Sexuality" held at my university. Students responded anonymously and provided a wide range of answers that I found very interesting. Two comments were of particular interest to me since they concerned the role instructors play in discussions about diversity. One student wrote, "I feel that if a professor is part of a minority the issue of diversity is more commonly discussed." This first student response is something I often face in my classes—or at least in my mind, it is often an issue. For example, as I have described in more detail in chapter 4, I try to include a wide variety of materials from a wide variety of writers in my writing courses. However, there is sometimes a perception that the material is organized around race or ethnicity, when in my mind it's organized around literacy or memory—and I think this is because of the way I look. Students see their Asian American teacher and assume an Asian American—or at least a diversity—agenda. Of course, I asked a class a few years back how they perceived me when I first entered the class—did they see an Asian teacher? "No—we just thought you were really young."

I don't think the student who made the response about "minority professors" and diversity was complaining—she was simply observing that teachers can provide different perspectives; that the teacher can have insight about diversity issues that can be beneficial to the classroom discussion. A second student response caught my attention because it seemed to reinforce the first response: " . . . sometimes I find [diversity] hard to discuss in classes because professors are not as informed on being a part of [a minority group], so it makes it complicated." This response is important to me because it highlights the need for a diverse teaching faculty. Even if the topic of a class is not "diversity" per se, having a teacher of a different background adds something to the classroom. This response also suggests that we need to be responsible in our discussions about diversity. We cannot simply introduce topics about diversity and assume students will make the connections that we see. We need to be overt in our discussions—that does not mean we need to preach. If we talk about diversity badly, we make all of our jobs more difficult.

There is, then, a need to re/vision our teaching. We need to understand why we bring discussions about diversity into our classrooms, especially the writing classroom. We need to ask the following questions: How do teachers position themselves in these discussions about diversity? How do students perceive teachers in these discussions? As teachers, what are our responsibilities in facilitating these kinds of discussions? With these and other questions in mind, I wonder what my and our future will be as we think about the changing face of our classrooms, of our teachers, and of our nation, as we negotiate a changing discourse about diversity.

Re/Visions of Citizenship: Being Ethnic, Becoming American?

On a July evening in the summer of 2000, I sat at a conference table at my local public library. I had been invited to facilitate a discussion about Maxine Hong Kingston's *Woman Warrior* for a program called "Being Ethnic, Becoming American." I was happy to participate, especially because I see the public library as an important public space that can support diverse literacy practices, and because I feel a responsibility to provide opportunities to discuss Asian American literature when possible. But I was a little troubled by the program title—"Being Ethnic, Becoming American." Certainly this is a common theme in America and in American literature, as people from many cultures still continue to come to America for what it can offer. But in my case and in the case of many people born in America, this theme does not quite fit. In fact, the inverse is probably a more apt description—"Being American, Becoming Ethnic"—as many people born and raised in America seek to understand their identities by exploring their cultural backgrounds. There is a hint in "Being Ethnic, Becoming American" that those who are marked by ethnicity or race are not part of American culture just yet, that we are somehow in the process of becoming American. Perhaps in thinking about what it means to be a citizen, we must think about the ways in which we are always becoming part of a community, whether it is one that we are born into, or one that we join through the use of language, culture, or other community practices that we continually negotiate.

In his essay "Notes of a Native Speaker" from his collection *The*

Accidental Asian, Eric Liu begins with a list of some of the ways he could say he is "white":

I listen to National Public Radio.
I wear khaki Dockers.
I own brown suede bucks.
I eat gourmet greens.
I have few close friends "of color."
I married a white woman.
I am a child of the suburbs.
I furnish my condo a la Crate & Barrel.
I vacation in charming bed-and-breakfasts.
I have never once been the victim of blatant discrimination.
I am a member of several exclusive institutions.
I have been in the inner sanctums of political power.
I have been there as something other than an attendant.
I have the ambition to return.
I am a producer of the culture.
I expect my voice to be heard.
I speak flawless, unaccented English.
I subscribe to *Foreign Affairs.*
I do not mind when editorialists write in the first person plural.
I do not mind how white the television casts are.
I am not too ethnic.
I am wary of minority militants.
I consider myself neither in exile nor opposition.
I am considered "a credit to my race." (33–34)

Liu provides this list and acknowledges that because he fits this profile he has become "white." But he is ambivalent about his assimilation, noting that to whites he is an "honorary white," and to other Asians he is a "banana," yellow on the outside, white on the inside. This ambivalence strikes me as "normal," as many Asian Americans try to understand where they fit in the complicated web of American culture. In American cultural politics, race often refers to black- and brown-skinned people. When a situation like the recent alleged spying of scientist Wen Ho Lee emerges, American culture is more likely to construct him as foreign and not American, despite his American citizenship.

I read Eric Liu's list and wonder to myself, "How different am I really from him?" And I look at the list again and think, "These are also some of the ways I am Asian American." While I have been fortunate enough to grow up in a setting where multi-ethnic culture was the condition of my everyday life, I find that I have had to discover a new framework for my experience as I live in a place now that makes me more conscious of my position as an Asian American. Perhaps I do many of the things on Eric Liu's list now because they are convenient. But does that make me "white?"

A few years ago, I met with the Asian American student group at my university. They were looking for an adviser, and I happened to be doing an independent study with a student from their group. I met with them one evening and described what I saw as the potential and purpose of their group. I talked about trying to lobby the administration for courses about Asian Americans: literature, history, and so on. In the wake of recent unrest regarding racist graffiti at the African American cultural center, I suggested to the students that they should be as concerned about racism as the African American students were, that they needed to be out there with those students instead of waiting to be the victims of racism themselves. I don't think I was ranting, but at that moment I began to understand the importance of becoming Asian American. I wasn't Asian American solely because of my racial condition. I was becoming Asian American because I had started to understand the necessity of addressing issues of racism, of knowing the history and culture of Asian Americans, because those things are most at stake when they are innocuously absent, when they are not a "critical" concern yet.

I have no romantic memory of sit-ins or picket lines or other protests for Asian American issues—that has not been part of my experience. But when those Asian American students resisted the idea that they could be victims of racism, I did not know what else to say. They explained that their group was about fostering community, not about being activists. I thanked them for their time, and as I left, I wondered how those two things could be exclusive of each other. They were minority students, but they were not willing to become minor. In some ways I was disappointed in these students because they seemingly were not coming to some critical consciousness. But in other ways, I saw myself in these students, who must feel an anxiety about their place in the university and in American culture when they are told in a variety of ways that they have already made it, that they are on their way to fulfilling the American Dream.

The more I think about this experience with these students and my time in the Midwest, the more I come to understand the difficulties of being minor and of developing and using a minority discourse. What was available to me in Hawai'i was a language, a historicized and theorized discourse that operated to deterritorialize dominant discourse, to connect minor subjects to political action, and to provide collective experiences of a growing multi-ethnic culture that often viewed itself in tension with the rest of the United States. Whether it was through Pidgin, or perhaps now Native Hawaiian, the presence of a viable alternative discourse, of a viable alternative cultural citizenship, was a very real experience for me and remains a very real experience for those who continue to live in Hawai'i. But what are the alternatives for those of us who now live within spaces where certain kinds of minority discourse become increasingly difficult to imagine and even more difficult to use within dominant culture?

Recently, I had presented to me the opportunity to return home to Hawai'i to live and teach. Working with students like me, trying to address the larger structural issues about literacy and education in a context like Hawai'i, and being with family and friends were all reasons to return home. In graduate school, I had prepared myself to return home to teach and to do research about the literacy and literary issues that were particular to Hawai'i. My many seminar papers and conference presentations and my dissertation had focused on Hawai'i. I faced a difficult decision as I struggled to figure out what returning home meant, what staying in the Midwest meant, what staying on the "mainland" meant. To the surprise of many, and perhaps to myself as well, I decided to stay in the Midwest for now, but not because I did not want to return home. In fact the possibility of serving the community that I grew up in was almost too important to pass up. And yet, I believe my presence where I am now is perhaps even more critical. In part I decided to stay because I have begun to re/vision the work I do in a place like the Midwest. I have begun to understand that becoming minor is a rhetorical and political act that does not rely on the ostensible categories of difference alone. Rather, it is about re/vision, the cultural work of unpacking hidden histories about literacy, race, and citizenship, of reading and writing these narratives to create full and complex portraits of American culture. As America enters the twenty-first century and many institutions, including our educational institutions, move to address issues of diversity and the intellectual value of examining our many American cultures, there is a need for vigilance and action in making sure that our minor narratives do not remain between the drafts of the American Story. And in my particular story, I narrate a partial history of Asian Americans so that they are not relegated to being the invisible presence, to being part of the landscape but not part of the conversation. I am in the continual process of becoming American—just as we all are—and in becoming Asian American, a minor re/vision that has allowed me to better understand the ways I do research, teach, and participate in our community.

Coda: American Re/Visions

. . . we talked about what *race* matters have meant in the
American past and how much race *matters* in the American
present. And I vowed to be more vigilant and virtuous in
my efforts to meet the formidable challenges posed by Plato
and Du Bois. For me, it is an urgent question of power and
morality; for others, it is an everyday matter of life and death.
— Cornel West, *Race Matters*

Why racial identity—why now? Because it is still a radical act
to stand in my shoes and speak when someone who looks like
me is not supposed to do what I do. This is resistance.
— Mari J. Matsuda, *Where Is Your Body?*

You ask me to write something about war, peace and race, but I
cannot. Words fail me.
— Jessica Hagedorn, "Notes from a New York Diary"

On 12 September 2001, the day after the terrorist attack on the
World Trade Center in New York City, I sat in front of my advanced
composition class, not quite sure what to do. It seemed wrong to
carry on as if nothing had happened. But it also seemed wrong for
me to act as a "therapist" when I have no training as one and,
frankly, was terrified about what might be said when emotions were
running high and many people, students and teachers, were looking
to the classroom to become a space where some kind of understanding could come out of the chaos. I could only do what I had
been planning to do as if it had been just any other day—we write.

I turned to the class and asked them to take out their journals.
"Over the last twenty-four hours, you've experienced a wide range

of emotions," I began, "make a list of all of these emotions you've felt." I watched the students dutifully take out their journals and pens but almost as if they were in slow motion. After a minute of writing and another, I continued, "Go back over your list and circle the emotions you felt most strongly, or the ones you are most confused by." The students pondered over their lists. "Freewrite about these emotions you have circled, describe how these emotions made you feel physically, psychologically." I turned to my own journal:

> I'm depressed—my body feels heavy, my eyes sting, I'm tired. My head hurts. I can't process what's going on. I don't know what to do—I just want to shut myself off. I want my body to feel alive again. I want to not feel so cold. The shock is real—there is not a way to deal with this. I can't believe this is happening—it is so horrible, it's so hard to imagine. There have been other disasters but somehow I felt I could grieve—there was hope as we saw some people being rescued right away. But to see the towers collapse, knowing there were all those people is too much to bear. The only way I can process this is to understand how this could happen. I also feel conflicted—because now Americans know what the rest of the world feels—we suffer as they suffer. Will this make us a more compassionate people?

I looked up to the class and watched as they continued to scrawl in their journals. "One more minute, finish your last thought." I thought about what to do next. We continued to write, we struggle for words.

I open this Coda with the two epigraphs from Cornel West and Mari Matsuda because they both remind me that race matters, whether we are the victims of blatant racism or discrimination, or believe that in American culture we can have faith in democracy, equality, and civil liberties. But race matters. Race matters in writing because, as I have argued, literacy and language have been used to discriminate against people of color but has also provided people of color with the means to respond to racism, to write their own stories and to write themselves into the American Story. Race matters in learning because it provides a framework to understanding how our experiences are different and similar, how our interactions in culture are generated and assessed. And race matters in teaching because what I do in the classroom is motivated by what I have experienced in my life. And my presence in the classroom will have an effect on the students who must interact with their Asian American teacher.

I include the epigraph from the Filipino American and New York writer Jessica Hagedorn because in the aftermath of September 11, 2001, issues of literacy, race, and citizenship have become even more critical in American culture. In trying to write about September 11, Hagedorn struggles to find the words, struggles to think about why race matters, why we need to think about war and peace. She struggles not because these are not critical issues but rather because the enormity of what has happened has raised the stakes in the ways we think about war, peace, and race. Questions about the status of Arabs and Arab Americans abound as we all look for some understanding about these events and worry about who our neighbors are. Comparisons are made to Pearl Harbor and the Japanese attack on America. The government cracks down on foreign students and others who may not have the "right" papers. Analogies are made to Japanese American internment camps as reports of racial profiling increase, while others assure the public that the camps would never happen again. And our anxiety about an uncertain future feeds the discourse of nationalism and need for nostalgia.

A re/vision of America has taken place. While I have argued throughout this book that re/vision is a central trope and practice that provides people of color and others in minor positions to narrate themselves into the American Story, we have seen a change in the cultural imagination that has made re/vision a more difficult prospect. Anxiety and nostalgia have become more prevalent as American culture looks to resolve its fear and confusion in more comforting discourses of nationalism. The tensions that I argue for as moments of critical awareness, as opportunities for re/vision, are being overwritten by narratives that again push minor stories between the drafts. It is in these moments when the minor is at risk of being lost that we must be even more vigilant in reading and writing our minor narratives about literacy, race, and citizenship. While we struggle for words now, as we try to write, like Hagedorn, about war, peace, and race, we must not let words fail us completely. We have faced the enormity of pain, anger, confusion, and even hopelessness, but in understanding the idea of America and what it can provide, we must continue to re/vision America, to challenge what we see as social injustice, and to embrace and demand social justice for all.

In the weeks and months after September 11, 2001, many Americans have taken the time to reflect on what it means to be American, and each holiday or day of remembrance brings new and different meanings to our lives. I myself have thought long and hard about what being American means to me. And I have wondered how my argument about literacy, race, and citizenship is affected by a changed American context. What I have learned from writing this book and in teaching and learning in these times is that I have faith in the idea of America, that despite troubling times when there are people who still face racism or discrimination of other kinds, there are those who will act to challenge racism and discrimination. I have also realized that as a teacher I have faith in my students to understand these complex issues and difficult times. When I read the journals from my advanced composition course and came across the entries for 12 September 2001, I embraced the words of more than a few students who expressed their own fears about the event itself but also about the aftermath and its consequences for our community, who still desire social justice for those often displaced and lost in events like this, who hoped that America would not fall into a chasm of racism or lose sight of what is good about our country. I read complicated responses to a difficult event and saw these students use writing to bring voice to what was almost unspeakable. When I read the writing of students, I become more aware of what these students are teaching me and what I hope to share with them.

When I examine the literacy artifacts from my own life, reread my stories, and begin to write my own literacy narrative, I see both the virtue and the danger in my performance as an elementary student some twenty-odd years ago, as a college sophomore a dozen years back, and as a teacher today. How can I not be nostalgic, as I'm sure my mother was whenever she placed something in the file, as I look back at what I achieved at five or six years old and consider the cumulative effect of these collected literacy moments. No wonder I am a professor of English and teach writing or courses on the teaching of writing. But I also read artifacts and compose memories here in order to move beyond the literacy myths that have structured my life, from the early awareness in my childhood that English Standard schools existed (and were apparently a good thing) to the amazement I felt (or was it shock) when my eighth-grade English teacher read the class a story written in Pidgin, to the work I do now in researching literacy across our many American cultures. In doing this work, I am also subject to anxiety because of the contradictory experiences in my life that have told me that despite my literacy, I am open to being questioned and challenged or to being held up as a model of assimilation. Perhaps it is my destiny, as my horoscope told me to live a life with words. In writing my own literacy narrative here, I have begun to understand the many layers of experience and the many layers of culture that make up my life. It is this understanding and these experiences that become the foundation for my life as a teacher and a scholar as I continue to read the literacy narratives in my classroom and in our culture, to write my own life's story, and to re/vision America.

Notes

Works Cited

Index

Notes

Introduction

1. 107th Congressional Record. H2722 (25 May 2001). (Statement of David Wu.)

2. The Chinese Exclusion Act of 1882 passed by the U.S. Congress prevented immigration of Chinese laborers to the United States for a period of ten years. This was the first in a series of acts by Congress to bar Chinese laborers from entering the country, and it was not until 1943 that these exclusions acts were repealed. The Immigration Act of 1917 created the "Asiatic Barred Zone," which excluded immigration from an area covering South Asia from Arabia to Indochina and included India, Burma, Siam, Malaysia, the East Indian islands, Asiatic Russia, the Polynesian islands, and parts of Arabia and Afghanistan. See Angelo N. Ancheta, *Race, Rights, and the Asian American Experience* (25–26).

3. In a series of U.S. Supreme Court decisions in the late nineteenth and early twentieth centuries *(United States v. Wong Kim Ark; Ozawa v. United States; United States v. Thind)*, the Court held that Asians not born in the United States were ineligible for naturalization because they did not fit the category of "free white person" established under the Nationality Act of 1790 or under the Fourteenth Amendment, which was enacted to allow "aliens of African nativity and persons of African descent" to become naturalized citizens. It was not until 1943 that Chinese became eligible to be naturalized, 1946 for Indians and Filipinos, and finally in 1952, Congress removed the racial limitation on naturalized citizenship. See Angelo N. Ancheta, *Race, Rights, and the Asian American Experience* (23–24).

4. In 1942, President Franklin Delano Roosevelt issued Executive Order 9066, which authorized the secretary of war to create military areas from which people could be excluded in the interest of national defense. While in theory this act could have been applied to those of German or Italian ancestry, those of Japanese ancestry were targeted. This resulted in the relocation of over 110,000 Japanese Americans from the West Coast (an area protected in the interest of national defense) to internment camps. See Angelo N. Ancheta, *Race, Rights, and the Asian American Experience* (30–32) and Michi Weglyn, *Years of Infamy: The Untold Story of America's Concentration Camps.*

1. Re/Visions: Narrating Literacy and Citizenship

1. In the scenes of childhood memory, I use parenthetical phrases and roman type to delineate between a reflective present-day self and a past childhood self.

2. The dramatic increase in number of "literacy" sessions can be attributed to the change in the way "Area Clusters" were defined. In the case of 1994, multiple choices for defining a literacy area were provided on the submission form. After 1994, a general category of "Institutional Contexts for Writing and Literacy" was used on the proposal form though several literacy subcatagories were used in the program.

3. In a personal communication, Peter Mortensen confirmed that as far as he knew, he and Janet Carey Eldred entered the term "literacy narrative" into the critical discourse of literacy and composition studies. However, he also noted that the "literacy narrative" was an idea that was much discussed though unnamed at the time they wrote their essay.

4. It is interesting that Kaplan does not refer to Eldred and Mortensen's essay "Reading Literacy Narratives" even though it appeared in *College English* in 1992 and Kaplan's essay appears in 1994. This seems to me to be a problem of disciplinary (perhaps generic) boundaries, which keeps related works from interacting with each other.

5. "Contact zone" has come into common usage in literary and composition studies since Pratt's essay appeared in 1991. Raymond Williams's use of "community" appeared in 1977.

2. Reading Literacy Narratives: Connecting Literacy, Race, and Citizenship Through the Stories of Others

1. See David Bleich's essay "Collaboration and the Pedagogy of Disclosure" for a discussion of the strategies theorized around acts of disclosure in the classroom.

2. See Ramon Saldivar's *Chicano Narrative* and Raymund Paredes's "Autobiography and Ethnic Politics" for further discussions of Rodriguez's construction of race/ethnicity as a public/private dichotomy.

3. See "Service Learning and the Literacy Connection" by Emily Nye and Morris Young for a fuller description of the service-learning course mentioned here.

4. Finch's critique of Rockwell's *Freedom of Speech* is that it presents too idealistic and naive a portrait. In Finch's view, the expressions of wonder and admiration on the faces of the central speaker and the surrounding audience caricature the idea of "freedom of speech" by presenting it in such a melodramatic way (168).

5. Bulosan's essay is clearly a version of his earlier poem, "If You Want to Know What We Are," which was published in the Philippines in 1940 and later in 1951 (Bulosan, "If You" 9). The poem is much more radical in its call for revolution and its images of violence against laborers. For example, the final line of the *Saturday Evening Post* essay is: "If you want to know what we are— We are Marching!" The final line of the poem is: "If you want to know what we are—WE ARE REVOLUTION!"

6. Elaine Kim describes the attention Bulosan received during World War II in her *Asian American Literature* (45). Kim lists Bulosan's works and discusses how some of these pieces were broadcast to American armed forces during World War II to create sympathy for American allies in the Pacific. She also mentions Rockwell's portrait and that it was displayed in the examination room of the Federal Building in San Francisco. Kim does not offer any critique of the appropriation of Bulosan by American culture as part of the war effort. This lack of critique seems to buy into the construction of the good immigrant who will believe in America and yet accept being marginalized as a price of being in America: the possibility and promise of liberty is more powerful than the reality.

7. Michelle Cruz Skinner revised her undergraduate honors thesis, which was then published as a collection of stories, *Balikbayan: A Filipino Homecoming* (1988). R. Zamora Linmark's collection of short stories, *Rolling the R's*, was published in 1995. His work has also appeared in the Asian American literature anthologies *Charlie Chan Is Dead: An Anthology of Contemporary Asian American Fiction* (1993) and *Flippin': Filipinos on America* (1996).

8. See Anne Ruggles Gere and Morris Young, "Cultural Institutions: Reading(s) (of) Zora Neale Hurston, Leslie Marmon Silko, and Maxine Hong Kingston," for a discussion about the cultivation of audience desire for the "exotic" and the institutionalized discourses about women writers of color.

9. This is perhaps Frank Chin's biggest complaint about Asian American literature that in his judgement does not articulate an Asian American sensibility through the use of language and subject matter. Chin argues that any writing by Asian Americans that fits into the Western genres of confession or autobiography cannot be considered Asian American writing since it relies upon Western literary conventions. While I understand the argument, I disagree with Chin since such a rigid definition denies the fact that Asian Americans born and raised in America operate in Western subjectivities and can create "new" cultural forms through their Asian backgrounds and American lives. See Frank Chin's essay, "Come All Ye Asian American Writers of the Real and the Fake."

10. Kim differs from Chin in that she accepts what she calls the "inclusive and characteristically Asian American genre of autobiography or personal history dedicated to the task of promoting cultural goodwill and understanding" (47). Again, while I understand Kim's impulse to define a type of autobiography as an Asian American genre, I disagree with her reading of this genre since it

does not seem to take into account the potentially subversive readings available in the texts.

11. The question of citizenship is complicated by the Philippines's status as a U.S. territory from 1898 through 1934, when Filipinos were considered U.S. nationals but not U.S. citizens. The passage of the Tydings-McDuffie Act in 1934 by the U.S. Congress granted commonwealth status to the Philippines and led to its independence in 1946 but also divested Filipinos of their status as U.S. nationals. This resulted in Filipinos being subjected to U.S. immigration laws, which limited their immigration to the U.S. and also made them ineligible to become naturalized citizens because of the bar against Asians. See Angelo Ancheta, *Race, Rights, and the Asian American Experience* (26–27).

12. See James Crawford, ed., *Language Loyalties* (252) and L. Ling-chi Wang, *"Lau v. Nichols"* (243). Wang goes as far to say that "Not since the Brown v. Board of Education decision in 1954 which outlawed school segregation was there such an important decision handed down on education by the Supreme Court" (243).

13. See Hyung-chan Kim, "An Overview" (65) and Philip T. Nash (904). Kim says Justice William Douglas, who wrote the *Lau v. Nichols* decision, used Section 601 of the Civil Rights Act of 1964 because it directly prohibits discrimination based "on the grounds of race, color, or national origin."

14. Opponents of bilingual education might argue that *Lau v. Nichols* actually reinforced the silencing of students because bilingual education can maintain the separation of non-English speakers and English speakers. This inversion of *Lau v. Nichols* is an interesting move because it suggests that language minorities want to maintain their linguistic separation and reinforces racial stereotypes.

3. Reading Hawai'i's Asian American Literacy Narratives: Re/Visions of Resistance, Schooling, and Citizenship

1. "American" was the term used to refer to "white Americans or those of Anglo-Saxon ancestry" by the bureau of vital statistics, Territorial Board of Health. See Riley H. Allen, "Education and Race Problems in Hawaii."

2. See Eileen Tamura's *Americanization, Acculturation, and Ethnic Identity* and John N. Hawkins's "Politics, Education, and Language Policy: The Case of Japanese Language Schools in Hawaii" for discussions of the U.S. Supreme Court decision on *Farrington v. Tokushige*.

3. The 2000 census allows individuals to identify themselves as mixed-race. In Hawai'i, 21.4 percent of the population identified themselves as mixed-race; however, the census report does not identify the combinations of racial backgrounds, so while it is likely that these mixed-race identifications include

an "identity of color," it cannot be determined definitively from the census report.

4. For further discussion of the development of Hawai'i Creole English/ Pidgin, see work by John E. Reinecke, Suzanne Romaine, and Charlene Sato.

5. For further discussion of the impact of imported plantation labor on the Native Hawaiian community, see the special issue of *Amerasia Journal* 26.2 (2000), "Asian Settler Colonialism in Hawai'i," edited by Candace Fujikane and Jonathan Y. Okamura.

6. See Norman Meller, appendix A, for examples of the oral English examination.

7. The baby luau (celebration) is an event typically held for a baby's first birthday. The *yakudoshi* is a Japanese tradition of having a large celebration on certain birthdays to ward off bad luck. The pounding of *mochi* (rice cake) takes place to celebrate the New Year.

8. See Stephen Sumida's chapter "Hawaii's Local Literary Tradition" in his *And the View from the Shore* for a discussion of the production of various cultural texts in Hawai'i.

9. While this Pidgin debate was underway, the issue of same-sex marriage was being contested in Hawai'i, after the Hawai'i State Supreme Court ruled that the state must show a "compelling reason" why same-sex couples cannot be issued a marriage license. In response to the Hawai'i case, states across the country as well as the federal government acted to legislate against same-sex marriage.

4. Teaching Literacy Narratives: Reading, Writing, and Re/Vision

1. I use pseudonyms for the students described here.

2. Used with permission of the author. This journal was written for English 380V, "Learning Communities: Explorations in Literacy, Education, and Service" (Spring 2002). I have used pseudonyms for the children.

Works Cited

Allen, Riley H. "Education and Race Problems in Hawaii." *American Review of Reviews* Dec. 1921: 613–24.

Alquizola, Marilyn. "The Fictive Narrator of *America Is in the Heart*." *Frontiers of American Studies: Writing, Research, and Commentary.* Ed. Gail M. Nomura, Russell Endo, Stephen H. Sumida, and Russell C. Leong. Pullman: Washington State UP, 1989. 211–17.

———. "Subversion or Affirmation: The Text and Subtext of *America Is in the Heart*." *Asian Americans: Comparative and Global Perspectives.* Ed. Shirley Hune, Hyung-chan Kim, Stephen S. Fugita, and Amy Ling. Pullman: Washington State UP, 1991. 199–209.

American Council on Education. *Hawaiian Schools: A Curriculum Survey, 1944–45.* Washington, D.C.: American Council on Education, 1946.

Ancheta, Angelo N. *Race, Rights, and the Asian American Experience.* New Brunswick: Rutgers UP, 1998.

Bacchilega, Cristina. "Pro-Vocations: Multivocality and Local Literature." "The Reader's Guide." Hawai'i Literature Conference. 12 March 1994. 8–12.

Bammer, Angelika, ed. *Displacements: Cultural Identities in Question.* Bloomington: Indiana UP, 1994.

Beebee, Thomas O. *The Ideology of Genre: A Comparative Study of Generic Instability.* University Park: Pennsylvania State UP, 1994.

Beechert, Edward D. "Patterns of Resistance and the Social Relations of Production in Hawaii." *Plantation Workers: Resistance and Accommodation.* Ed. Brij V. Lal, Doug Munro, and Edward D. Beechert. Honolulu: U of Hawaii P, 1993. 45–67.

Berlant, Lauren. *The Anatomy of National Fantasy: Hawthorne, Utopia, and Everyday Life.* Chicago: U of Chicago P, 1991.

Bleich, David. "Collaboration and the Pedagogy of Disclosure." *College English* 57.1 (1995): 43–61.

Brandt, Deborah. *Literacy in American Lives.* Cambridge: Cambridge UP, 2001.

Brodkey, Linda. "Tropics of Literacy. *Journal of Education* 168 (1986): 47–54.

Bruner, Jerome. *Acts of Meaning.* Cambridge: Harvard UP, 1990.

Bullock, Richard, and John Trimbur, eds. *The Politics of Writing Instruction: Postsecondary.* Portsmouth: Boynton, 1991.

Bulosan, Carlos. *America Is in the Heart: A Personal History.* Harcourt, 1946. Seattle: U of Washington P, 1973.

———. "Freedom from Want." *The Saturday Evening Post* 6 Mar. 1943: 12–13.

———. "If You Want to Know What We Are." *If You Want to Know What We Are: A Carlos Bulosan Reader.* Ed. E. San Juan Jr. Minneapolis: West End, 1983. 78–79.

———. "The Story of a Letter." *If You Want to Know What We Are: A Carlos Bulosan Reader.* Ed. E. San Juan Jr. Minneapolis: West End, 1983. 39–44.

———. "The Writer as Worker." *On Becoming Filipino: Selected Writings of Carlos Bulosan.* Ed. E. San Juan Jr. Philadelphia: Temple UP, 1995. 143–44.

Bunker, Frank F. "The Education of the Child of the American-Born Parent in Hawaii." *Hawaii Education Review* Sept. 1922: 1–2.

Campomanes, Oscar V., and Todd S. Gernes. "Two Letters from America: Carlos Bulosan and the Act of Writing." *MELUS* 15 (1988): 15–46.

Chang, Thelma. "Revisiting Pidgin." *The Honolulu Advertiser* 30 Oct. 1994: B-1+.

Chesire, Jenny, ed. *English Around the World.* Cambridge: Cambridge UP, 1991.

Cheung, King-Kok. *Articulate Silences: Hisaye Yamamoto, Maxine Hong Kingston, Joy Kogawa.* Ithaca: Cornell UP, 1993.

Chin, Frank. "Come All Ye Asian American Writers of the Real and the Fake." *The Big Aiiieeeee: An Anthology of Chinese American and Japanese American Literature.* New York: Meridian, 1991. 1–92.

Chock, Eric, and Darrell Lum, eds. *Paké: Writings by Chinese in Hawaii.* Honolulu: Bamboo Ridge, 1989.

Clark, Gregory, and S. Michael Halloran, eds. *Oratorical Culture in Nineteenth-Century America: Transformations in the Theory and Practice of Rhetoric.* Carbondale: Southern Illinois UP, 1993.

Coles, Robert. *The Call of Stories: Teaching and the Moral Imagination.* Boston: Houghton, 1989.

Conference on College Composition and Communication. 1990 Program. *Strengthening Community Through Diversity.* 22–24 Mar. 1990, Chicago.

———. 1991 Program. *Times of Trial, Reorientation, and Reconsiderations: A Fin de Siècle Review/Prophecy.* 21–23 Mar. 1991, Boston.

———. 1992 Program. *Contexts, Communities, and Constraints: Sites of Composing and Communicating.* 19–21 Mar. 1992, Cincinnati.

———. 1993 Program. *Twentieth-Century Problems, Twenty-First Century Solutions: Issues, Answers, Actions.* 1–3 Apr. 1993, San Diego.

———. 1994 Program. *Common Concerns, Uncommon Realities: Teaching, Research, and Scholarship in a Complex World.* 16–19 Mar. 1994, Nashville.

———. 1995 Program. *Literacies, Technologies, Responsibilities.* 22–25 Mar. 1995, Washington, D.C.

———. 1996 Program. *Transcending Boundaries.* 27–30 Mar. 1996, Milwaukee.

———. 1997 Program. *Just Teaching, Just Writing: Reflection and Responsibility.* 12–15 Mar. 1997, Phoenix.

————. 1998 Program. *Ideas, Historias y Cuentos: Breaking with Precedent.* 1–4 Apr. 1998, Chicago.

————. 1999 Program. *Visible Students, Visible Teachers.* 24–27 Mar. 1999, Atlanta.

————. 2000 Program. *Educating the Imagination, Re-imagining Education.* 12–15 Apr. 2000, Minneapolis.

————. 2001 Program. *Composing Community.* 14–17 Mar. 2001, Denver.

Courts, Patrick L. *Literacy and Empowerment: The Meaning Makers.* New York: Bergin, 1991.

Crawford, James, ed. *Language Loyalties: A Sourcebook on the Official English Controversy.* Chicago: U of Chicago P, 1992.

Cushman, Ellen. "Rhetorician as Agent of Social Change." *College Composition and Communication* 47.1 (1996): 7–28.

Davidson, Cathy N. *Revolution and the Word: The Rise of the Novel in America.* New York: Oxford UP, 1986.

Deleuze, Gilles, and Felix Guattari. *Kafka: Toward a Minor Literature.* Trans. Dana Polan. Minneapolis: U of Minnesota P, 1986.

Douglass, Frederick. *Narrative of the Life of Frederick Douglass, An American Slave, Written by Himself.* Eds. William L. Andrews and William S. McFeely. New York: Norton, 1997.

Eldred, Janet Carey. "Narratives of Socialization: Literacy in the Short Story." *College English* 53.6 (1991): 686–700.

Eldred, Janet Carey, and Peter Mortensen. "Reading Literacy Narratives." *College English* 54.5 (1992): 512–39.

Finch, Christopher. *Norman Rockwell's America.* New York: Abrams, 1975.

Fleischer, Cathy, and David Schaasma, eds. *Literacy and Democracy: Teacher Research and Composition Studies in Pursuit of Habitable Spaces.* Urbana: NCTE, 1998.

Flores, William V., and Rina Benmayor, eds. *Latino Cultural Citizenship: Claiming Identity, Space, and Rights.* Boston: Beacon, 1997.

Francia, Luis H., and Eric Gamalinda, eds. *Flippin': Filipinos on America.* New York: The Asian American Writers' Workshop, 1996.

Fujikane, Candace. "Reimagining Development and the Local in Lois-Ann Yamanaka's *Saturday Night at the Pahala Theatre.*" *Social Process in Hawai'i* 38 (1997): 42–61.

Fujikane, Candace, and Jonathan Y. Okamura. "Whose Vision? Asian Settler Colonialism in Hawai'i." Spec. issue of *Amerasia Journal* 26.2 (2000).

Gee, Emma, ed. *Counterpoint.* Los Angeles: Asian American Studies Center, UCLA, 1976.

Gere, Anne Ruggles. *Intimate Practices: Literacy and Cultural Work in U.S. Women's Clubs, 1880–1920.* Urbana: U of Illinois P, 1997.

Gere, Anne Ruggles, and Morris Young. "Cultural Institutions: Reading(s) (of)

Zora Neale Hurston, Leslie Marmon Silko, and Maxine Hong Kingston." *Critical Theory and the Teaching of Literature: Politics, Curriculum, Pedagogy.* Ed. James Slevin and Art Young. Urbana: NCTE, 1996. 153–71.

Gilyard, Keith. *Voices of the Self: A Study of Language Competence.* Detroit: Wayne State UP, 1991.

Giroux, Henry. *Schooling and the Struggle for Public Life: Critical Pedagogy in the Modern Age.* Minneapolis: U of Minnesota P, 1988.

Graff, Harvey J. *The Literacy Myth: Literacy and Social Structure in the Nineteenth-Century City.* New York: Academic, 1979.

Hagedorn, Jessica, ed. *Charlie Chan Is Dead: An Anthology of Contemporary Asian American Fiction.* New York: Penguin, 1993.

———. "Notes from a New York Diary." *Amerasia* 27.3 (2001)/28.1 (2002): 13–16.

Hall, Jon. Letter. *The Honolulu Advertiser.* 4 Oct. 1994: A-12.

Hara, Marie. *Bananaheart and Other Stories.* Honolulu: Bamboo Ridge, 1994.

———. "Fourth Grade Ukus." *Bananaheart and Other Stories.* Honolulu: Bamboo Ridge, 1994. 47–62.

Hawaii English Program: Project End Evaluation Report, 1970–1971. Honolulu: Hawaii State Dept. of Education, 1971.

Hawkins, John. "Politics, Education, and Language Policy: The Case of Japanese Language Schools in Hawaii." *The Asian American Educational Experience: A Source Book for Teachers and Students.* Ed. Don T. Nakanishi and Tina Yamamoto Nishida. New York: Routledge, 1995. 30–41.

Hoggart, Richard. *The Uses of Literacy.* Essential, 1957. New Brunswick: Transaction, 1992.

Horning, Alice, and Ron Sudol, eds. *The Literacy Connection.* Creeskill: Hampton, 1999.

Hune, Shirley, Hyung-chan Kim, Stephen S. Fugita, and Amy Ling, eds. *Asian Americans: Comparative and Global Perspectives.* Pullman: Washington State UP, 1991. 199–209.

Hybolics 1 (1999).

Infante, Esme M. "Pidgin—Happy Talk or Something Unspeakable?" *Honolulu Advertiser* 14 May 1995: A-1.

JanMohamed, Abdul R., and David Lloyd. "Introduction: Toward a Theory of Minority Discourse: What Is To Be Done?" *The Nature and Context of Minority Discourse.* New York: Oxford UP, 1990. 1–16.

———, eds. *The Nature and Context of Minority Discourse.* New York: Oxford UP, 1990.

Kaplan, Alice Yeager. "On Language Memoir." *Displacements: Cultural Identities in Question.* Ed. Angelika Bammer. Bloomington: Indiana UP, 1994. 59–70.

Kawamoto, Kevin Y. "Hegemony and Language Politics in Hawaii." *World Englishes.* 12.2 (1993): 193–207.

Kim, Elaine H. *Asian American Literature: An Introduction to the Writings and Their Social Context.* Philadelphia: Temple UP, 1982.

Kim, Hyung-chan, ed. *Asian Americans and the Supreme Court: A Documentary History.* New York: Greenwood, 1992.

———. "An Overview." In *Asian Americans and the Supreme Court: A Documentary History.* New York: Greenwood, 1992. 1–76.

Kincaid, Jamaica. *Annie John.* New York: Noonday, 1997.

Kingston, Maxine Hong. *China Men.* Knopf, 1980. New York: Vintage, 1989.

———. "Personal Statement." *Approaches to Teaching Kingston's The Woman Warrior.* Ed. Shirley Geok-lin Lim. 23–25.

———. *The Woman Warrior: Memoirs of a Girlhood among Ghosts.* Knopf, 1976. New York: Vintage, 1989.

Kintgen, Eugene R., Barry M. Kroll, and Mike Rose. *Perspectives on Literacy.* Carbondale: Southern Illinois UP, 1988.

Kirsch, Gesa E., and Joy S. Ritchie. "Beyond the Personal: Theorizing a Politics of Location in Composition Research." *College Composition and Communication* 46.1 (1995): 7–29.

Lau v. Nichols. 414 U.S. 563–72. U.S. Supr. Ct. 1974.

Libretti, Tim. "*America Is in the Heart* by Carlos Bulosan." *A Resource Guide to Asian American Literature.* Ed. Sau-ling Cynthia Wong and Stephen H. Sumida. New York: MLA, 2001. 21–31.

Lim, Shirley Geok-lin, ed. *Approaches to Teaching Kingston's The Woman Warrior.* New York: MLA 1991.

Linmark, R. Zamora. *Rolling the R's.* New York: Kaya, 1995.

Lipsitz, George. *Time Passages: Collective Memory and American Popular Culture.* Minneapolis: U of Minnesota P, 1990.

Liu, Eric. *The Accidental Asian: Notes of a Native Speaker.* New York: Vintage, 1998.

Lowe, Lisa. *Immigrant Acts: On Asian American Cultural Politics.* Durham, Duke UP, 1996.

Lung, Lisa-Anne. Letter. *The Honolulu Advertiser.* 29 Jan. 1995: B-3.

Lynch, William S. "Loyalty in Spite of All." *Saturday Review of Literature* 9 Mar. 1946: 7–8.

MacCaughey, Vaughn. "The School Year 1919–20 in Hawaii." *Hawaii Educational Review* 9.1 (1920): 1–31.

Maitino, John R., and David R. Peck, eds. *Teaching American Ethnic Literatures: Nineteen Essays.* Albuquerque: U of New Mexico P, 1996.

Malkin, Michelle. "When Everyone's a Winner Our Students Are the Losers." *Seattle Times* 4 June 1996: B4.

Marquez, Antonio C. "Richard Rodriguez's *Hunger of Memory* and New Perspectives on Ethnic Autobiography." *Teaching American Ethnic Literatures: Nineteen Essays.* Ed. John R. Maitino and David R. Peck. Albuquerque: U of New Mexico P, 1996. 237–54.

Matsuda, Mari J. *"Where Is Your Body?" and Other Essays on Race, Gender, and the Law.* Boston: Beacon, 1996.

Matsunaga, Mark. "Pidgin: Unique Language Seeks to Find Its Place in Both Classroom, Boardroom." *Honolulu Advertiser* 15 May 1995: B1.

Meller, Norman. "Hawaii's English Standard Schools." Report No. 3, 1948. Honolulu: Hawaii Territorial Legislature.

Nakanishi, Don T., and Tina Yamamoto Nishida, eds. *The Asian American Educational Experience: A Source Book for Teachers and Students.* New York: Routledge, 1995.

Nash, Philip T. "Asian Americans and their Rights for Employment and Education." *Asian Americans and the Supreme Court: A Documentary History.* Ed. Hyung-chan Kim. New York: Greenwood, 1992. 897–908.

National Center for Education Statistics. "Race/Ethnicity of College Faculty." Fast Facts. <www.nces.ed.gov>.

National Council of Teachers of English. "On the Critical Shortage of Minority Educators." Resolution, NCTE Annual Business Meeting, 1990, Atlanta.

Nomura, Gail M., Russell Endo, Stephen H. Sumida, and Russell C. Leong, eds. *Frontiers of American Studies: Writing, Research, and Commentary.* Pullman: Washington State UP, 1989.

Nunberg, Geoffrey. "Afterword: The Official English Movement: Reimagining America." *Language Loyalties: A Sourcebook on the Official English Controversy.* Ed. James Crawford. Chicago: U of Chicago P, 1992. 479–94.

Nye, Emily, and Morris Young. "Service-Learning and the Literacy Connection." *The Literacy Connection.* Ed. Alice Horning and Ron Sudol. Creeskill: Hampton, 1999. 69–96.

Omi, Michael, and Howard Winant. *Racial Formation in the United States: From the 1960s to the 1980s.* New York: Routledge, 1986.

107th Congressional Record. H2722 (25 May 2001). (Statement of David Wu.)

Paredes, Raymund. "Autobiography and Ethnic Politics." *Multicultural Autobiography.* Ed. James Robert Payne. Knoxville: U of Tennessee P, 1992. 280–96.

Pratt, Mary Louise. "Arts of the Contact Zone." *Profession 91* (1991): 33–40.

———. "Daring to Dream: Re-Visioning Culture and Citizenship." *Critical Theory and the Teaching of Literature: Politics, Curriculum, Pedagogy.* Ed. James F. Slevin and Art Young. Urbana: NCTE, 1996. 3–20.

Reinecke, John E. *Language and Dialect in Hawaii: A Sociolinguistic History to 1935.* Ed. Stanley M. Tsuzaki. Honolulu: U of Hawaii P, 1969.

Rivera, Tomas. "Richard Rodriguez's *Hunger of Memory* as Humanistic Antithesis." *MELUS* 11.4 (1984): 5–13.

Robinson, Jay. "Literacy and Lived Lives: Reflections on the Responsibilities of Teachers." *Literacy and Democracy: Teacher Research and Composition Studies in Pursuit of Habitable Spaces.* Ed. Cathy Fleischer and David Schaasma. Urbana: NCTE, 1998. 1–27.

Rockwell, Norman. Illustration. "Freedom from Want." *Saturday Evening Post*

6 March 1943: 13. Rpt. in *Norman Rockwell's America* by Christopher Finch. New York: Abrams, 1975. Plate #206.

Rodriguez, Richard. *Hunger of Memory: The Education of Richard Rodriguez.* New York: Bantam, 1982.

Romaine, Suzanne. "Changing Attitudes to Hawai'i Creole English: Fo' Find One Good Job, You Gotta Know How fo' Talk like One Haole." *Creole Genesis, Attitude and Discourse.* Ed. John R. Rickford and Suzanne Romaine. Amsterdam: Benjamins, 1999. 285–301.

————. "Hawai'i Creole English as a Literary Language." *Language in Society* 23.4 (1994): 527–54.

Rosaldo, Renato. "Cultural Citizenship, Inequality, and Multiculturalism." *Latino Cultural Citizenship: Claiming Identity, Space, and Rights.* Ed. William V. Flores and Rina Benmayor. Boston: Beacon, 1997. 27–38.

Rose, Mike. *Lives on the Boundary.* New York: Penguin, 1990.

Rosen, Harold. "The Importance of Story." *Language Arts* 63.3 (1986): 226–37.

Roskelly, Hephzibah. "On Becoming a Teacher." *College English* 57.6 (1995): 713–22.

Rouse, P. Joy. "Margaret Fuller: A Rhetoric of Citizenship in Nineteenth-Century America." *Oratorical Culture in Nineteenth-Century America: Transformations in the Theory and Practice of Rhetoric.* Ed. Gregory Clark and S. Michael Halloran. Carbondale: Southern Illinois UP, 1993. 110–36.

Saldivar, Ramon. *Chicano Narrative: The Dialectics of Difference.* Madison: U of Wisconsin P, 1990.

Sanders, Scott Russell. *Writing from the Center.* Bloomington: Indiana UP, 1995.

San Juan, E., Jr., ed. *If You Want to Know What We Are: A Carlos Bulosan Reader.* Minneapolis: West End, 1983.

————. "Searching for the Heart of 'America.'" *Teaching American Ethnic Literatures: Nineteen Essays.* Ed. John R. Maitino and David R. Peck. Albuquerque: U of New Mexico P, 1996. 259–72.

Sato, Charlene J. "Linguistic Inequality in Hawaii: The Post-Creole Dilemma." *Language of Inequality.* Ed. Nessa Wolfson and Joan Manes. Berlin: Mouton, 1985. 255–72.

————. "Sociolinguistic Variation and Language Attitudes in Hawai'i." *English Around the World.* Ed. Jenny Chesire. Cambridge: Cambridge UP, 1991. 647–63.

Schutz, Albert J. *The Voices of Eden: A History of Hawaiian Language Studies.* Honolulu: U of Hawaii P, 1996.

Scribner, Sylvia. "Literacy in Three Metaphors." *Perspectives on Literacy.* Ed. Eugene R. Kintgen, Barry M. Kroll, and Mike Rose. Carbondale: Southern Illinois UP, 1988. 71–81.

Shannon, Patrick. "The Struggle for Control of Literacy Lessons." *Language Arts* 66.6 (1989): 625–34.

Shaw, Bernard. *Pygmalion.* New York: Penguin, 1957.

Simonson, Rick, and Scott Walker, eds. *The Graywolf Annual Five: Multicultural Literacy: Opening the American Mind.* St. Paul: Graywolf, 1988.

Skinner, Michelle Cruz. *Balikbayan: A Filipino Homecoming.* Honolulu: Bess, 1988.

Slevin, James, and Art Young, eds. *Critical Theory and the Teaching of Literature: Politics, Curriculum, Pedagogy.* Urbana: NCTE, 1996.

Sommers, Nancy. "Between the Drafts." *College Composition and Communication* 43.1 (1992): 23–31.

Stoddard, Maynard Good. "The Four Freedoms Live On." *Saturday Evening Post* May/June 1995: 60–64.

Street, Brian V. *Social Literacies: Critical Approaches to Literacy in Development, Ethnography, and Education.* London: Longman, 1995.

Stueber, Ralph. "Hawaii: A Case Study in Development Education, 1778–1960." Diss., U of Wisconsin, 1964.

Sumida, Stephen H. *And the View from the Shore: Literary Traditions of Hawai'i.* Seattle: U of Washington P, 1991.

Takaki, Ronald. *A Different Mirror: A History of Multicultural America.* Boston: Back Bay, 1993.

———. *Strangers from a Different Shore: A History of Asian Americans.* Revised Edition. Boston: Little, 1998.

Tamura, Eileen H. *Americanization, Acculturation, and Ethnic Identity: The Nisei Generation in Hawaii.* Urbana: U of Illinois P, 1994.

Tonouchi, Lee A. *Da Word.* Honolulu: Bamboo Ridge, 2001.

Trimbur, John. "Literacy and the Discourse of Crisis." *The Politics of Writing Instruction: Postsecondary.* Ed. Richard Bullock and John Trimbur. Portsmouth: Boynton, 1991. 277–95.

Tsai, Michael. "Pondering Pidgin." *Honolulu Weekly.* 4 Jan. 1995.

TuSmith, Bonnie. "The Cultural Translator: Toward an Ethnic Womanist Pedagogy." *MELUS* 16 (1989–1990): 17–29.

United States Census 2000. United States Census Bureau. 25 May 2001. <http://www.census.gov>.

United States Department of the Interior. Bureau of Education. *A Survey of Education in Hawaii.* Bulletin 1920, No. 16. Washington, D.C.: GPO, 1920.

University of Hawai'i Style Guide. Honolulu: Office of the Vice President for External Affairs and University Relations, 2002.

Van Gelder, Lawrence. "D'Amato Mocks Ito and Sets Off Furor." *New York Times.* 6 Apr. 1995: B1+.

Villanueva, Victor, Jr. *Bootstraps: From an American Academic of Color.* Urbana: NCTE, 1993.

———. "On the Rhetoric and Precedents of Racism." *College Composition and Communication* 50.4 (1999): 645–61.

Wang, L. Ling-chi. "*Lau v. Nichols:* History of a Struggle for Equal and Quality

Education." *Counterpoint.* Ed. Emma Gee. Los Angeles: Asian American Studies Center, UCLA, 1976. 240–63.

Weglyn, Michi Nishimura. *Years of Infamy: The Untold Story of American's Concentration Camps.* Seattle: U of Washington P, 1976, 1996.

West, Cornel. *Race Matters.* New York: Vintage, 1993.

White, Hayden. *Tropics of Discourse: Essays in Cultural Criticism.* Baltimore: Johns Hopkins UP, 1978.

Williams, Raymond. *Keywords: A Vocabulary of Culture and Society.* London: Fontana, 1976.

———. *Marxism and Literature.* Oxford: Oxford UP, 1977.

Wist, Benjamin O. *A Century of Public Education in Hawaii, 1840–1940.* Honolulu: Hawaii Educational Review, 1940.

Wong, Sau-ling Cynthia. "Denationalization Reconsidered: Asian American Cultural Criticism at a Theoretical Crossroads. *Amerasia* 21 (1995): 1–27.

———. *Reading Asian American Literature: From Necessity to Extravagance.* Princeton: Princeton UP, 1993.

Yagelski, Robert P. *Literacy Matters: Writing and Reading the Social Self.* New York: Teachers College P, 2000.

Yamanaka, Lois-Ann. *Saturday Night at the Pahala Theatre.* Honolulu: Bamboo Ridge, 1993.

———. *Wild Meat and the Bully Burgers.* New York: Farrar, 1996.

"Year's Fifty Best Books." *Look.* 5 Aug. 1947: 98–99.

Yee, Wai Chee Chun. "For You a Lei." *Paké: Writings by Chinese in Hawaii.* Ed. Eric Chock and Darrell Lum. Honolulu: Bamboo Ridge, 1989. 68–88.

Index

academics, 15–16, 68–72, 76–77, 144–49, 184–85. *See also* writers
accent, foreign, 5–6
Accidental Asian (Liu), 189–90
achievement, pain of, 109
Adaptation (Scribner term), 23–24, 34, 37
African Americans, 57, 151
agriculture, 118–19
aliens: Asian Americans as, 48–49; resident, 45
Allen, Riley H., 113
Alquizola, Marilyn, 85, 86
America: re/vision of, 195–97; translation of, 85. *See also* citizenship; culture
America Is in the Heart (Bulosan), 13–14, 81–89, 90, 92, 94, 108; cultural translation in, 83–89, 96; as narrative of assimilation, 81, 83–86; on relationship of people of color to literacy in, 54–58; Young's reading of, 82. *See also* Carlos
American Council of Education, 114
American Dream, 89, 106, 130, 148, 191; promise of, 9, 16, 23. *See also* American Story
Americanization, 29, 63, 107–8, 122, 125–26, 170. *See also* assimilation; citizenship; culture; identity
American Story, 13, 15, 30, 51–52, 67, 112; minor narratives in, 192; race in, 16, 193, 195; re/vision of, 109, 134. *See also* American Dream
Ann Arbor, Michigan, 57, 82
Anzaldua, Gloria, 158
Arabs, 195
artifacts, of literacy, 20–23, 24, 172–

82, 197; report card as, 172–77, 181–82; worksheet as, 177–80, 181–82
Asian American Literature: An Introduction to the Writings and Their Social Context (Kim), 86
Asian Americans, 14, 79, 190; Filipinos as, 45, 84–86, 91, 93, 95; Koreans as, 92; literacy, race, and citizenship of, 43–44, 48–49, 81–82, 107–8; literacy narratives of, 2, 10, 111; as Orientals, 83, 103, 107, 113, 115, 121–122; as writers, 80–82, 98, 100. *See also* other; people of color; race
assimilation, 66, 81, 83–86; or unassimilability, 123
Association for Asian American Studies, 2
autobiography, 12, 32–34, 59–60, 66
autoethnography, 36–37, 50, 60–61

Bacchilega, Cristina, 110
Baldwin, James, 148, 152
Bamboo Ridge Press, 135
basalization, of literacy, 180
Beebee, Thomas O., 33
"Being Ethnic, Becoming American" (public discussion facilitated by Young), 188
Berlant, Lauren, 29
"Beyond the Personal" (Kirsch and Ritchie), 182
bigotry, 69. *See also* discrimination
bildungsroman, 13
bilingualism, 97, 204n. 14
Black and White, 14, 56. *See also* people of color; race; white

health card, school, 20
hegemony, 41–43, 63, 75
Hirsch, E. D., 52
history, context of, 157
Hoggart, Richard, 25, 26, 64
Honolulu Advertiser, 135–38
Honolulu Weekly, 138
"How I Started to Write" (Fuente), 158
hula, 126
Hunger of Memory (Rodriguez), 13–14,
    54–58, 61, 66–68, 108, 158
Hybolic magazine, 139

identity, 127, 158, 160; American, 63;
    children's, 104–6; claiming, 170; in
    Hawai'i, 39, 165, 169–70; literacy as
    part of, 2; normal, 130; role of lan-
    guage in, 132–33
ideology, 25–26; of Americanization,
    107–8; forms of, 177, 179; of Stan-
    dard English, 128–29
"If I Could Write This in Fire, I Would
    Write This in Fire" (Cliff), 148
Immigrant Acts (Lowe), 48
immigration, 48–50, 201n. 2. *See also*
    citizenship; multiculturalism; *indi-
    vidual nationalities*
Imus, Don, 4
individual, and collective, 72, 77–78.
    See also personal
institutions, cultural, 116–17
interpretation, 150, 155. *See also* trans-
    lation
Intimate Practices (Gere), 10
"Invisibility Blues" (Wallace), 148
Ito, Judge Lance, 4–5

JanMohamed, Abdul, 13, 40–41, 42
Japanese, 121, 201n. 4
"Journey into Speech, A" (Cliff), 148

Kafka, Franz, 40
Kang, Younghill, 92–93
Kaplan, Alice Yeager, 32–34
Kim, Elaine, 86
kindergarten, 102–3, 172

King-Kok Cheung, 98–99, 107
Kingston, Maxine Hong, 100, 157,
    188; on citizenship, race and literacy,
    54–57, 81–82, 96, 98, 108; use of
    personal and private by, 12–14
Kirsch, Gesa, 182
Koreans, 92

language: Chinese, 103–4, 107; Creole,
    110, 117–18, 177; educational rights
    for minority, 96–97; in Hawai'i, 110–
    15, 118, 134–39; official, 51; per-
    sonal and private, 59–63, 65–68;
    Pidgin, 14–15, 110–12, 117–18,
    128–32, 134–39; politics of, 134;
    polyglot, 46; in relationship to citi-
    zenship, 63–65; silence in, 98–99,
    102–3, 107, 112; vocalization of, 18–
    19, 100–101, 105–7, 123, 135, 198–
    99. *See also* English
"Language Memoir, On" (Kaplan), 32
Latin Americans, 14, 56, 57
Lau, Kinney Kinmon, 97
Lau v. Nichols, 96–99, 100, 102
learning, literacy, 180
Lee, Wen Ho, 190
legitimacy, 2, 6; of citizenship, 46–47;
    of culture, 135–37
Lincoln School, 122–23
Linmark, R. Zamora, 82
Lipsitz, George, 35–36
literacy, 9–11, 24–26, 140, 148–53,
    172–82; access to, 151, 166; arti-
    facts of, 20–23, 24, 172–82, 197;
    consciousness on issues of, 29–31,
    78, 94; re/vision of, 167–68; teach-
    ing of, 180; as transformation, 29.
    See also citizenship: relationship be-
    tween race, literacy, and; narratives:
    literacy
Literacy Matters (Yagelski), 11
Literacy Myth, The (Graff), 24, 25
Literacy Narrative writing project,
    158–62
literature: Asian American, 82; of the
    contact zone, 32, 36; minor, 40

MORRIS YOUNG is an associate professor of English at Miami University in Oxford, Ohio. His research and teaching focuses on the teaching of writing, the literacy and rhetorical practices of communities of colors, and the continuing development of Asian Pacific American literature. His work has appeared in *College English* and the *Journal of Basic Writing* and in the collections *The Literacy Connection; Critical Theory and the Teaching of Literature: Politics, Curriculum, Pedagogy;* and *Personal Effects: The Social Character of Scholarly Writing.*

Studies in Writing & Rhetoric

In 1980 the Conference on College Composition and Communication established the Studies in Writing & Rhetoric (SWR) series as a forum for monograph-length arguments or presentations that engage general compositionists. SWR encourages extended essays or research reports addressing any issue in composition and rhetoric from any theoretical or research perspective as long as the general significance to the field is clear. Previous SWR publications serve as models for prospective authors; in addition, contributors may propose alternate formats and agendas that inform or extend the field's current debates.

SWR is particularly interested in projects that connect the specific research site or theoretical framework to contemporary classroom and institutional contexts of direct concern to compositionists across the nation. Such connections may come from several approaches, including cultural, theoretical, field-based, gendered, historical, and interdisciplinary. SWR especially encourages monographs by scholars early in their careers, by established scholars who wish to share an insight or exhortation with the field, and by scholars of color.

The SWR series editor and editorial board members are committed to working closely with prospective authors and offering significant developmental advice for encouraged manuscripts and prospectuses. Editorships rotate every five years. Prospective authors intending to submit a prospectus during the 2002 to 2007 editorial appointment should obtain submission guidelines from Robert Brooke, SWR editor, University of Nebraska-Lincoln, Department of English, P.O. Box 880337, 202 Andrews Hall, Lincoln, NE 68588-0337.

General inquiries may also be addressed to Sponsoring Editor, Studies in Writing & Rhetoric, Southern Illinois University Press, P.O. Box 3697, Carbondale, IL 62902-3697.